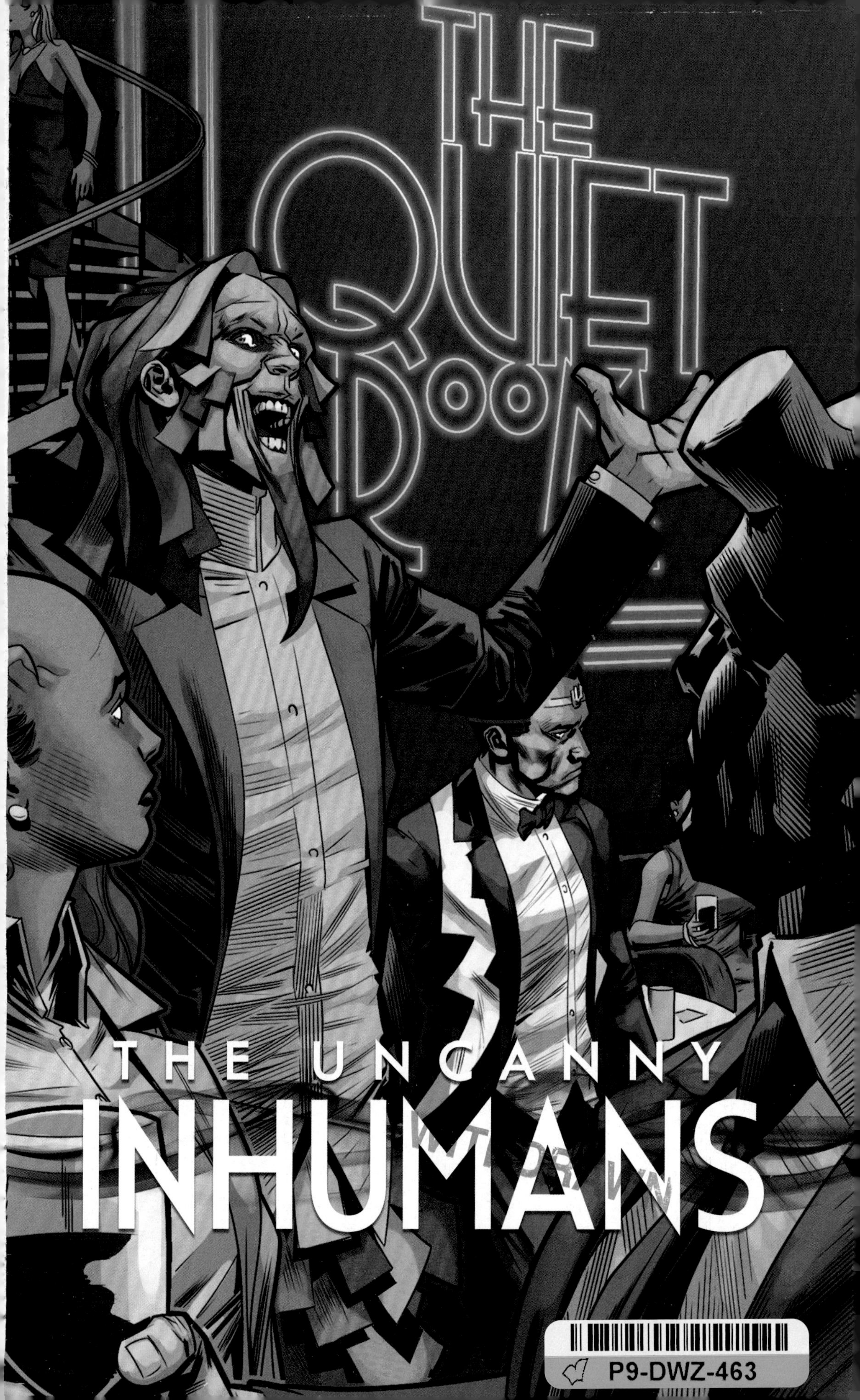
THE QUIET ROOM
THE UNCANNY
INHUMANS

After releasing colossal clouds of Terrigen Mist into Earth's atmosphere and transforming many unwitting Inhuman descendants, Black Bolt, the King of the Inhumans, went into hiding. Upon his return, Queen Medusa forced the king to abdicate the throne becoming sole sovereign heir of New Attilan.

Having recently rescued their son Ahura from the clutches of Kang the Conqueror, the pair must now readjust to their new dynamic as separated co-parents.

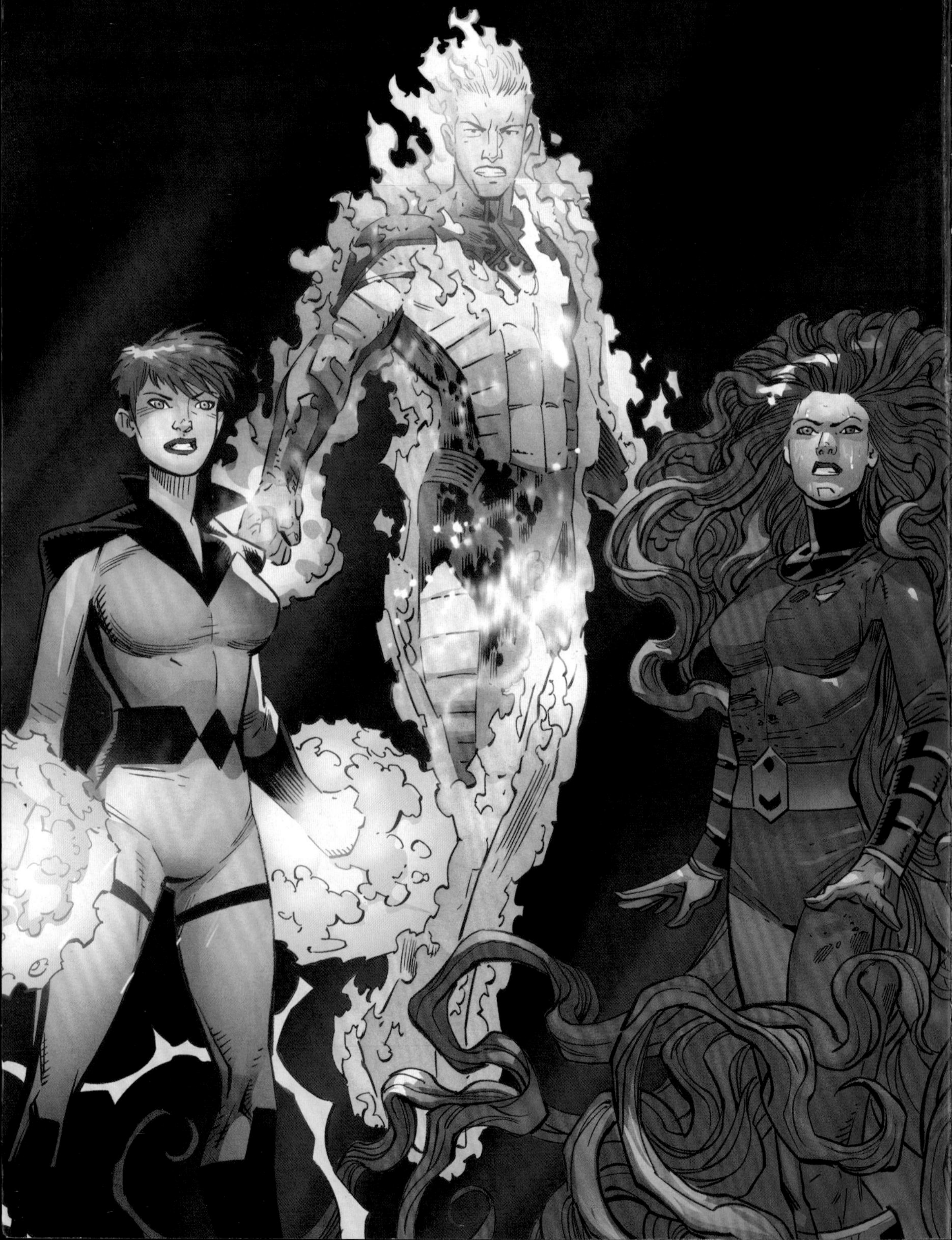

Thousands of years ago aliens experimented on cavemen, super-charging their evolution, and then mysteriously left their experiments behind. These men and women built the city of Attilan and discovered a chemical called Terrigen that unlocked secret super-powers in their modified DNA, making them...

THE UNCANNY INHUMANS

THE QUIET ROOM

CHARLES SOULE
WRITER

ISSUES #5-7

BRANDON PETERSON
ARTIST

JAVA TARTAGLIA
COLOR ARTIST

BRANDON PETERSON (#5-6) & STACEY LEE (#7)
COVER ARTISTS

ISSUES #8-10

KEV WALKER
PENCILER

SCOTT HANNA
INKER

DAVID CURIEL
COLOR ARTIST

MAHMUD ASRAR & DAVE McCAIG (#8-9) AND GIUSEPPE CAMUNCOLI & ANDRES MOSSA (#10)
COVER ARTISTS

VC'S CLAYTON COWLES
LETTERER

CHARLES BEACHAM
ASSISTANT EDITOR

DARREN SHAN
ASSOCIATE EDITOR

NICK LOWE
EDITOR

INHUMANS CREATED BY STAN LEE & JACK KIRBY

COLLECTION EDITOR: JENNIFER GRÜNWALD
ASSOCIATE EDITOR: SARAH BRUNSTAD
ASSOCIATE MANAGING EDITOR: ALEX STARBUCK
EDITOR, SPECIAL PROJECTS: MARK D. BEAZLEY

VP, PRODUCTION & SPECIAL PROJECTS: JEFF YOUNGQUIST
SVP PRINT, SALES & MARKETING: DAVID GABRIEL
BOOK DESIGN: JAY BOWEN

EDITOR IN CHIEF: AXEL ALONSO
CHIEF CREATIVE OFFICER: JOE QUESADA
PUBLISHER: DAN BUCKLEY
EXECUTIVE PRODUCER: ALAN FINE

UNCANNY INHUMANS VOL. 2: THE QUIET ROOM. Contains material originally published in magazine form as UNCANNY INHUMANS #5-10. First printing 2016. ISBN# 978-0-7851-9707-2. Published by MARVEL WORLDWIDE, INC., a subsidiary of MARVEL ENTERTAINMENT, LLC. OFFICE OF PUBLICATION: 135 West 50th Street, New York, NY 10020. **Printed in Canada.** ALAN FINE, President, Marvel Entertainment; DAN BUCKLEY, President, TV, Publishing & Brand Management; JOE QUESADA, Chief Creative Officer; TOM BREVOORT, SVP of Publishing; DAVID BOGART, SVP of Business Affairs & Operations, Publishing & Partnership; C.B. CEBULSKI, VP of Brand Management & Development, Asia; DAVID GABRIEL, SVP of Sales & Marketing, Publishing; JEFF YOUNGQUIST, VP of Production & Special Projects; DAN CARR, Executive Director of Publishing Technology; ALEX MORALES, Director of Publishing Operations; SUSAN CRESPI, Production Manager; STAN LEE, Chairman Emeritus. For information regarding advertising in Marvel Comics or on Marvel.com, please contact Vit DeBellis, Integrated Sales Manager, at vdebellis@marvel.com. For Marvel subscription inquiries, please call 888-511-5480. **Manufactured between 6/10/2016 and 7/18/2016 by SOLISCO PRINTERS, SCOTT, QC, CANADA.**

10 9 8 7 6 5 4 3 2 1

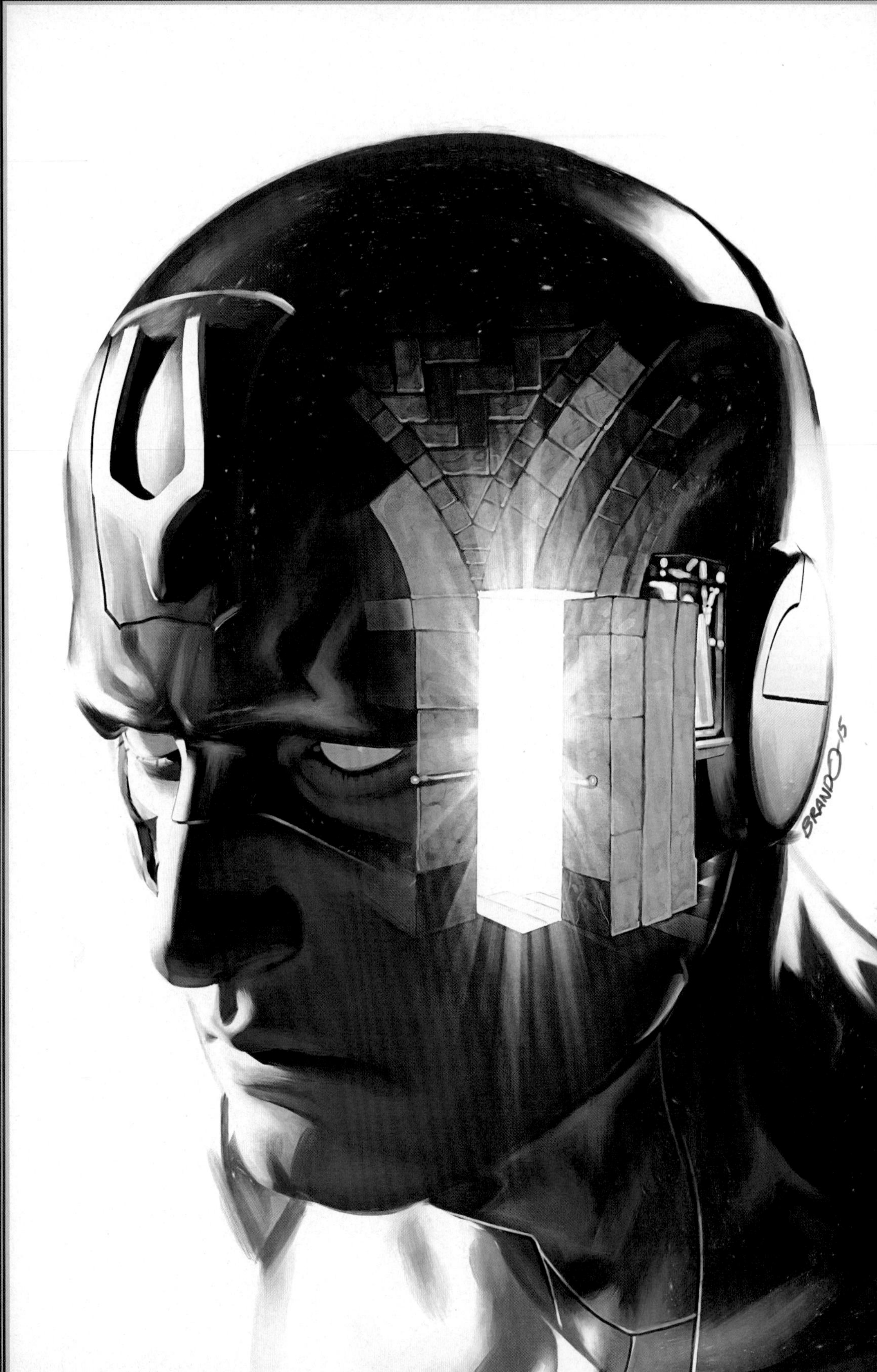
BRANDO-15

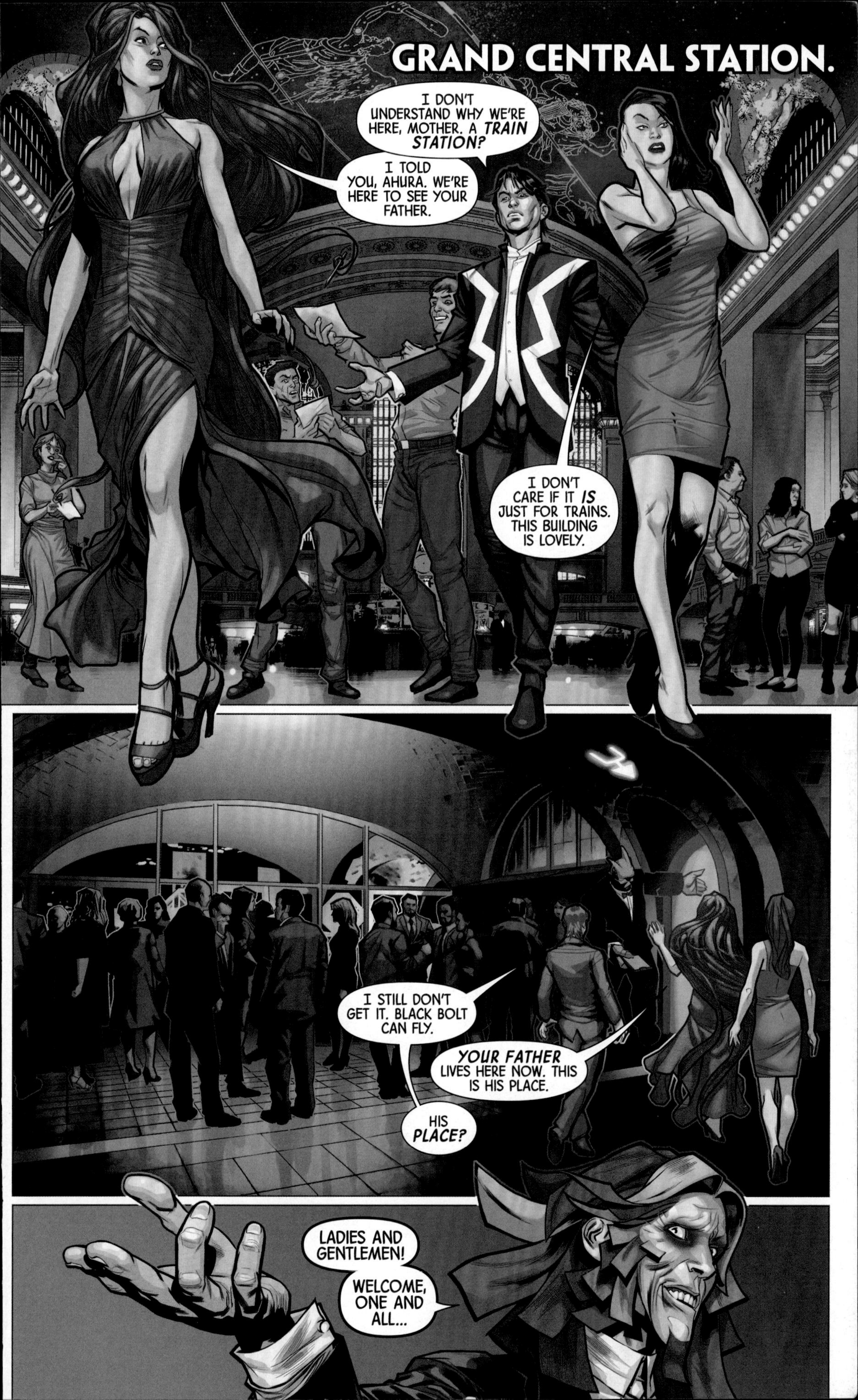
GRAND CENTRAL STATION.
I DON'T UNDERSTAND WHY WE'RE HERE, MOTHER. A TRAIN STATION?
I TOLD YOU, AHURA. WE'RE HERE TO SEE YOUR FATHER.
I DON'T CARE IF IT IS JUST FOR TRAINS. THIS BUILDING IS LOVELY.
I STILL DON'T GET IT. BLACK BOLT CAN FLY.
YOUR FATHER LIVES HERE NOW. THIS IS HIS PLACE.
HIS PLACE?
LADIES AND GENTLEMEN!
WELCOME, ONE AND ALL...

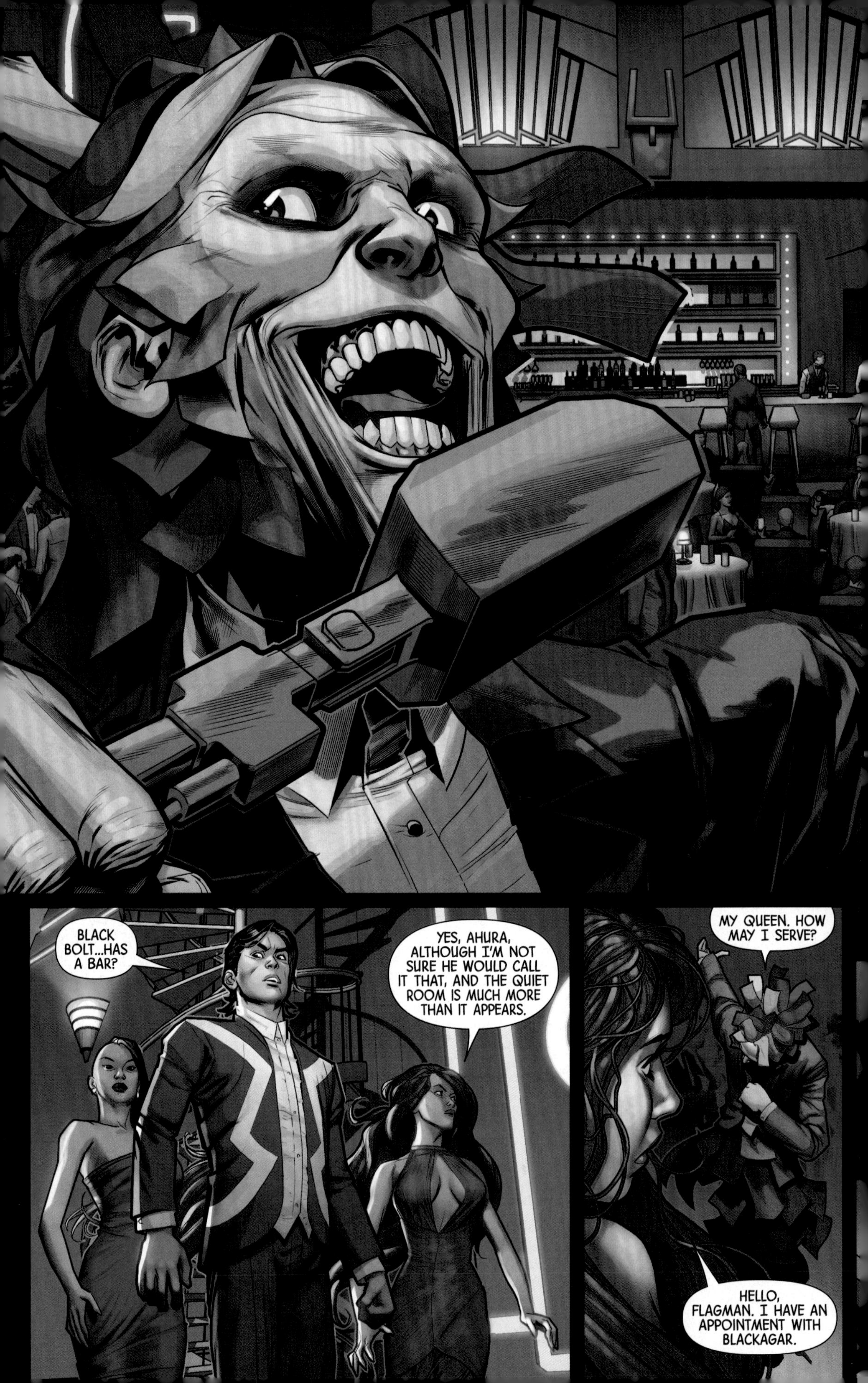
BLACK BOLT...HAS A BAR?
YES, AHURA, ALTHOUGH I'M NOT SURE HE WOULD CALL IT THAT, AND THE QUIET ROOM IS MUCH MORE THAN IT APPEARS.
MY QUEEN. HOW MAY I SERVE?
HELLO, FLAGMAN. I HAVE AN APPOINTMENT WITH BLACKAGAR.

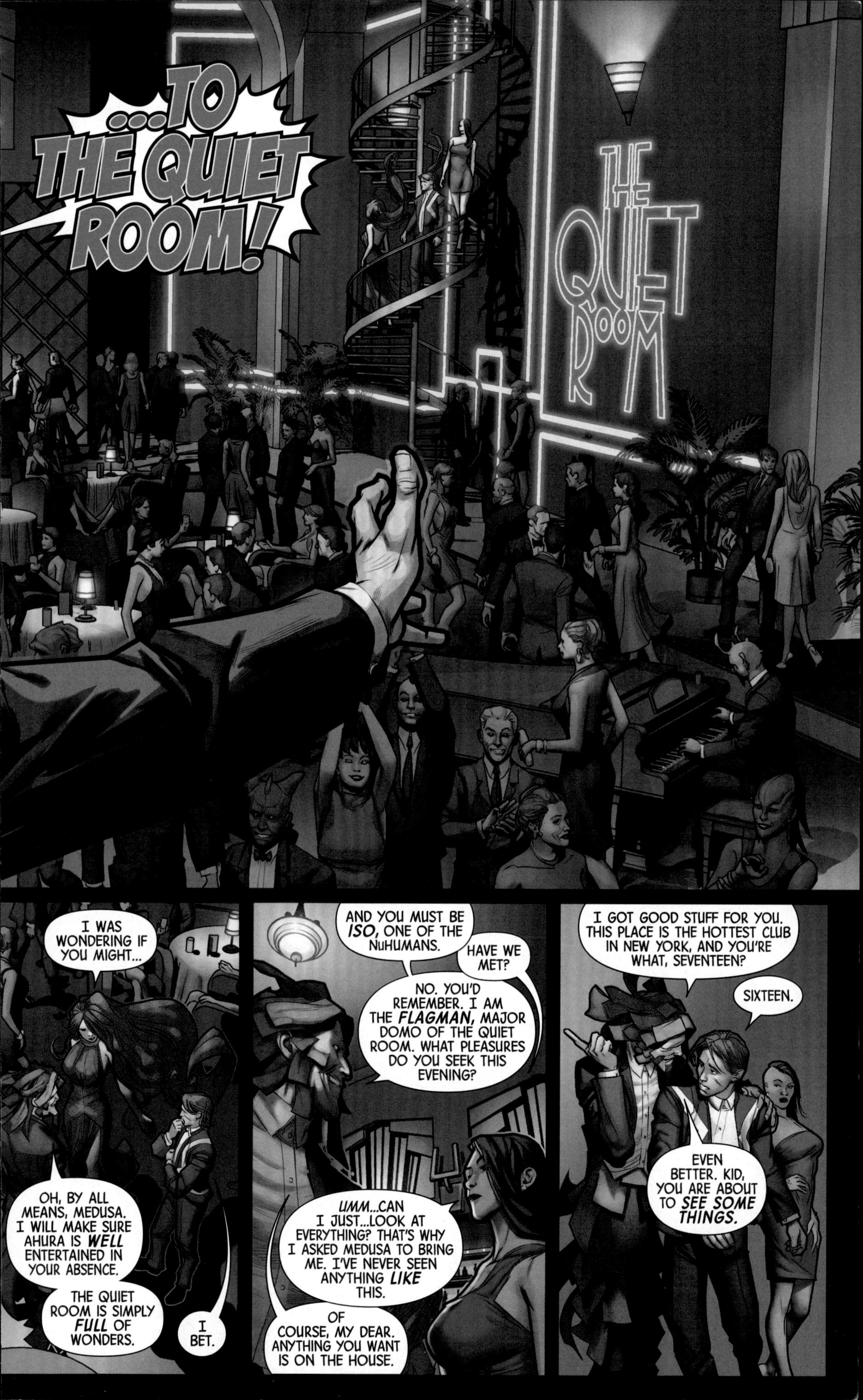
...TO THE QUIET ROOM!
THE QUIET ROOM
I WAS WONDERING IF YOU MIGHT...
OH, BY ALL MEANS, MEDUSA. I WILL MAKE SURE AHURA IS WELL ENTERTAINED IN YOUR ABSENCE.
THE QUIET ROOM IS SIMPLY FULL OF WONDERS.
I BET.
AND YOU MUST BE ISO, ONE OF THE NuHUMANS.
HAVE WE MET?
NO. YOU'D REMEMBER. I AM THE FLAGMAN, MAJOR DOMO OF THE QUIET ROOM. WHAT PLEASURES DO YOU SEEK THIS EVENING?
UMM...CAN I JUST...LOOK AT EVERYTHING? THAT'S WHY I ASKED MEDUSA TO BRING ME. I'VE NEVER SEEN ANYTHING LIKE THIS.
OF COURSE, MY DEAR. ANYTHING YOU WANT IS ON THE HOUSE.
I GOT GOOD STUFF FOR YOU. THIS PLACE IS THE HOTTEST CLUB IN NEW YORK, AND YOU'RE WHAT, SEVENTEEN?
SIXTEEN.
EVEN BETTER. KID, YOU ARE ABOUT TO SEE SOME THINGS.

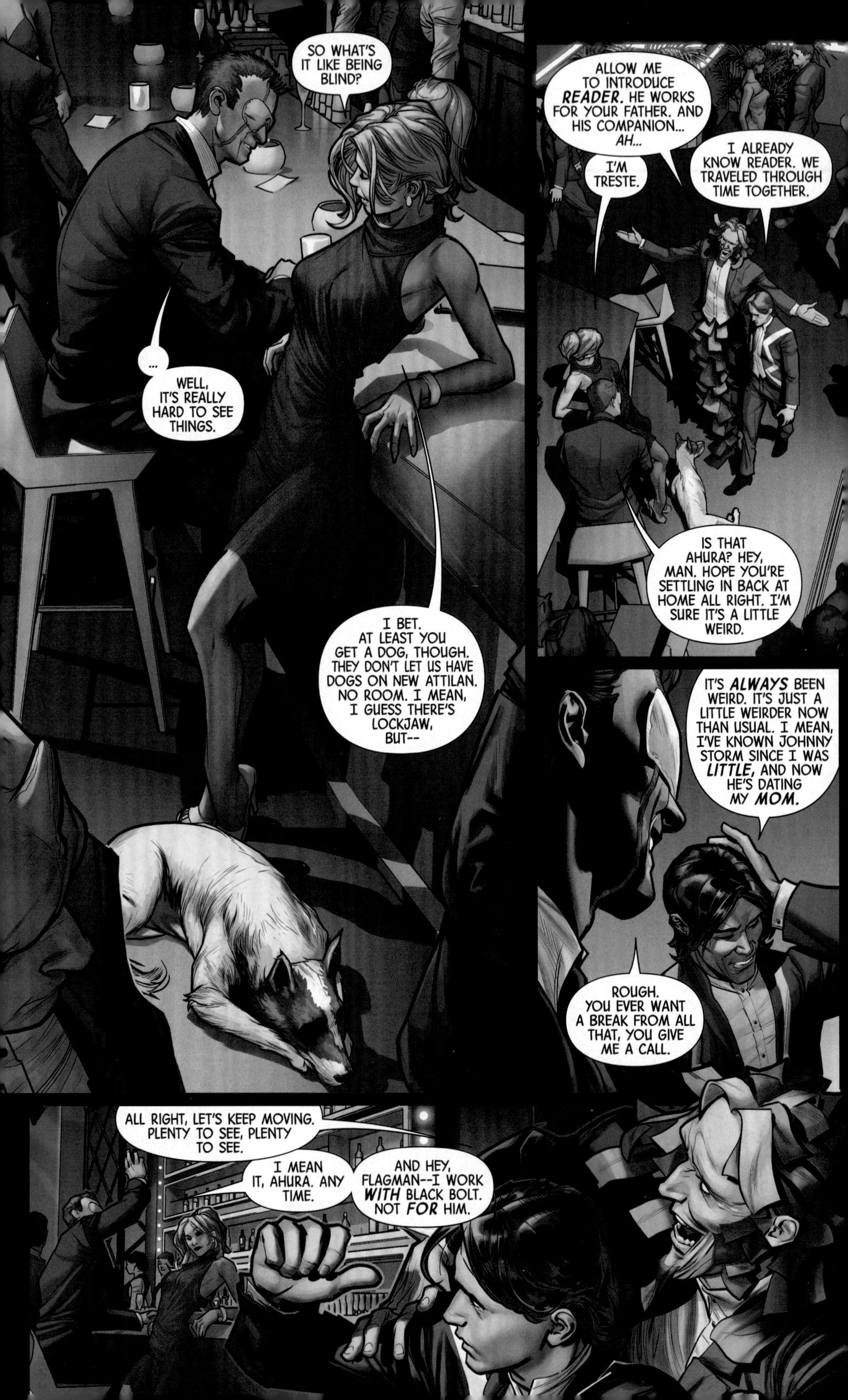
SO WHAT'S IT LIKE BEING BLIND?
... WELL, IT'S REALLY HARD TO SEE THINGS.
I BET. AT LEAST YOU GET A DOG, THOUGH. THEY DON'T LET US HAVE DOGS ON NEW ATTILAN. NO ROOM. I MEAN, I GUESS THERE'S LOCKJAW, BUT--
ALLOW ME TO INTRODUCE READER. HE WORKS FOR YOUR FATHER. AND HIS COMPANION... AH...
I'M TRESTE.
I ALREADY KNOW READER. WE TRAVELED THROUGH TIME TOGETHER.
IS THAT AHURA? HEY, MAN. HOPE YOU'RE SETTLING IN BACK AT HOME ALL RIGHT. I'M SURE IT'S A LITTLE WEIRD.
IT'S ALWAYS BEEN WEIRD. IT'S JUST A LITTLE WEIRDER NOW THAN USUAL. I MEAN, I'VE KNOWN JOHNNY STORM SINCE I WAS LITTLE, AND NOW HE'S DATING MY MOM.
ROUGH. YOU EVER WANT A BREAK FROM ALL THAT, YOU GIVE ME A CALL.
ALL RIGHT, LET'S KEEP MOVING. PLENTY TO SEE, PLENTY TO SEE.
I MEAN IT, AHURA. ANY TIME.
AND HEY, FLAGMAN--I WORK WITH BLACK BOLT. NOT FOR HIM.

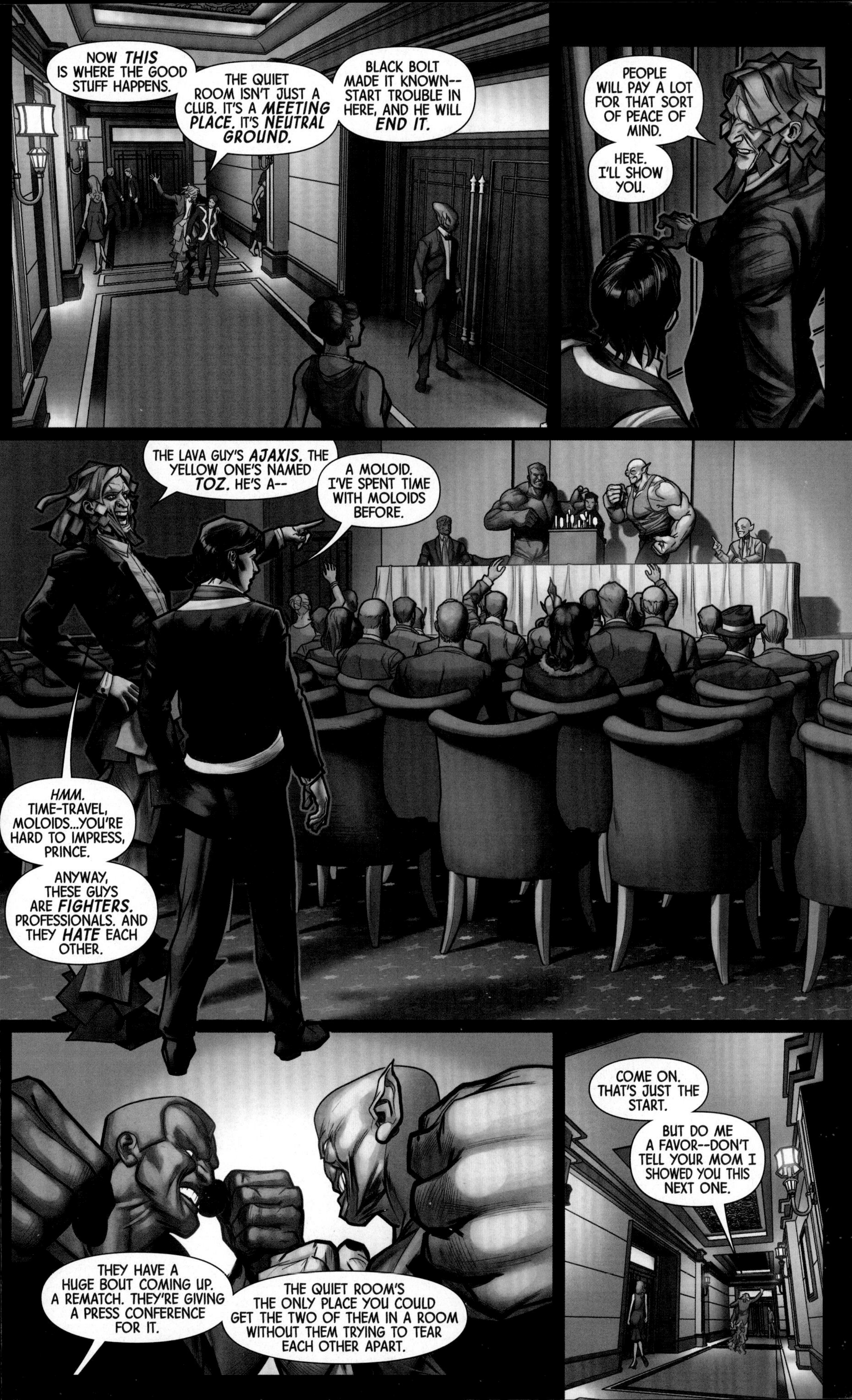
NOW THIS IS WHERE THE GOOD STUFF HAPPENS.
THE QUIET ROOM ISN'T JUST A CLUB. IT'S A MEETING PLACE. IT'S NEUTRAL GROUND.
BLACK BOLT MADE IT KNOWN-- START TROUBLE IN HERE, AND HE WILL END IT.
PEOPLE WILL PAY A LOT FOR THAT SORT OF PEACE OF MIND.
HERE. I'LL SHOW YOU.
THE LAVA GUY'S AJAXIS. THE YELLOW ONE'S NAMED TOZ. HE'S A--
A MOLOID. I'VE SPENT TIME WITH MOLOIDS BEFORE.
HMM. TIME-TRAVEL, MOLOIDS...YOU'RE HARD TO IMPRESS, PRINCE.
ANYWAY, THESE GUYS ARE FIGHTERS. PROFESSIONALS. AND THEY HATE EACH OTHER.
THEY HAVE A HUGE BOUT COMING UP. A REMATCH. THEY'RE GIVING A PRESS CONFERENCE FOR IT.
THE QUIET ROOM'S THE ONLY PLACE YOU COULD GET THE TWO OF THEM IN A ROOM WITHOUT THEM TRYING TO TEAR EACH OTHER APART.
COME ON. THAT'S JUST THE START.
BUT DO ME A FAVOR--DON'T TELL YOUR MOM I SHOWED YOU THIS NEXT ONE.

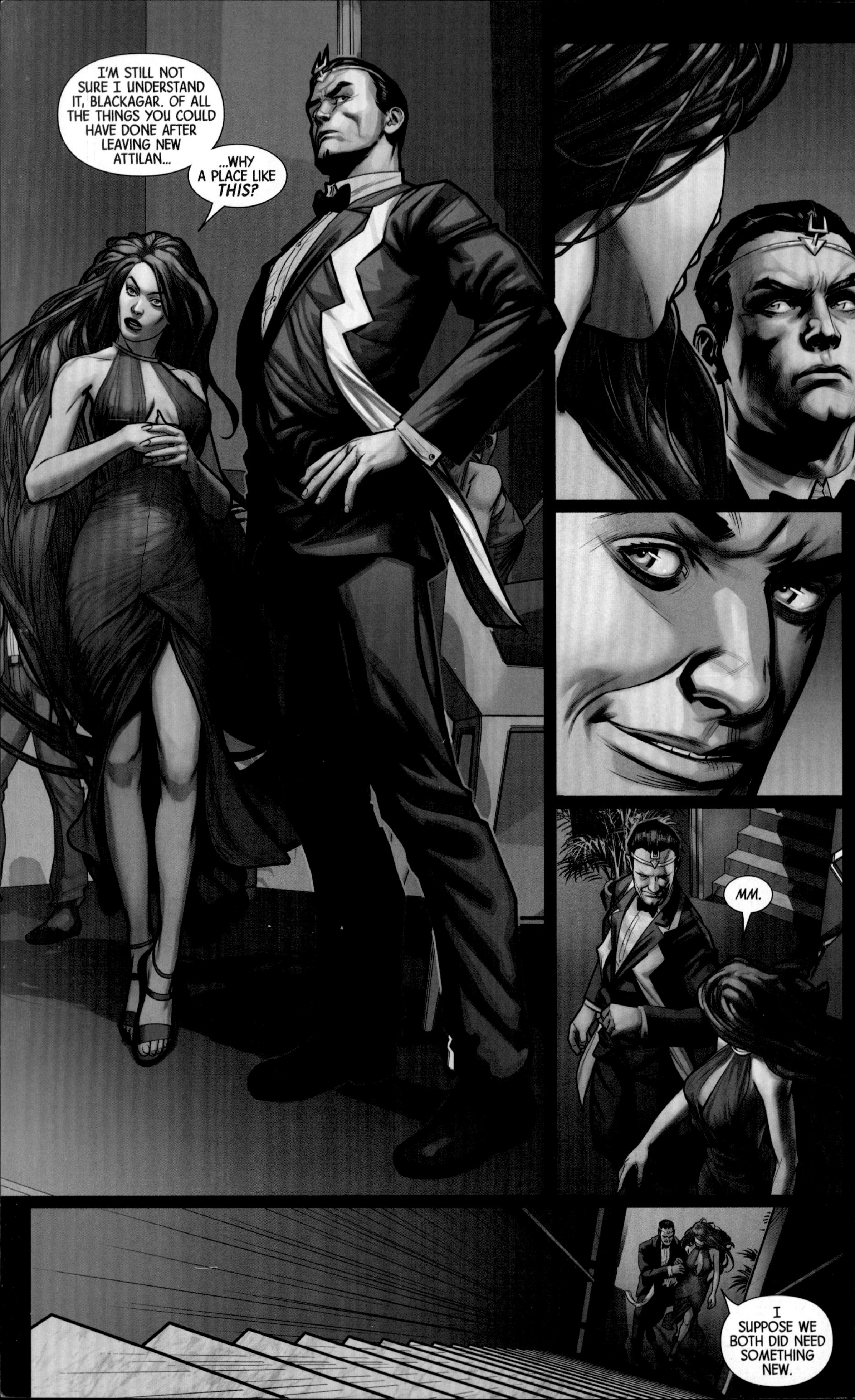
I'M STILL NOT SURE I UNDERSTAND IT, BLACKAGAR. OF ALL THE THINGS YOU COULD HAVE DONE AFTER LEAVING NEW ATTILAN...
...WHY A PLACE LIKE THIS?
MM.
I SUPPOSE WE BOTH DID NEED SOMETHING NEW.

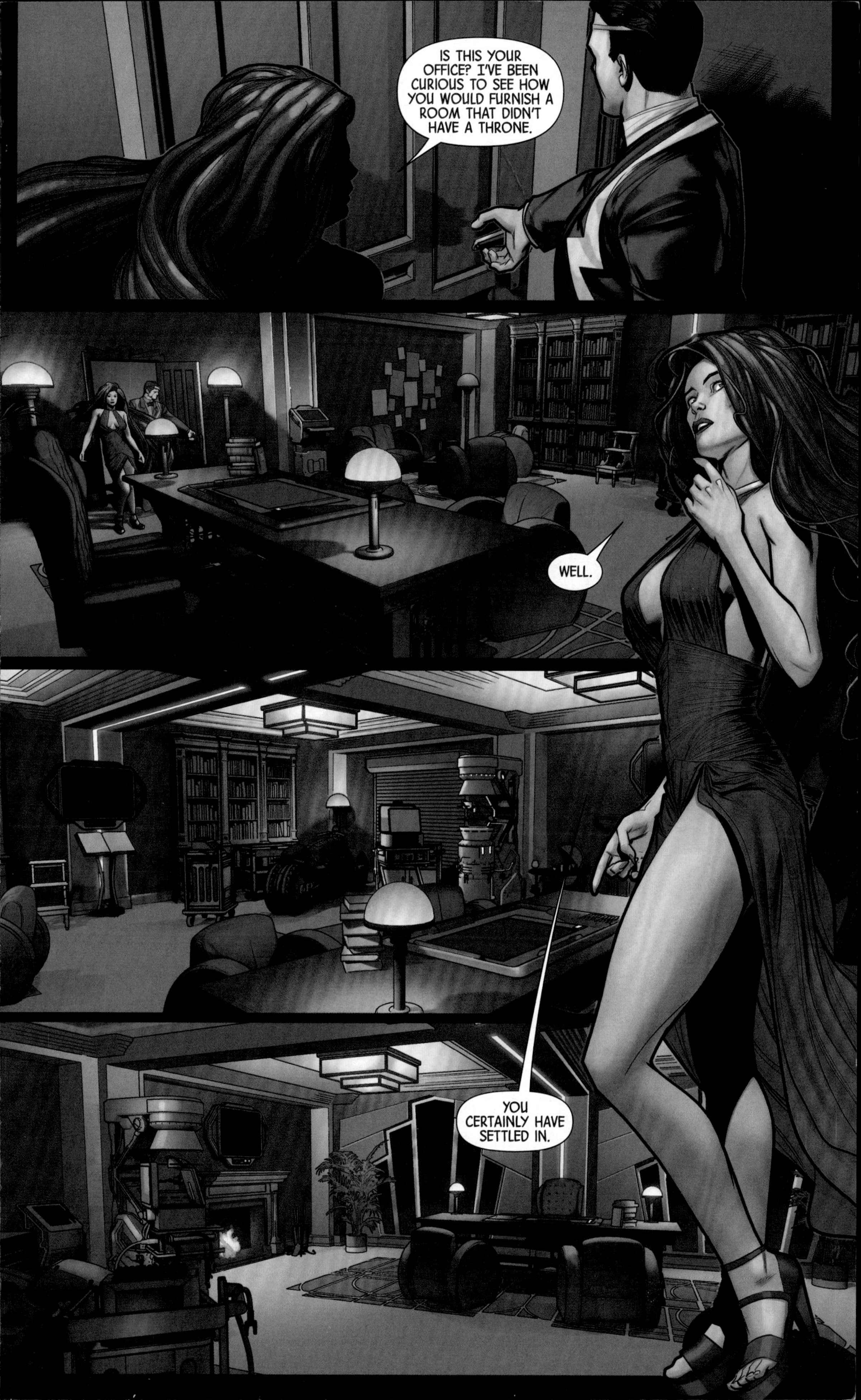
IS THIS YOUR OFFICE? I'VE BEEN CURIOUS TO SEE HOW YOU WOULD FURNISH A ROOM THAT DIDN'T HAVE A THRONE.
WELL.
YOU CERTAINLY HAVE SETTLED IN.

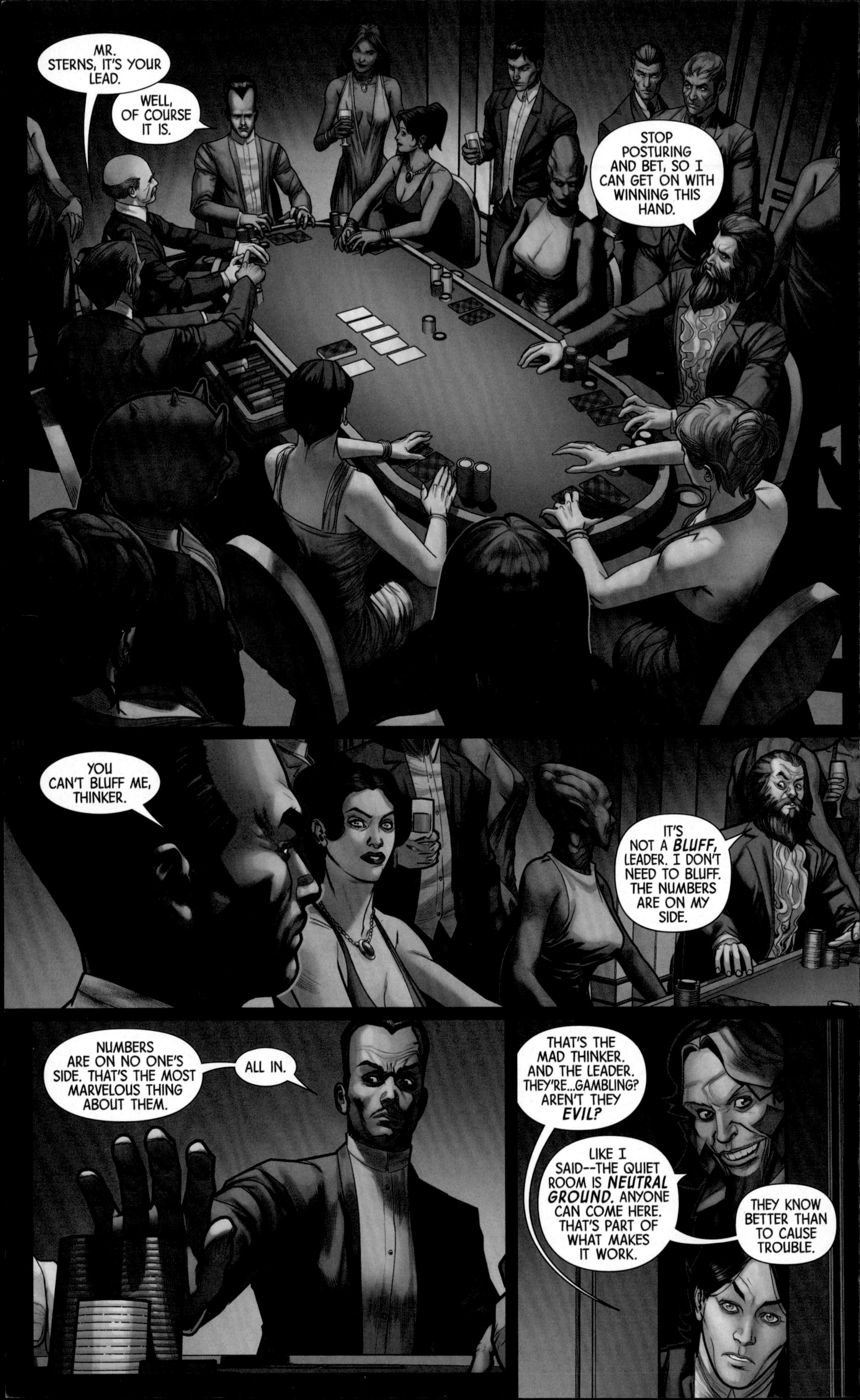
MR. STERNS, IT'S YOUR LEAD.
WELL, OF COURSE IT IS.
STOP POSTURING AND BET, SO I CAN GET ON WITH WINNING THIS HAND.
YOU CAN'T BLUFF ME, THINKER.
IT'S NOT A BLUFF, LEADER. I DON'T NEED TO BLUFF. THE NUMBERS ARE ON MY SIDE.
NUMBERS ARE ON NO ONE'S SIDE. THAT'S THE MOST MARVELOUS THING ABOUT THEM.
ALL IN.
THAT'S THE MAD THINKER. AND THE LEADER. THEY'RE...GAMBLING? AREN'T THEY EVIL?
LIKE I SAID--THE QUIET ROOM IS NEUTRAL GROUND. ANYONE CAN COME HERE. THAT'S PART OF WHAT MAKES IT WORK.
THEY KNOW BETTER THAN TO CAUSE TROUBLE.

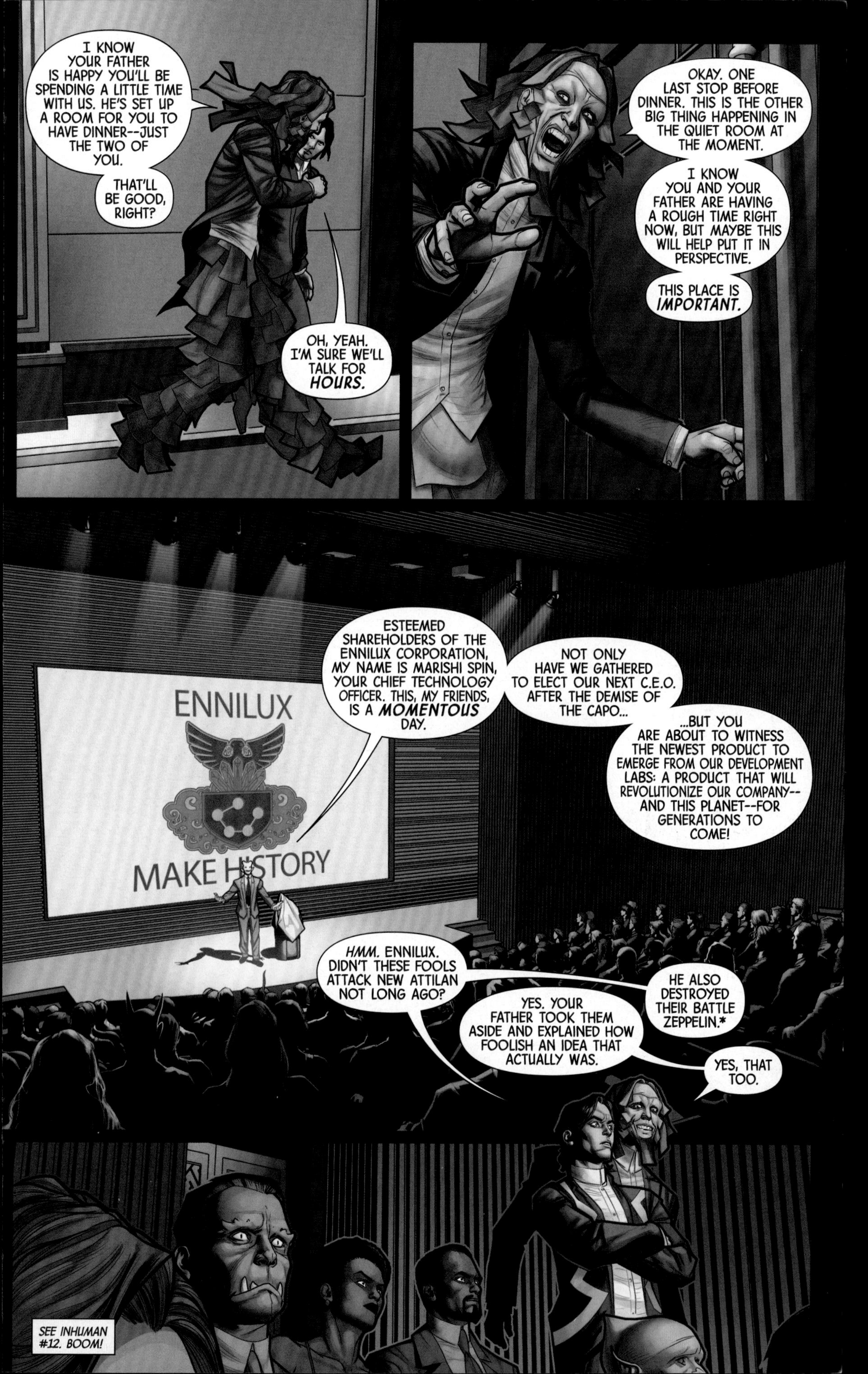
I KNOW YOUR FATHER IS HAPPY YOU'LL BE SPENDING A LITTLE TIME WITH US. HE'S SET UP A ROOM FOR YOU TO HAVE DINNER--JUST THE TWO OF YOU.
THAT'LL BE GOOD, RIGHT?
OH, YEAH. I'M SURE WE'LL TALK FOR HOURS.
OKAY. ONE LAST STOP BEFORE DINNER. THIS IS THE OTHER BIG THING HAPPENING IN THE QUIET ROOM AT THE MOMENT.
I KNOW YOU AND YOUR FATHER ARE HAVING A ROUGH TIME RIGHT NOW, BUT MAYBE THIS WILL HELP PUT IT IN PERSPECTIVE.
THIS PLACE IS IMPORTANT.
ENNILUX
MAKE HISTORY
ESTEEMED SHAREHOLDERS OF THE ENNILUX CORPORATION, MY NAME IS MARISHI SPIN, YOUR CHIEF TECHNOLOGY OFFICER. THIS, MY FRIENDS, IS A MOMENTOUS DAY.
NOT ONLY HAVE WE GATHERED TO ELECT OUR NEXT C.E.O. AFTER THE DEMISE OF THE CAPO...
...BUT YOU ARE ABOUT TO WITNESS THE NEWEST PRODUCT TO EMERGE FROM OUR DEVELOPMENT LABS: A PRODUCT THAT WILL REVOLUTIONIZE OUR COMPANY--AND THIS PLANET--FOR GENERATIONS TO COME!
HMM. ENNILUX. DIDN'T THESE FOOLS ATTACK NEW ATTILAN NOT LONG AGO?
YES. YOUR FATHER TOOK THEM ASIDE AND EXPLAINED HOW FOOLISH AN IDEA THAT ACTUALLY WAS.
HE ALSO DESTROYED THEIR BATTLE ZEPPELIN.*
YES, THAT TOO.
SEE INHUMAN #12. BOOM!

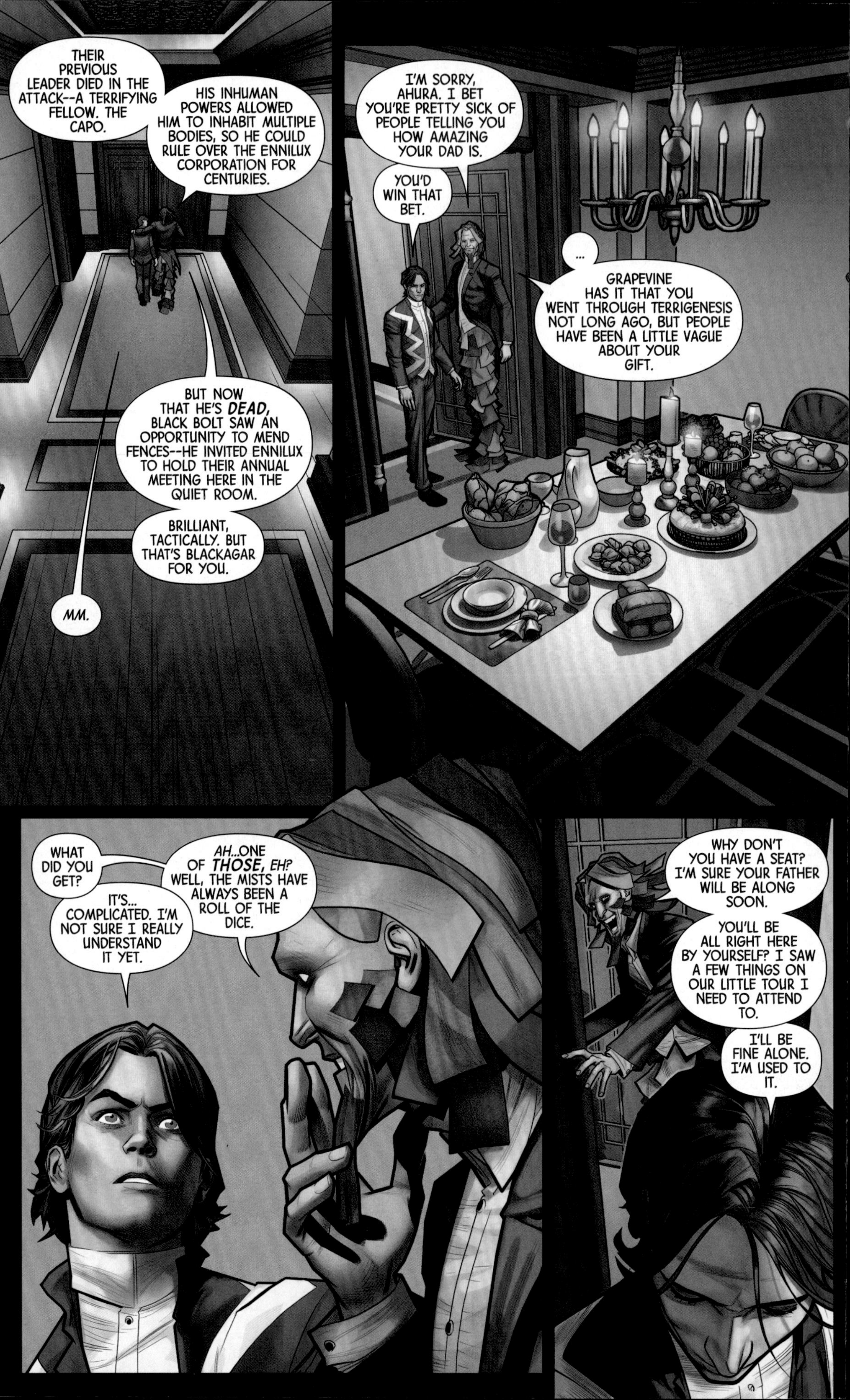
THEIR PREVIOUS LEADER DIED IN THE ATTACK--A TERRIFYING FELLOW. THE CAPO.
HIS INHUMAN POWERS ALLOWED HIM TO INHABIT MULTIPLE BODIES, SO HE COULD RULE OVER THE ENNILUX CORPORATION FOR CENTURIES.
BUT NOW THAT HE'S DEAD, BLACK BOLT SAW AN OPPORTUNITY TO MEND FENCES--HE INVITED ENNILUX TO HOLD THEIR ANNUAL MEETING HERE IN THE QUIET ROOM.
BRILLIANT, TACTICALLY. BUT THAT'S BLACKAGAR FOR YOU.
MM.
I'M SORRY, AHURA. I BET YOU'RE PRETTY SICK OF PEOPLE TELLING YOU HOW AMAZING YOUR DAD IS.
YOU'D WIN THAT BET.
...
GRAPEVINE HAS IT THAT YOU WENT THROUGH TERRIGENESIS NOT LONG AGO, BUT PEOPLE HAVE BEEN A LITTLE VAGUE ABOUT YOUR GIFT.
WHAT DID YOU GET?
IT'S... COMPLICATED. I'M NOT SURE I REALLY UNDERSTAND IT YET.
AH...ONE OF THOSE, EH? WELL, THE MISTS HAVE ALWAYS BEEN A ROLL OF THE DICE.
WHY DON'T YOU HAVE A SEAT? I'M SURE YOUR FATHER WILL BE ALONG SOON.
YOU'LL BE ALL RIGHT HERE BY YOURSELF? I SAW A FEW THINGS ON OUR LITTLE TOUR I NEED TO ATTEND TO.
I'LL BE FINE ALONE. I'M USED TO IT.

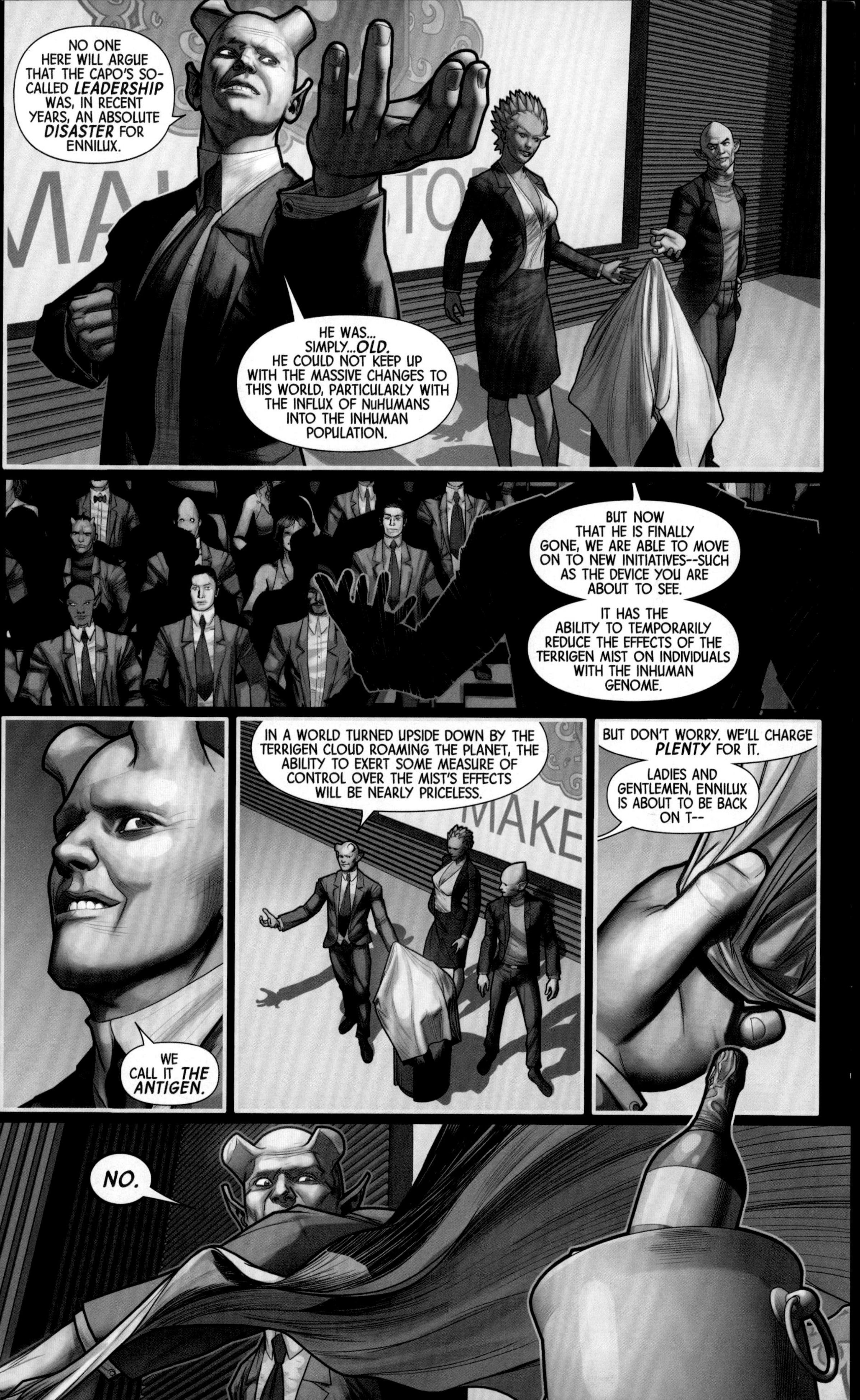
NO ONE HERE WILL ARGUE THAT THE CAPO'S SO-CALLED LEADERSHIP WAS, IN RECENT YEARS, AN ABSOLUTE DISASTER FOR ENNILUX.
HE WAS... SIMPLY...OLD. HE COULD NOT KEEP UP WITH THE MASSIVE CHANGES TO THIS WORLD, PARTICULARLY WITH THE INFLUX OF NuHUMANS INTO THE INHUMAN POPULATION.
BUT NOW THAT HE IS FINALLY GONE, WE ARE ABLE TO MOVE ON TO NEW INITIATIVES--SUCH AS THE DEVICE YOU ARE ABOUT TO SEE.
IT HAS THE ABILITY TO TEMPORARILY REDUCE THE EFFECTS OF THE TERRIGEN MIST ON INDIVIDUALS WITH THE INHUMAN GENOME.
WE CALL IT THE ANTIGEN.
IN A WORLD TURNED UPSIDE DOWN BY THE TERRIGEN CLOUD ROAMING THE PLANET, THE ABILITY TO EXERT SOME MEASURE OF CONTROL OVER THE MIST'S EFFECTS WILL BE NEARLY PRICELESS.
MAKE
BUT DON'T WORRY. WE'LL CHARGE PLENTY FOR IT.
LADIES AND GENTLEMEN, ENNILUX IS ABOUT TO BE BACK ON T--
NO.

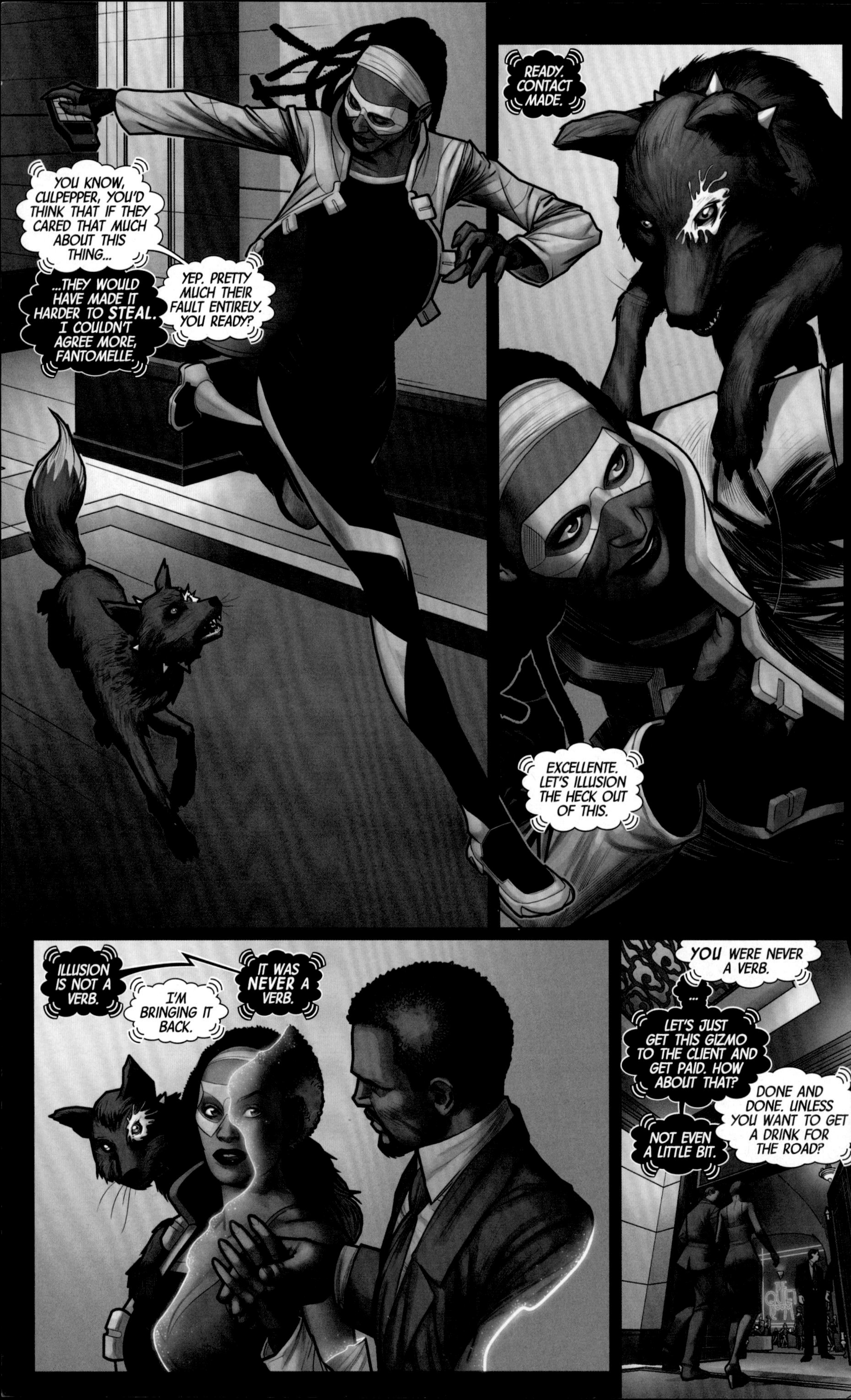
YOU KNOW, CULPEPPER, YOU'D THINK THAT IF THEY CARED THAT MUCH ABOUT THIS THING...
...THEY WOULD HAVE MADE IT HARDER TO STEAL. I COULDN'T AGREE MORE, FANTOMELLE.
YEP. PRETTY MUCH THEIR FAULT ENTIRELY. YOU READY?
READY. CONTACT MADE.
EXCELLENTE. LET'S ILLUSION THE HECK OUT OF THIS.
ILLUSION IS NOT A VERB.
I'M BRINGING IT BACK.
IT WAS NEVER A VERB.
YOU WERE NEVER A VERB.
...
LET'S JUST GET THIS GIZMO TO THE CLIENT AND GET PAID. HOW ABOUT THAT?
DONE AND DONE. UNLESS YOU WANT TO GET A DRINK FOR THE ROAD?
NOT EVEN A LITTLE BIT.

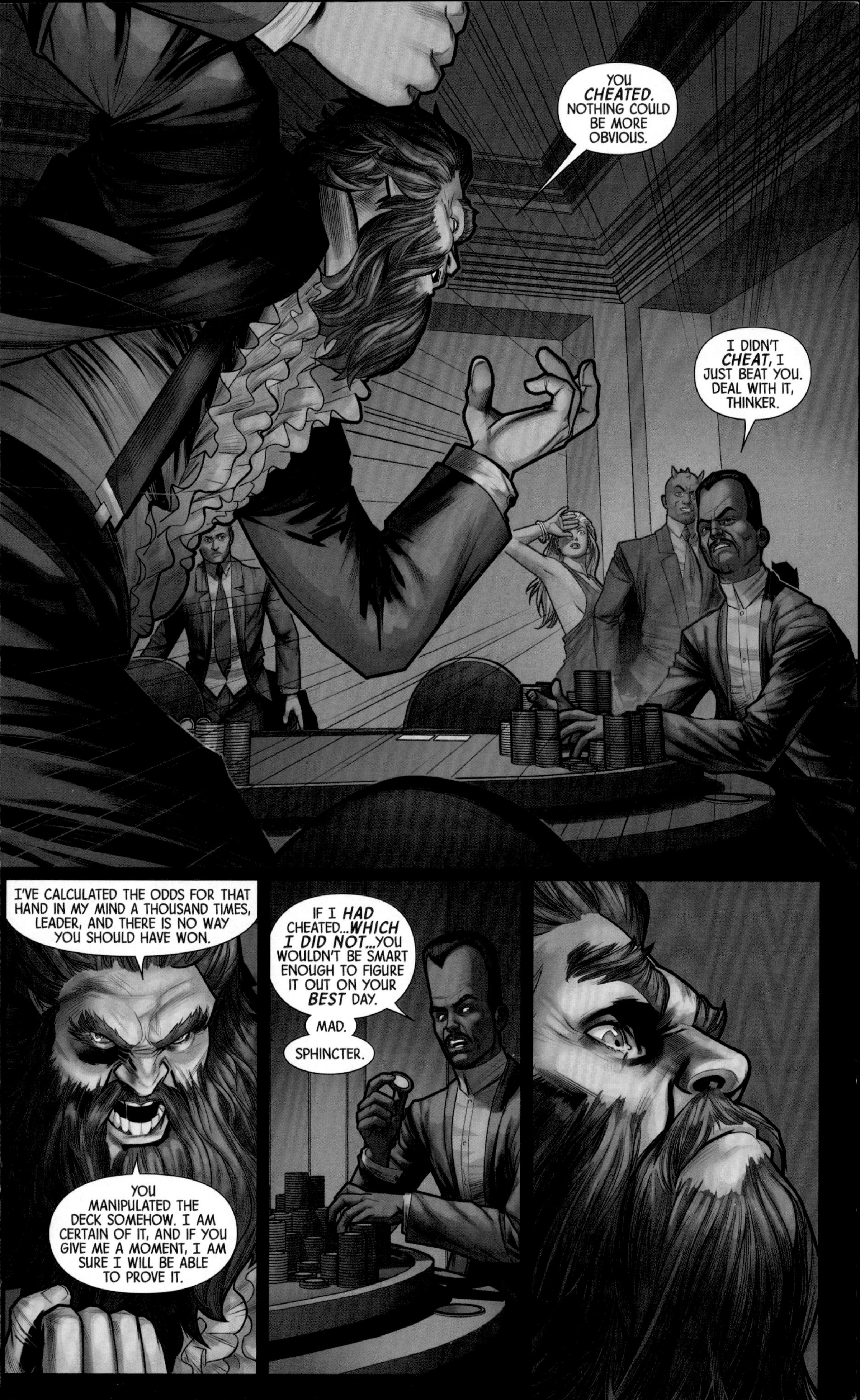
YOU CHEATED. NOTHING COULD BE MORE OBVIOUS.
I DIDN'T CHEAT, I JUST BEAT YOU. DEAL WITH IT, THINKER.
I'VE CALCULATED THE ODDS FOR THAT HAND IN MY MIND A THOUSAND TIMES, LEADER, AND THERE IS NO WAY YOU SHOULD HAVE WON.
YOU MANIPULATED THE DECK SOMEHOW. I AM CERTAIN OF IT, AND IF YOU GIVE ME A MOMENT, I AM SURE I WILL BE ABLE TO PROVE IT.
IF I HAD CHEATED...WHICH I DID NOT...YOU WOULDN'T BE SMART ENOUGH TO FIGURE IT OUT ON YOUR BEST DAY.
MAD.
SPHINCTER.

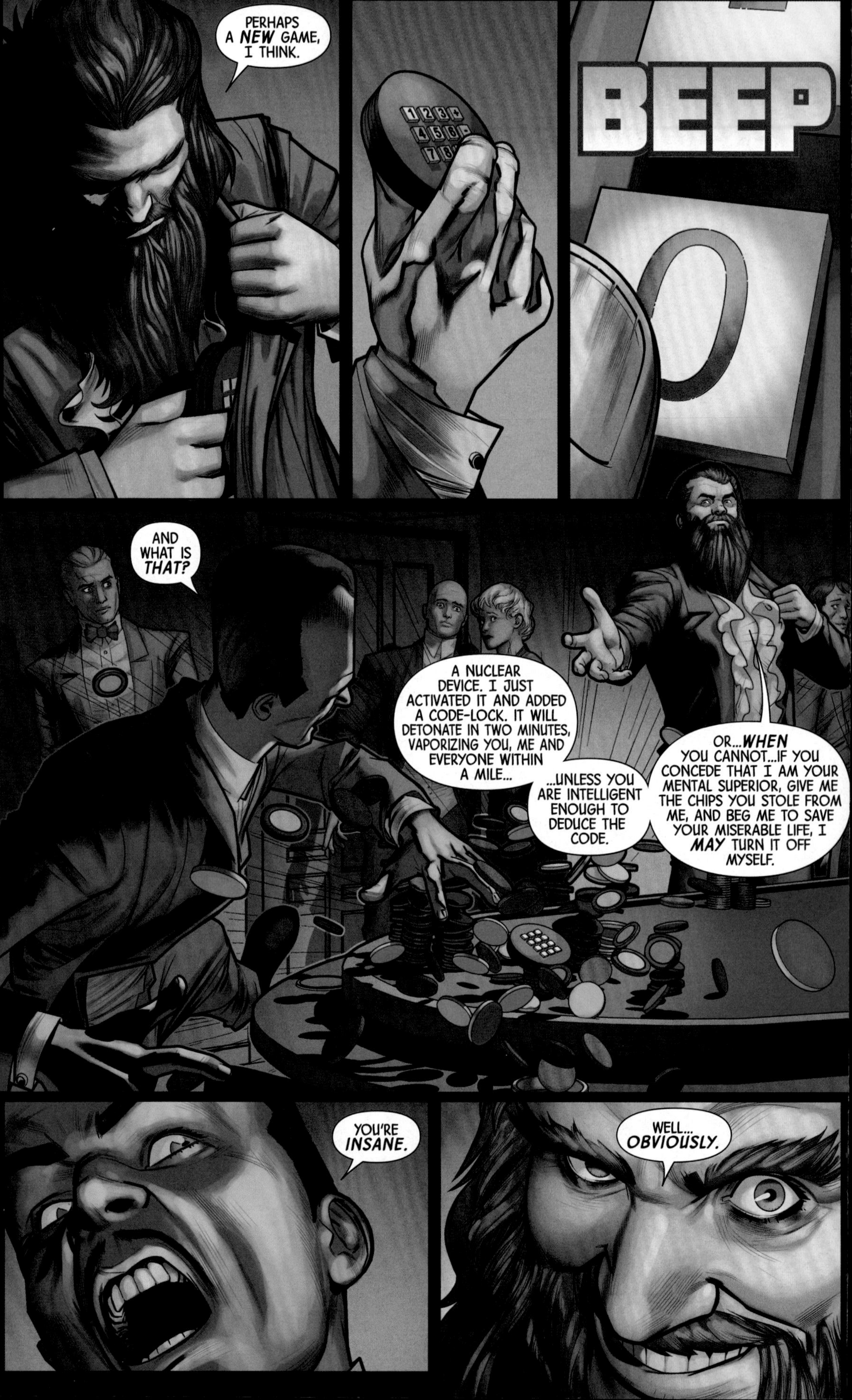
PERHAPS A NEW GAME, I THINK.
BEEP
AND WHAT IS THAT?
A NUCLEAR DEVICE. I JUST ACTIVATED IT AND ADDED A CODE-LOCK. IT WILL DETONATE IN TWO MINUTES, VAPORIZING YOU, ME AND EVERYONE WITHIN A MILE...
...UNLESS YOU ARE INTELLIGENT ENOUGH TO DEDUCE THE CODE.
OR...WHEN YOU CANNOT...IF YOU CONCEDE THAT I AM YOUR MENTAL SUPERIOR, GIVE ME THE CHIPS YOU STOLE FROM ME, AND BEG ME TO SAVE YOUR MISERABLE LIFE, I MAY TURN IT OFF MYSELF.
YOU'RE INSANE.
WELL... OBVIOUSLY.

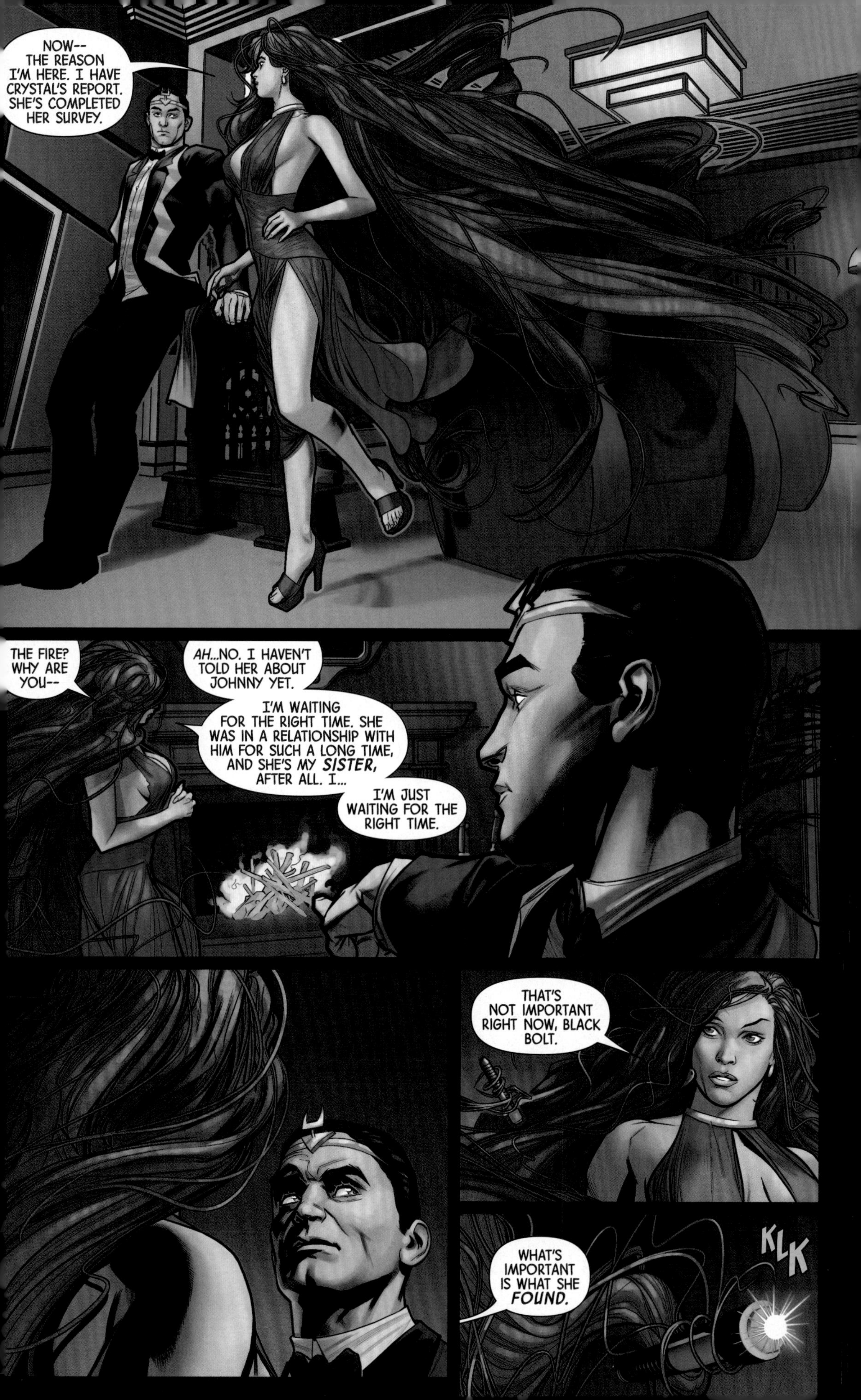
NOW-- THE REASON I'M HERE. I HAVE CRYSTAL'S REPORT. SHE'S COMPLETED HER SURVEY.
THE FIRE? WHY ARE YOU--
AH...NO. I HAVEN'T TOLD HER ABOUT JOHNNY YET.
I'M WAITING FOR THE RIGHT TIME. SHE WAS IN A RELATIONSHIP WITH HIM FOR SUCH A LONG TIME, AND SHE'S MY SISTER, AFTER ALL. I...
I'M JUST WAITING FOR THE RIGHT TIME.
THAT'S NOT IMPORTANT RIGHT NOW, BLACK BOLT.
WHAT'S IMPORTANT IS WHAT SHE FOUND.
KLK

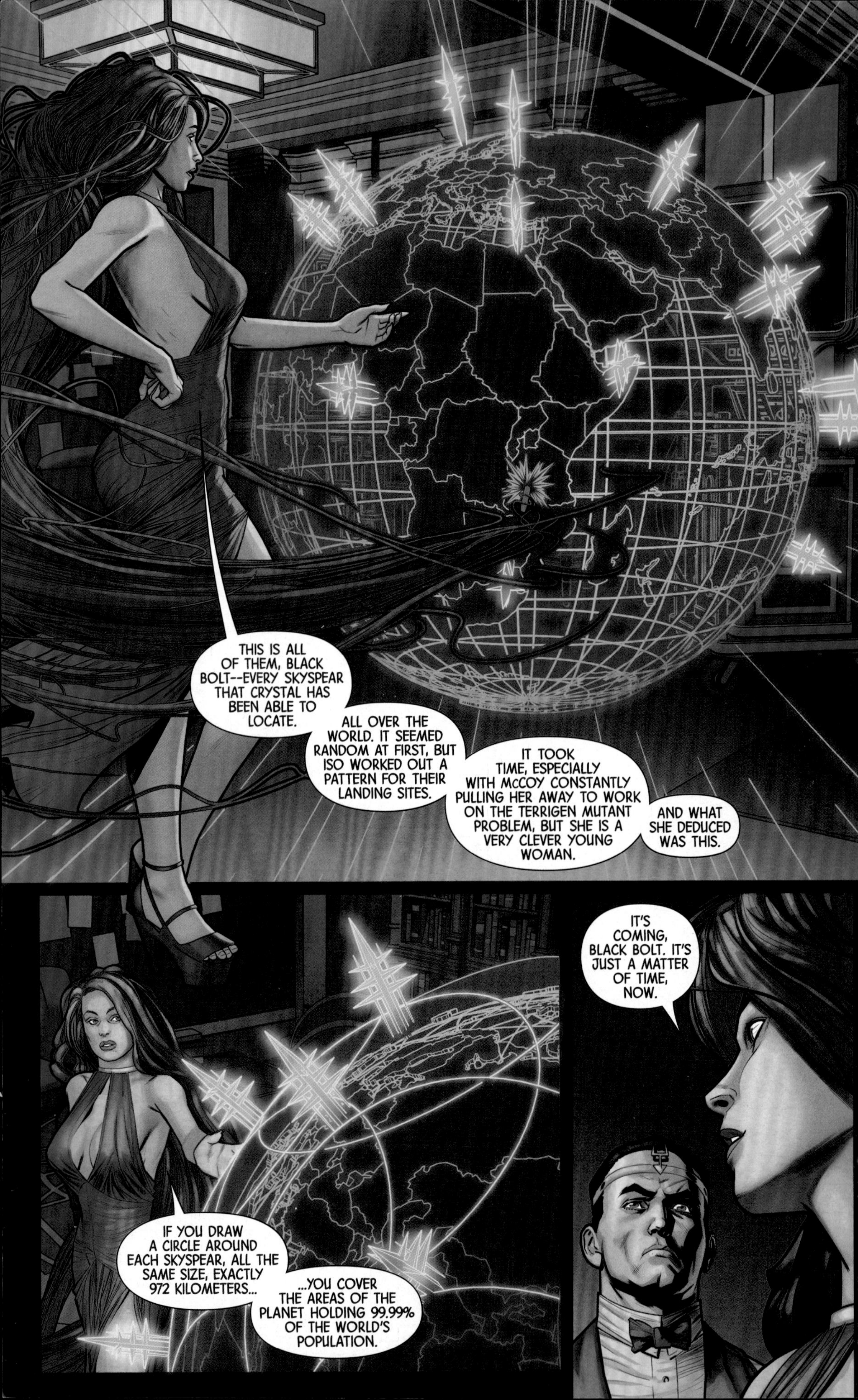
THIS IS ALL OF THEM, BLACK BOLT--EVERY SKYSPEAR THAT CRYSTAL HAS BEEN ABLE TO LOCATE.
ALL OVER THE WORLD. IT SEEMED RANDOM AT FIRST, BUT ISO WORKED OUT A PATTERN FOR THEIR LANDING SITES.
IT TOOK TIME, ESPECIALLY WITH McCOY CONSTANTLY PULLING HER AWAY TO WORK ON THE TERRIGEN MUTANT PROBLEM, BUT SHE IS A VERY CLEVER YOUNG WOMAN.
AND WHAT SHE DEDUCED WAS THIS.
IF YOU DRAW A CIRCLE AROUND EACH SKYSPEAR, ALL THE SAME SIZE, EXACTLY 972 KILOMETERS...
...YOU COVER THE AREAS OF THE PLANET HOLDING 99.99% OF THE WORLD'S POPULATION.
IT'S COMING, BLACK BOLT. IT'S JUST A MATTER OF TIME, NOW.

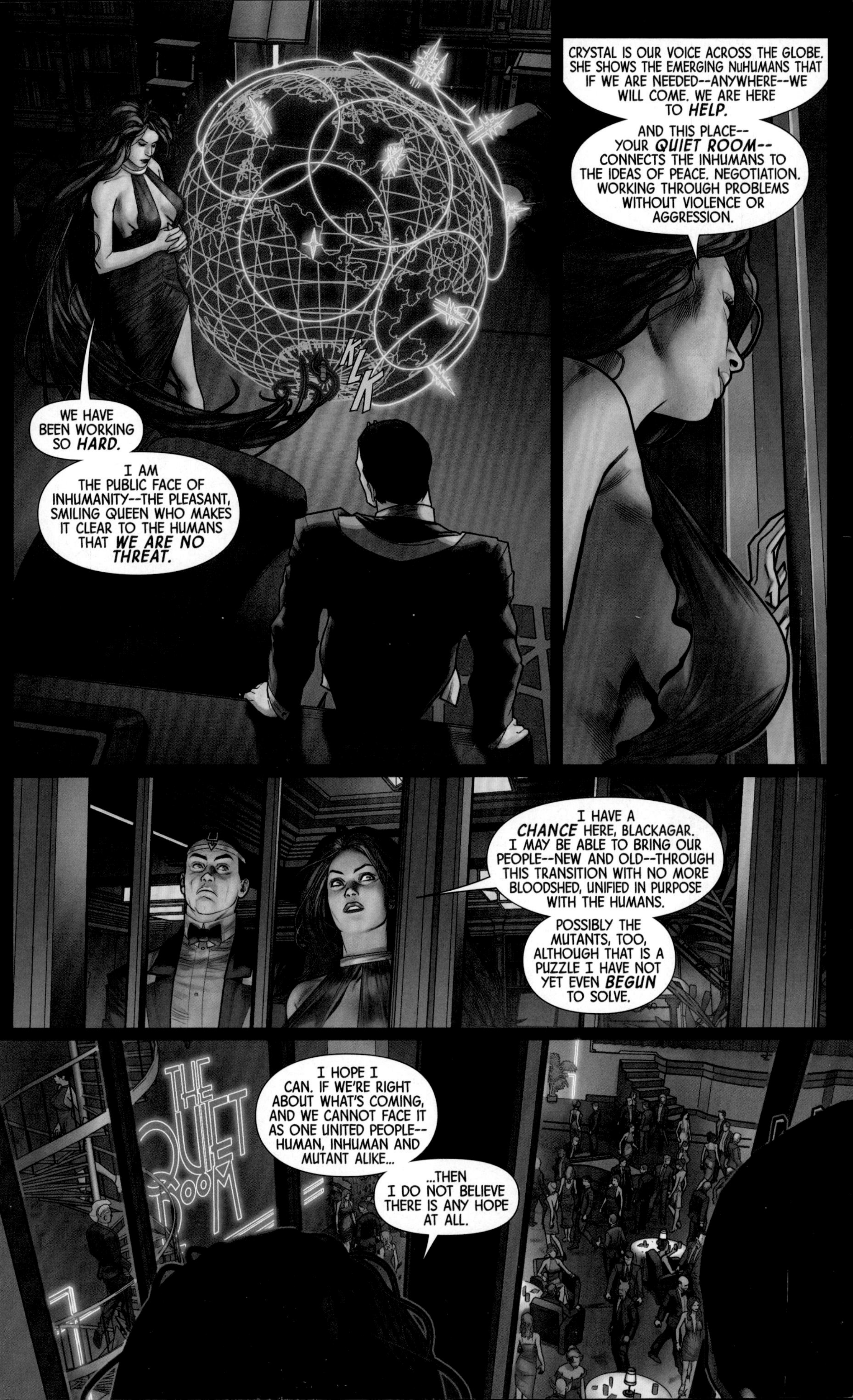
KLK
WE HAVE BEEN WORKING SO HARD.
I AM THE PUBLIC FACE OF INHUMANITY--THE PLEASANT, SMILING QUEEN WHO MAKES IT CLEAR TO THE HUMANS THAT WE ARE NO THREAT.
CRYSTAL IS OUR VOICE ACROSS THE GLOBE. SHE SHOWS THE EMERGING NuHUMANS THAT IF WE ARE NEEDED--ANYWHERE--WE WILL COME. WE ARE HERE TO HELP.
AND THIS PLACE-- YOUR QUIET ROOM-- CONNECTS THE INHUMANS TO THE IDEAS OF PEACE. NEGOTIATION. WORKING THROUGH PROBLEMS WITHOUT VIOLENCE OR AGGRESSION.
I HAVE A CHANCE HERE, BLACKAGAR. I MAY BE ABLE TO BRING OUR PEOPLE--NEW AND OLD--THROUGH THIS TRANSITION WITH NO MORE BLOODSHED, UNIFIED IN PURPOSE WITH THE HUMANS.
POSSIBLY THE MUTANTS, TOO, ALTHOUGH THAT IS A PUZZLE I HAVE NOT YET EVEN BEGUN TO SOLVE.
THE QUIET ROOM
I HOPE I CAN. IF WE'RE RIGHT ABOUT WHAT'S COMING, AND WE CANNOT FACE IT AS ONE UNITED PEOPLE-- HUMAN, INHUMAN AND MUTANT ALIKE...
...THEN I DO NOT BELIEVE THERE IS ANY HOPE AT ALL.

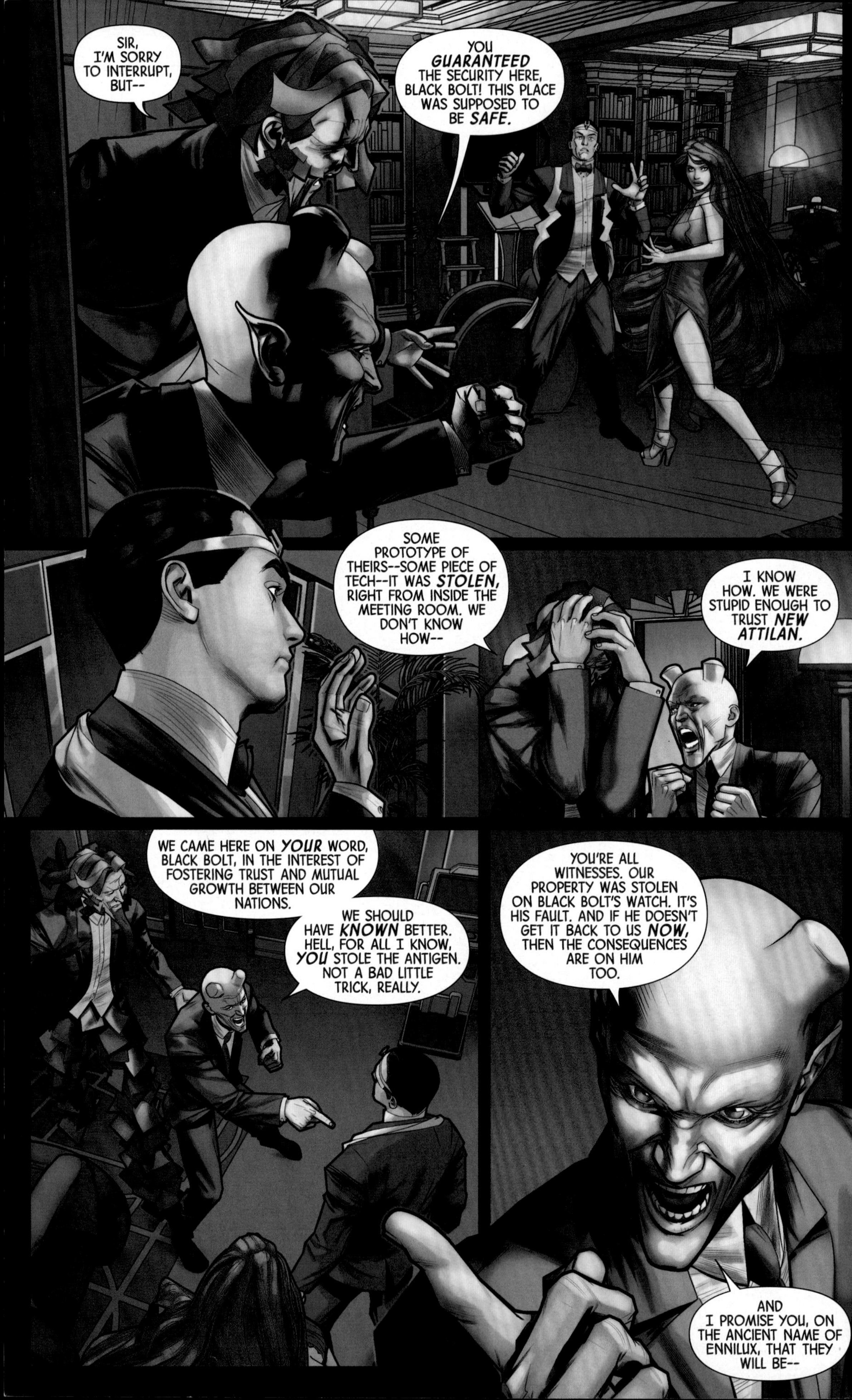
SIR, I'M SORRY TO INTERRUPT, BUT--
YOU GUARANTEED THE SECURITY HERE, BLACK BOLT! THIS PLACE WAS SUPPOSED TO BE SAFE.
SOME PROTOTYPE OF THEIRS--SOME PIECE OF TECH--IT WAS STOLEN, RIGHT FROM INSIDE THE MEETING ROOM. WE DON'T KNOW HOW--
I KNOW HOW. WE WERE STUPID ENOUGH TO TRUST NEW ATTILAN.
WE CAME HERE ON YOUR WORD, BLACK BOLT, IN THE INTEREST OF FOSTERING TRUST AND MUTUAL GROWTH BETWEEN OUR NATIONS.
WE SHOULD HAVE KNOWN BETTER. HELL, FOR ALL I KNOW, YOU STOLE THE ANTIGEN. NOT A BAD LITTLE TRICK, REALLY.
YOU'RE ALL WITNESSES. OUR PROPERTY WAS STOLEN ON BLACK BOLT'S WATCH. IT'S HIS FAULT. AND IF HE DOESN'T GET IT BACK TO US NOW, THEN THE CONSEQUENCES ARE ON HIM TOO.
AND I PROMISE YOU, ON THE ANCIENT NAME OF ENNILUX, THAT THEY WILL BE--

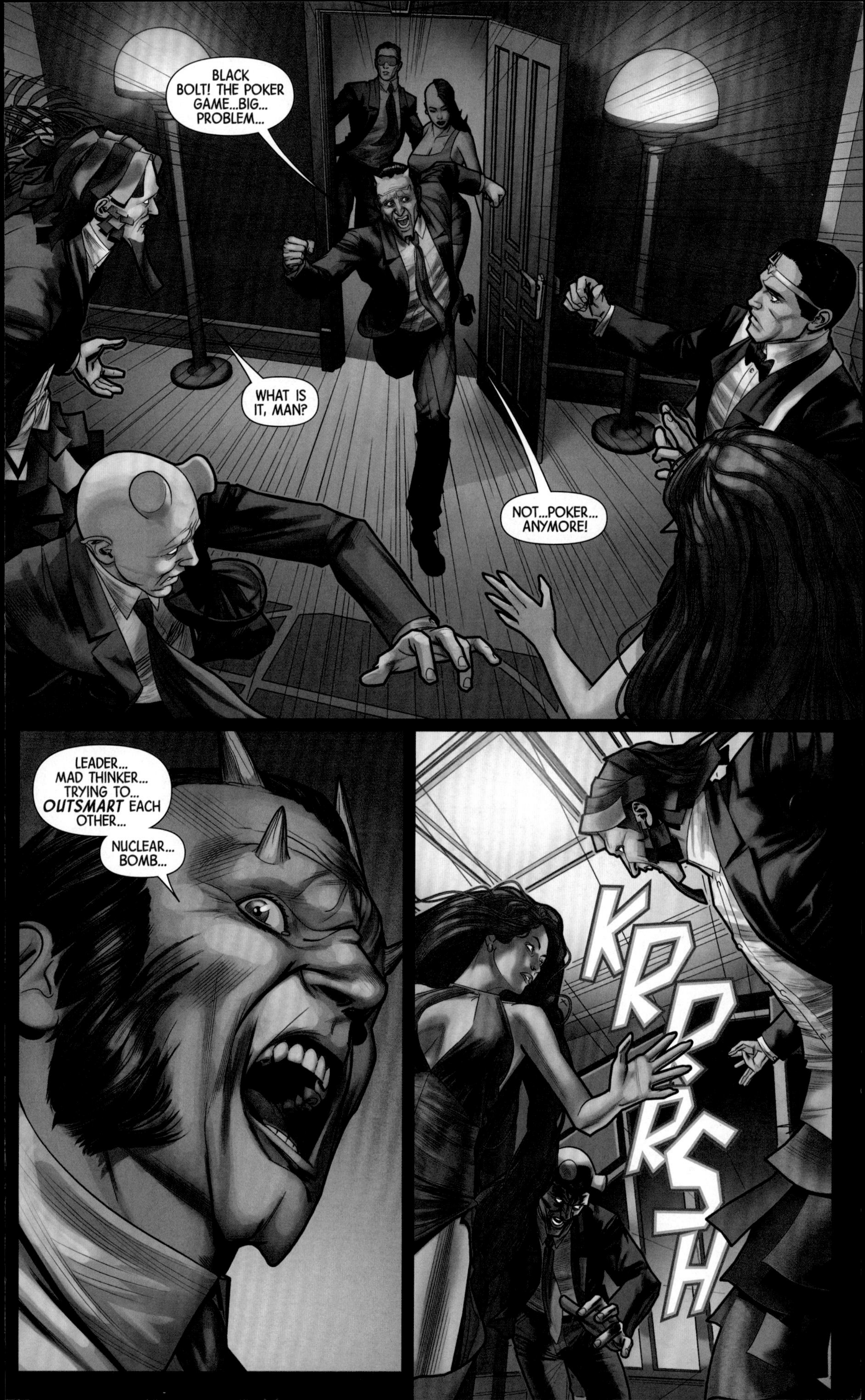
BLACK BOLT! THE POKER GAME...BIG... PROBLEM...
WHAT IS IT, MAN?
NOT...POKER... ANYMORE!
LEADER... MAD THINKER... TRYING TO... OUTSMART EACH OTHER...
NUCLEAR... BOMB...
KRRRSH

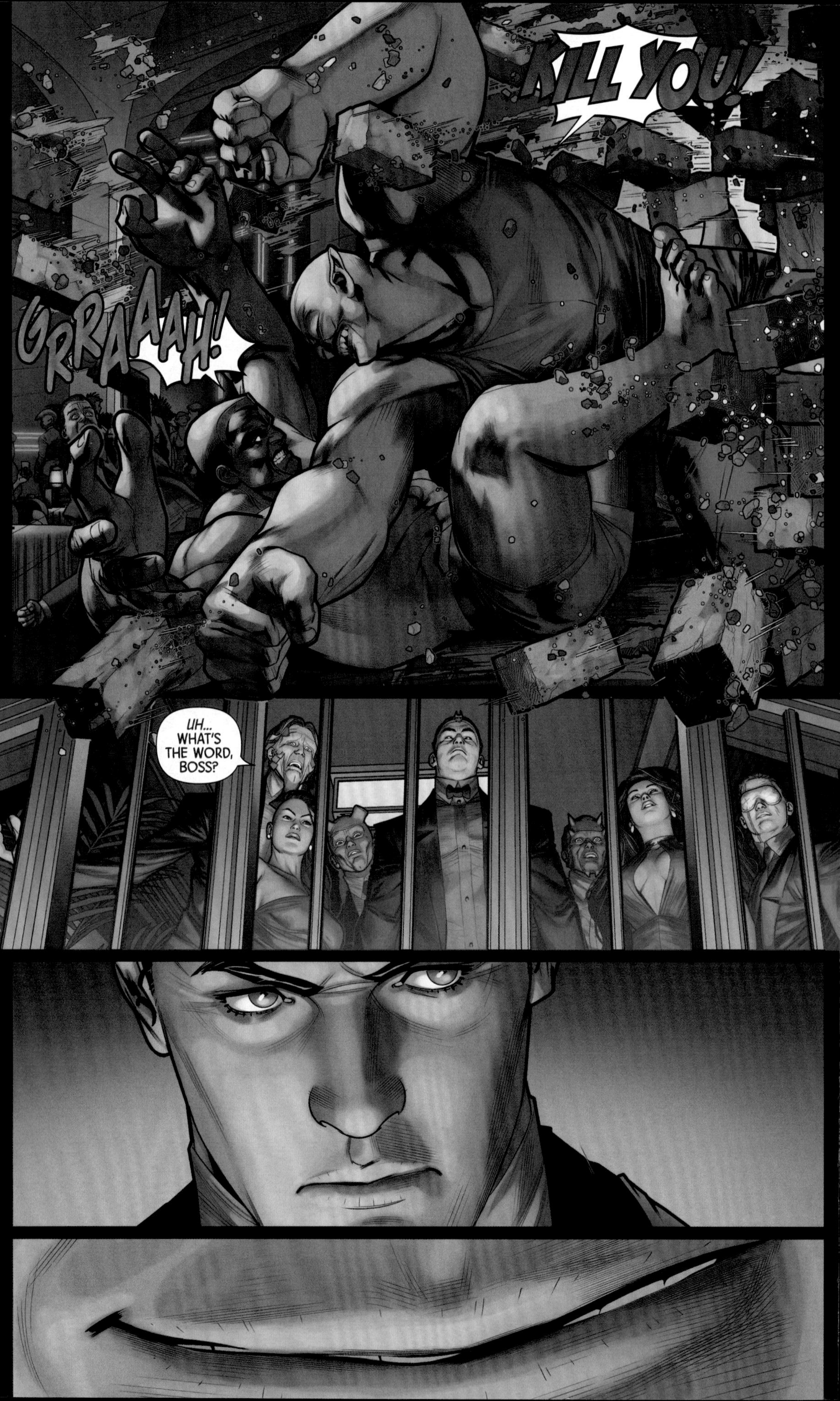
KILL YOU!
GRRAAAAH!
UH... WHAT'S THE WORD, BOSS?

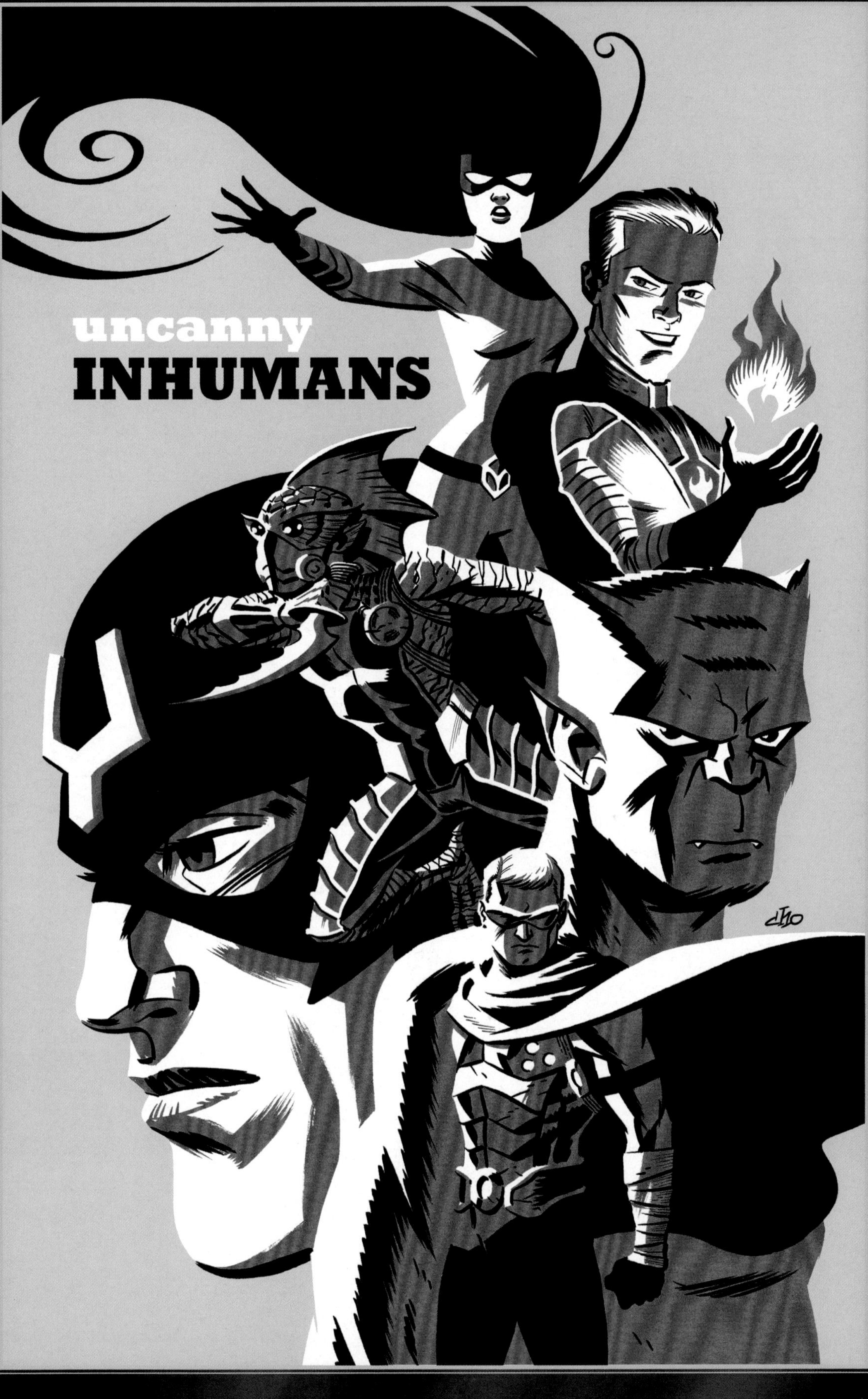
uncanny
INHUMANS
cho

#5 VARIANT BY MICHAEL CHO

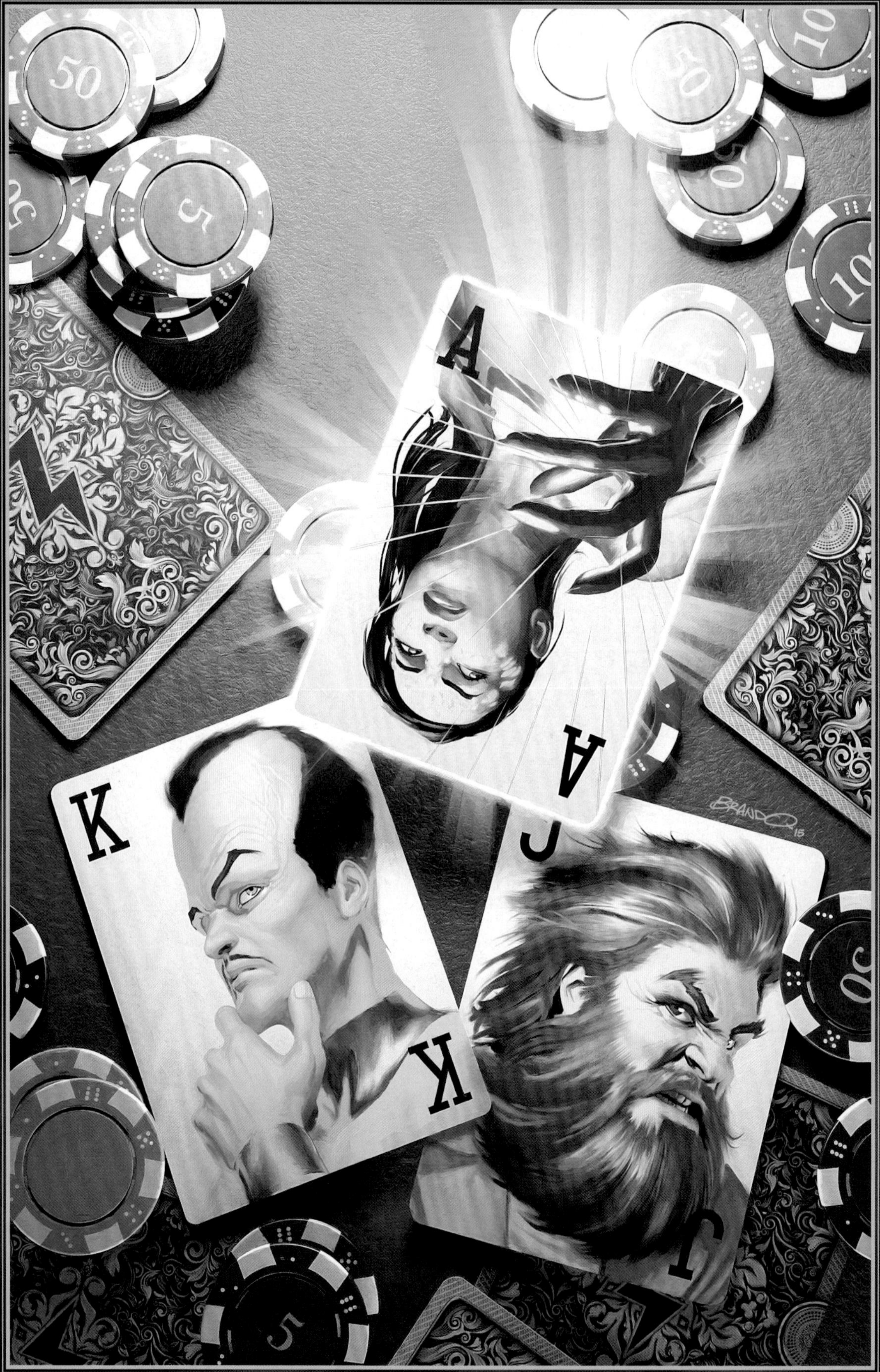

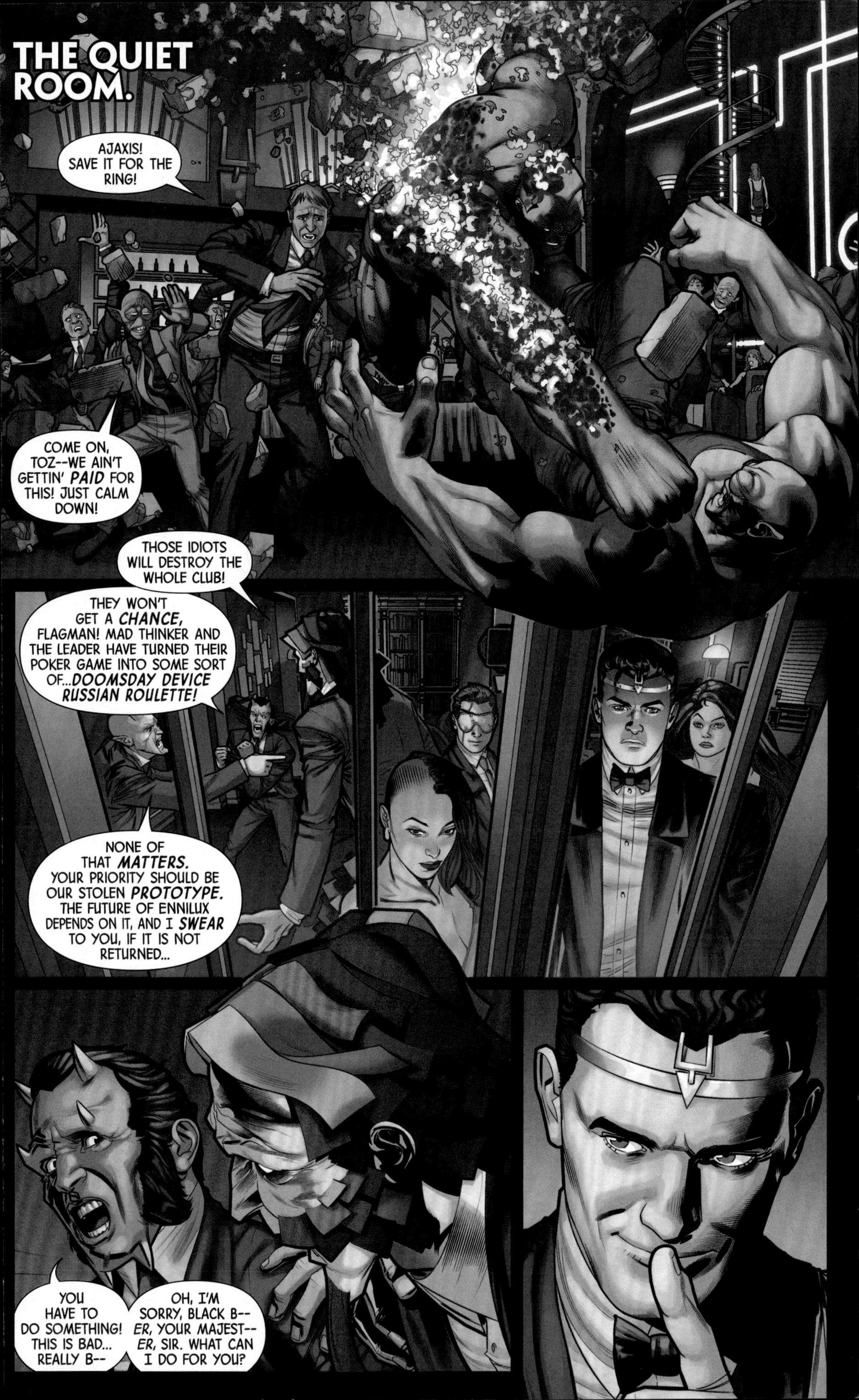
THE QUIET ROOM.
AJAXIS! SAVE IT FOR THE RING!
COME ON, TOZ--WE AIN'T GETTIN' PAID FOR THIS! JUST CALM DOWN!
THOSE IDIOTS WILL DESTROY THE WHOLE CLUB!
THEY WON'T GET A CHANCE, FLAGMAN! MAD THINKER AND THE LEADER HAVE TURNED THEIR POKER GAME INTO SOME SORT OF...DOOMSDAY DEVICE RUSSIAN ROULETTE!
NONE OF THAT MATTERS. YOUR PRIORITY SHOULD BE OUR STOLEN PROTOTYPE. THE FUTURE OF ENNILUX DEPENDS ON IT, AND I SWEAR TO YOU, IF IT IS NOT RETURNED...
YOU HAVE TO DO SOMETHING! THIS IS BAD... REALLY B--
OH, I'M SORRY, BLACK B-- ER, YOUR MAJEST-- ER, SIR. WHAT CAN I DO FOR YOU?

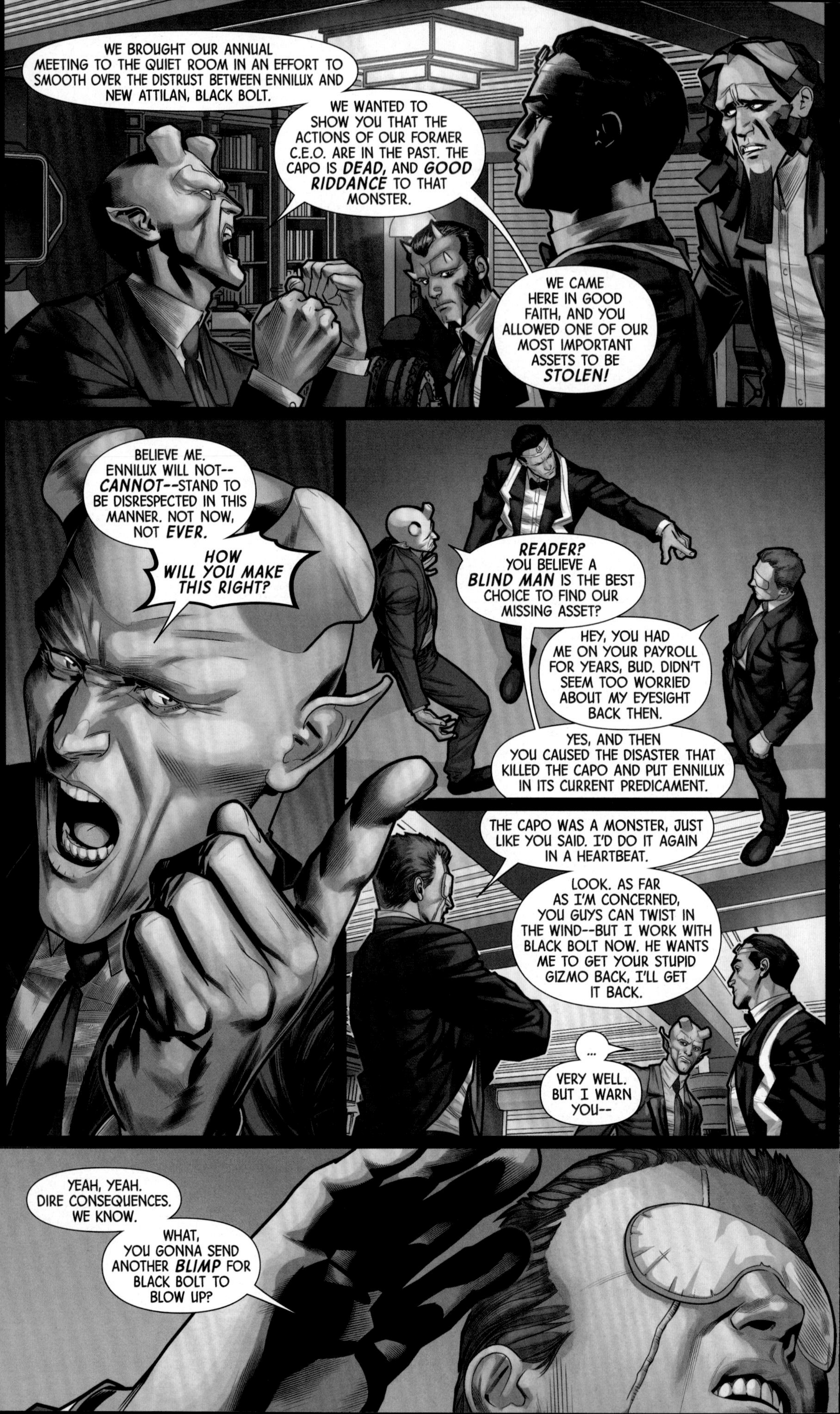
WE BROUGHT OUR ANNUAL MEETING TO THE QUIET ROOM IN AN EFFORT TO SMOOTH OVER THE DISTRUST BETWEEN ENNILUX AND NEW ATTILAN, BLACK BOLT.
WE WANTED TO SHOW YOU THAT THE ACTIONS OF OUR FORMER C.E.O. ARE IN THE PAST. THE CAPO IS DEAD, AND GOOD RIDDANCE TO THAT MONSTER.
WE CAME HERE IN GOOD FAITH, AND YOU ALLOWED ONE OF OUR MOST IMPORTANT ASSETS TO BE STOLEN!
BELIEVE ME. ENNILUX WILL NOT--CANNOT--STAND TO BE DISRESPECTED IN THIS MANNER. NOT NOW, NOT EVER.
HOW WILL YOU MAKE THIS RIGHT?
READER? YOU BELIEVE A BLIND MAN IS THE BEST CHOICE TO FIND OUR MISSING ASSET?
HEY, YOU HAD ME ON YOUR PAYROLL FOR YEARS, BUD. DIDN'T SEEM TOO WORRIED ABOUT MY EYESIGHT BACK THEN.
YES, AND THEN YOU CAUSED THE DISASTER THAT KILLED THE CAPO AND PUT ENNILUX IN ITS CURRENT PREDICAMENT.
THE CAPO WAS A MONSTER, JUST LIKE YOU SAID. I'D DO IT AGAIN IN A HEARTBEAT.
LOOK. AS FAR AS I'M CONCERNED, YOU GUYS CAN TWIST IN THE WIND--BUT I WORK WITH BLACK BOLT NOW. HE WANTS ME TO GET YOUR STUPID GIZMO BACK, I'LL GET IT BACK.
...
VERY WELL. BUT I WARN YOU--
YEAH, YEAH. DIRE CONSEQUENCES. WE KNOW.
WHAT, YOU GONNA SEND ANOTHER BLIMP FOR BLACK BOLT TO BLOW UP?

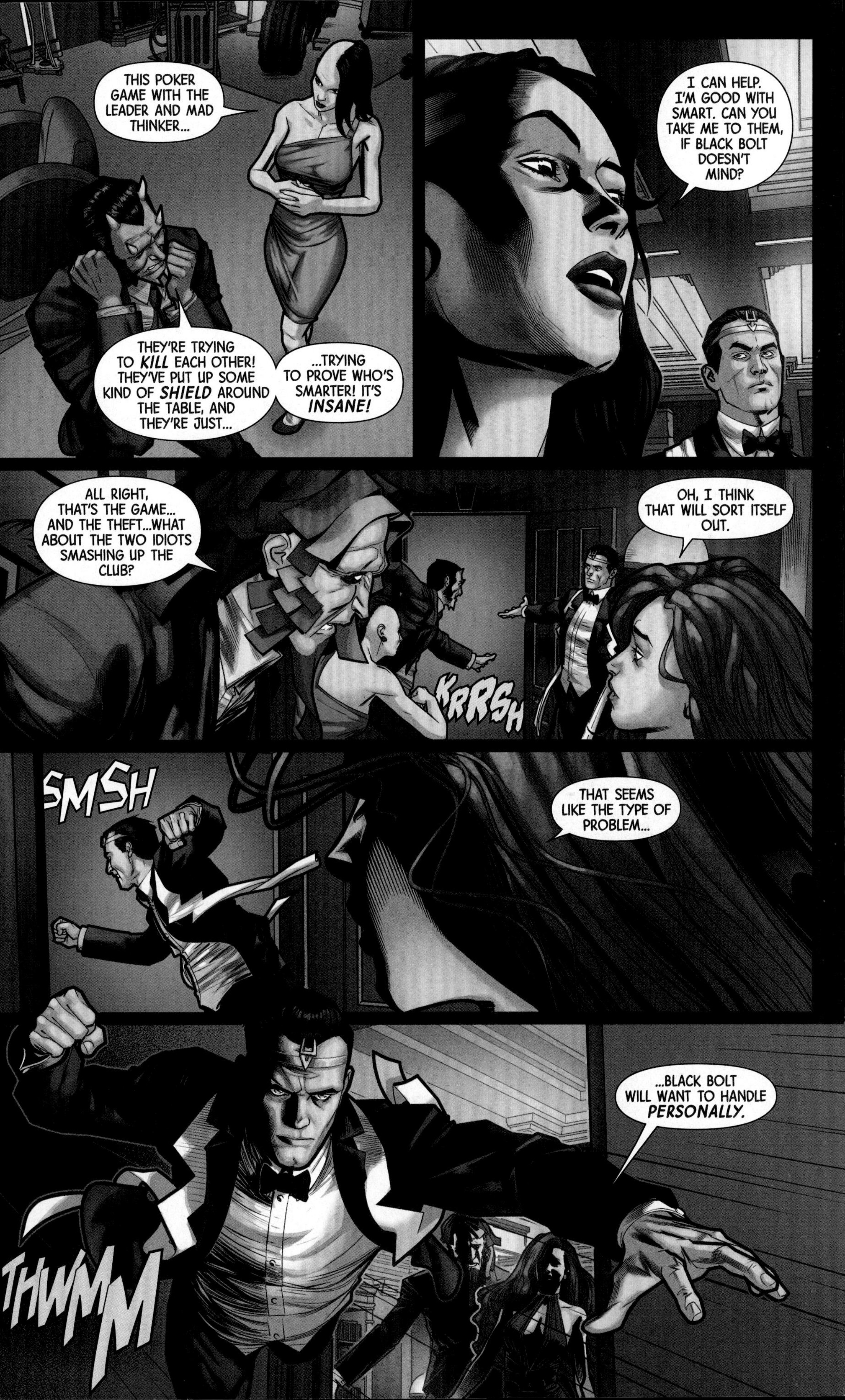
THIS POKER GAME WITH THE LEADER AND MAD THINKER...
THEY'RE TRYING TO KILL EACH OTHER! THEY'VE PUT UP SOME KIND OF SHIELD AROUND THE TABLE, AND THEY'RE JUST...
...TRYING TO PROVE WHO'S SMARTER! IT'S INSANE!
I CAN HELP. I'M GOOD WITH SMART. CAN YOU TAKE ME TO THEM, IF BLACK BOLT DOESN'T MIND?
ALL RIGHT, THAT'S THE GAME... AND THE THEFT...WHAT ABOUT THE TWO IDIOTS SMASHING UP THE CLUB?
OH, I THINK THAT WILL SORT ITSELF OUT.
KRRSH
SMSH
THAT SEEMS LIKE THE TYPE OF PROBLEM...
...BLACK BOLT WILL WANT TO HANDLE PERSONALLY.
THWMM

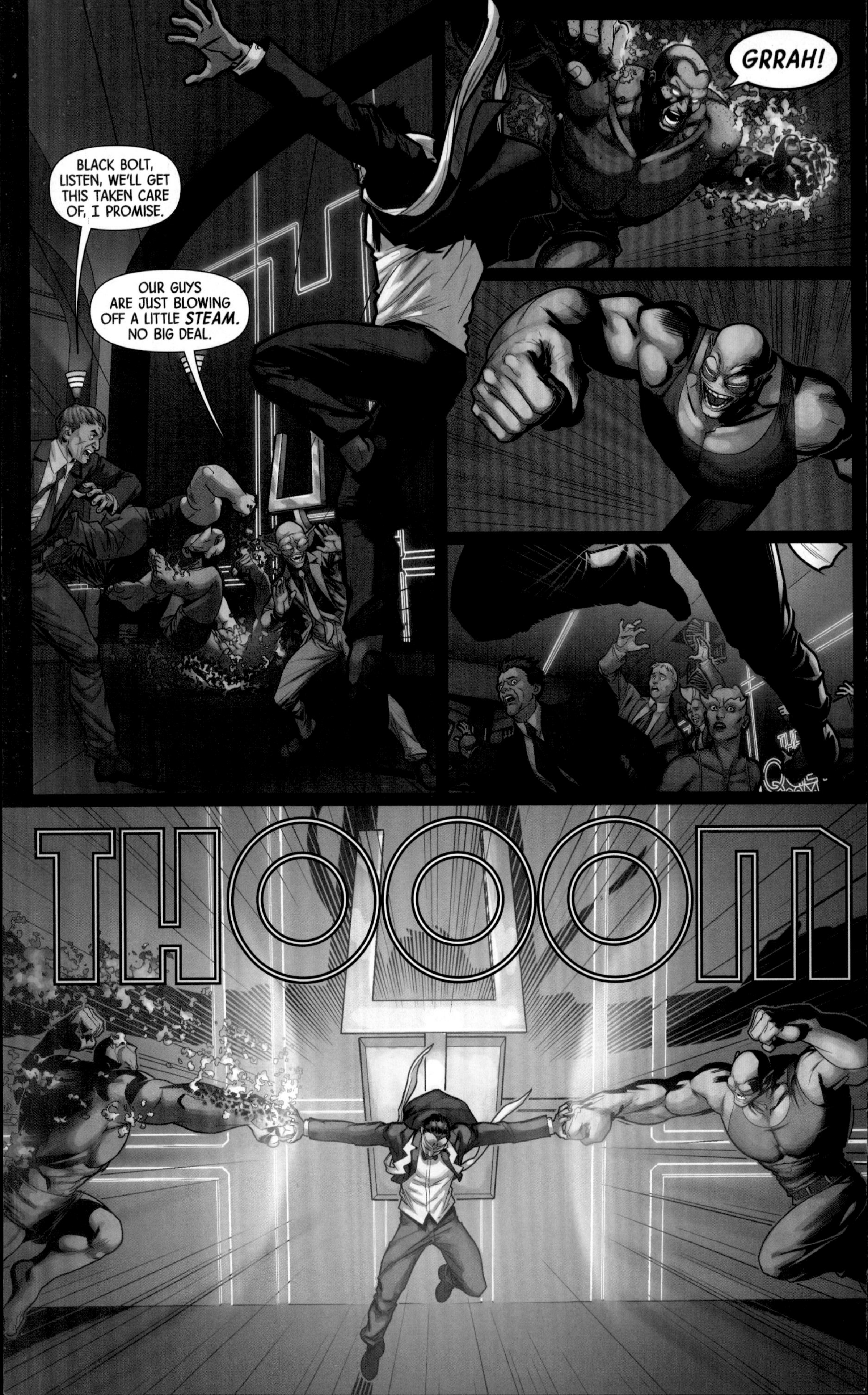
BLACK BOLT, LISTEN, WE'LL GET THIS TAKEN CARE OF, I PROMISE.
GRRAH!
OUR GUYS ARE JUST BLOWING OFF A LITTLE STEAM. NO BIG DEAL.
THOOOM

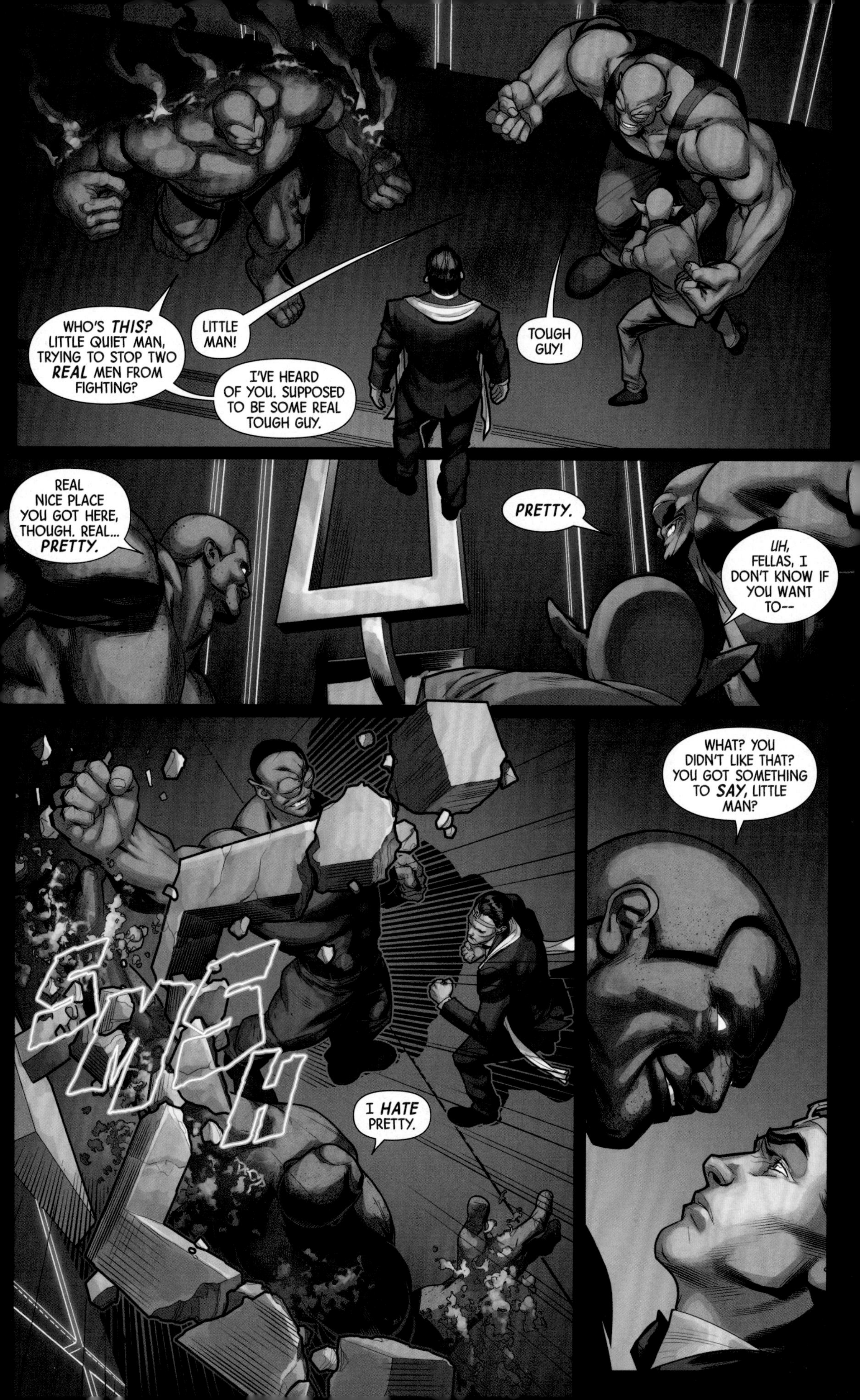
WHO'S THIS? LITTLE QUIET MAN, TRYING TO STOP TWO REAL MEN FROM FIGHTING?
LITTLE MAN!
I'VE HEARD OF YOU. SUPPOSED TO BE SOME REAL TOUGH GUY.
TOUGH GUY!
REAL NICE PLACE YOU GOT HERE, THOUGH. REAL... PRETTY.
PRETTY.
UH, FELLAS, I DON'T KNOW IF YOU WANT TO--
SMASH
I HATE PRETTY.
WHAT? YOU DIDN'T LIKE THAT? YOU GOT SOMETHING TO SAY, LITTLE MAN?

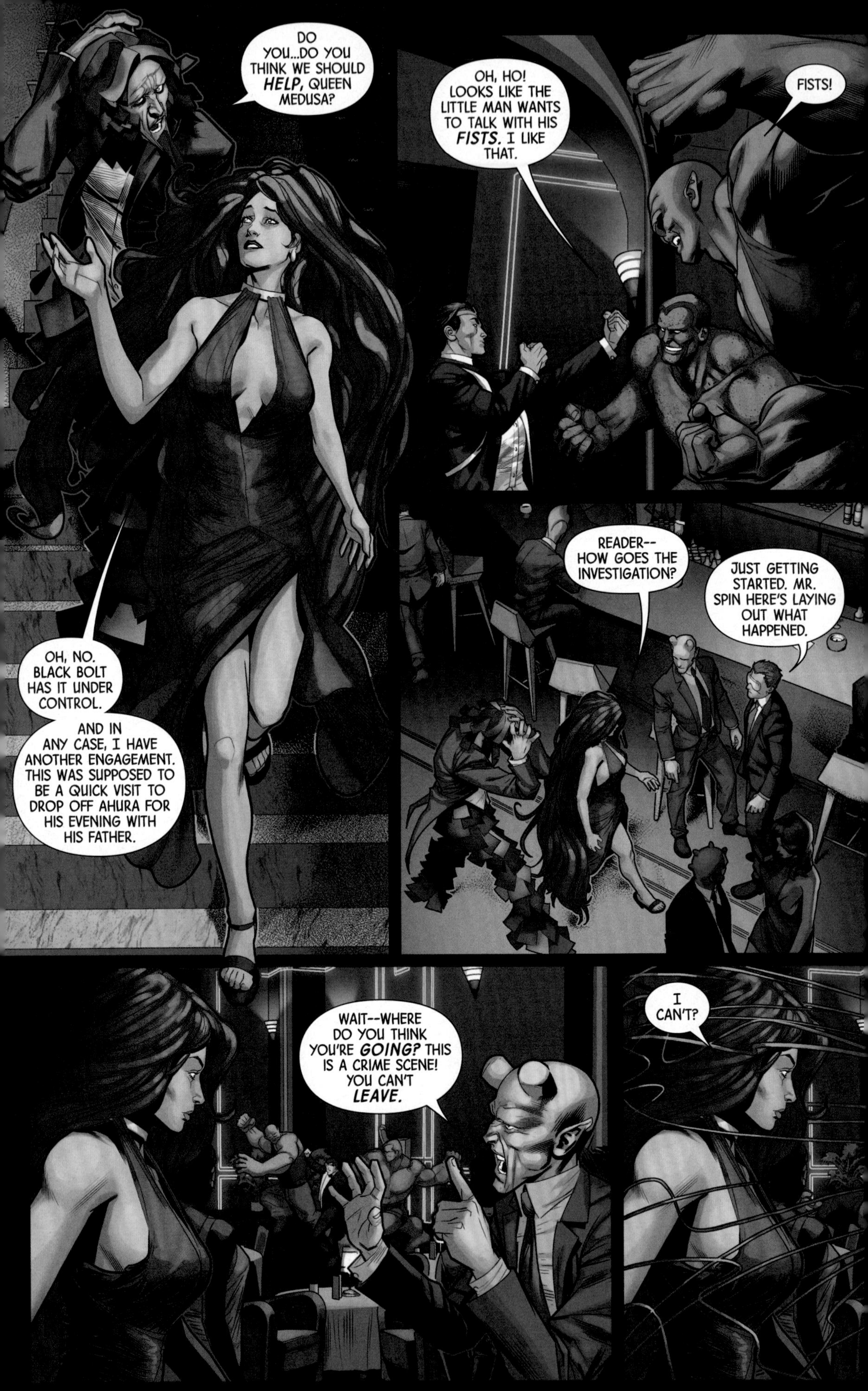
DO YOU...DO YOU THINK WE SHOULD HELP, QUEEN MEDUSA?
OH, NO. BLACK BOLT HAS IT UNDER CONTROL.
AND IN ANY CASE, I HAVE ANOTHER ENGAGEMENT. THIS WAS SUPPOSED TO BE A QUICK VISIT TO DROP OFF AHURA FOR HIS EVENING WITH HIS FATHER.
OH, HO! LOOKS LIKE THE LITTLE MAN WANTS TO TALK WITH HIS FISTS. I LIKE THAT.
FISTS!
READER-- HOW GOES THE INVESTIGATION?
JUST GETTING STARTED. MR. SPIN HERE'S LAYING OUT WHAT HAPPENED.
WAIT--WHERE DO YOU THINK YOU'RE GOING? THIS IS A CRIME SCENE! YOU CAN'T LEAVE.
I CAN'T?

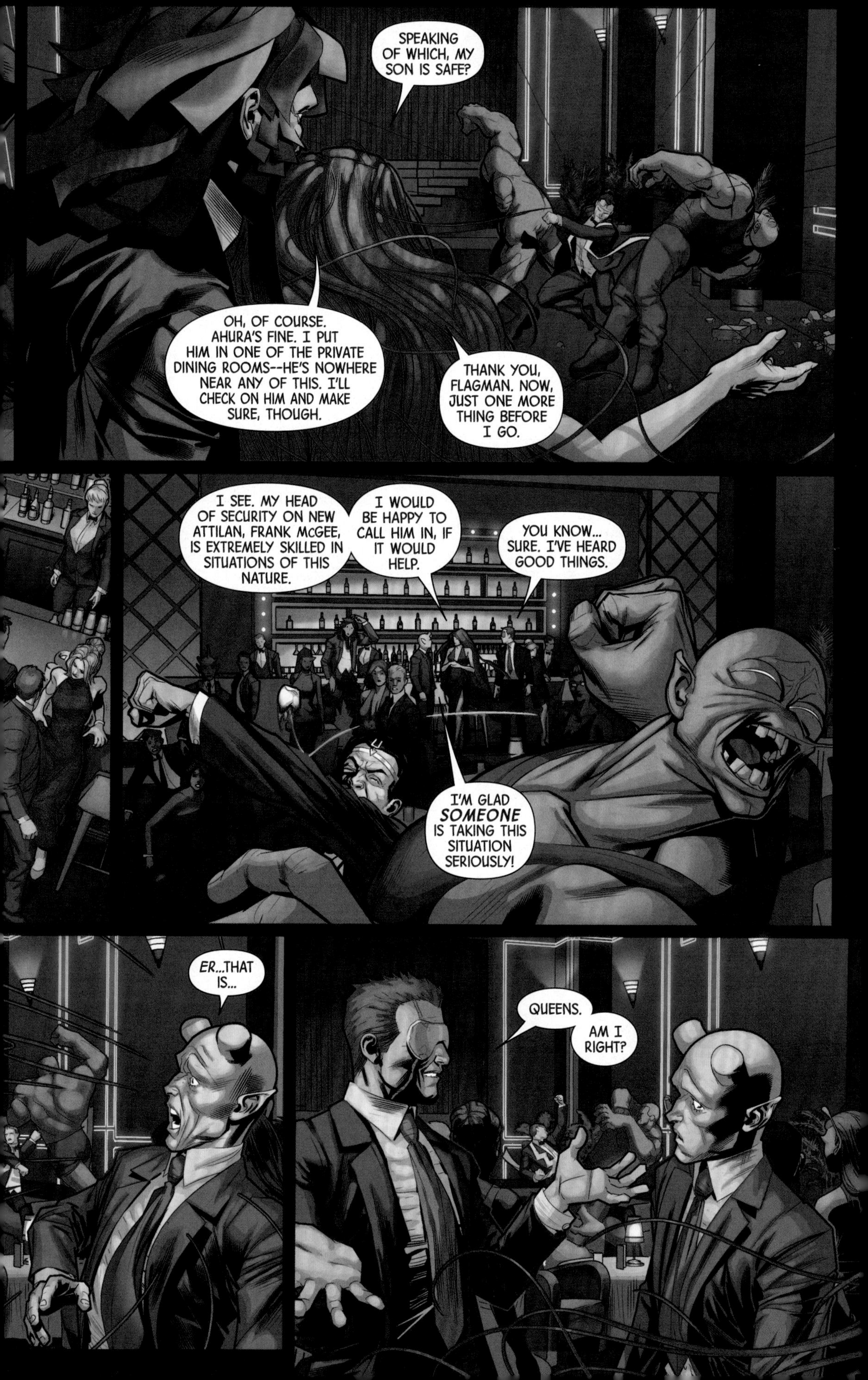
SPEAKING OF WHICH, MY SON IS SAFE?
OH, OF COURSE. AHURA'S FINE. I PUT HIM IN ONE OF THE PRIVATE DINING ROOMS--HE'S NOWHERE NEAR ANY OF THIS. I'LL CHECK ON HIM AND MAKE SURE, THOUGH.
THANK YOU, FLAGMAN. NOW, JUST ONE MORE THING BEFORE I GO.
I SEE. MY HEAD OF SECURITY ON NEW ATTILAN, FRANK McGEE, IS EXTREMELY SKILLED IN SITUATIONS OF THIS NATURE.
I WOULD BE HAPPY TO CALL HIM IN, IF IT WOULD HELP.
YOU KNOW... SURE. I'VE HEARD GOOD THINGS.
I'M GLAD SOMEONE IS TAKING THIS SITUATION SERIOUSLY!
ER...THAT IS...
QUEENS.
AM I RIGHT?

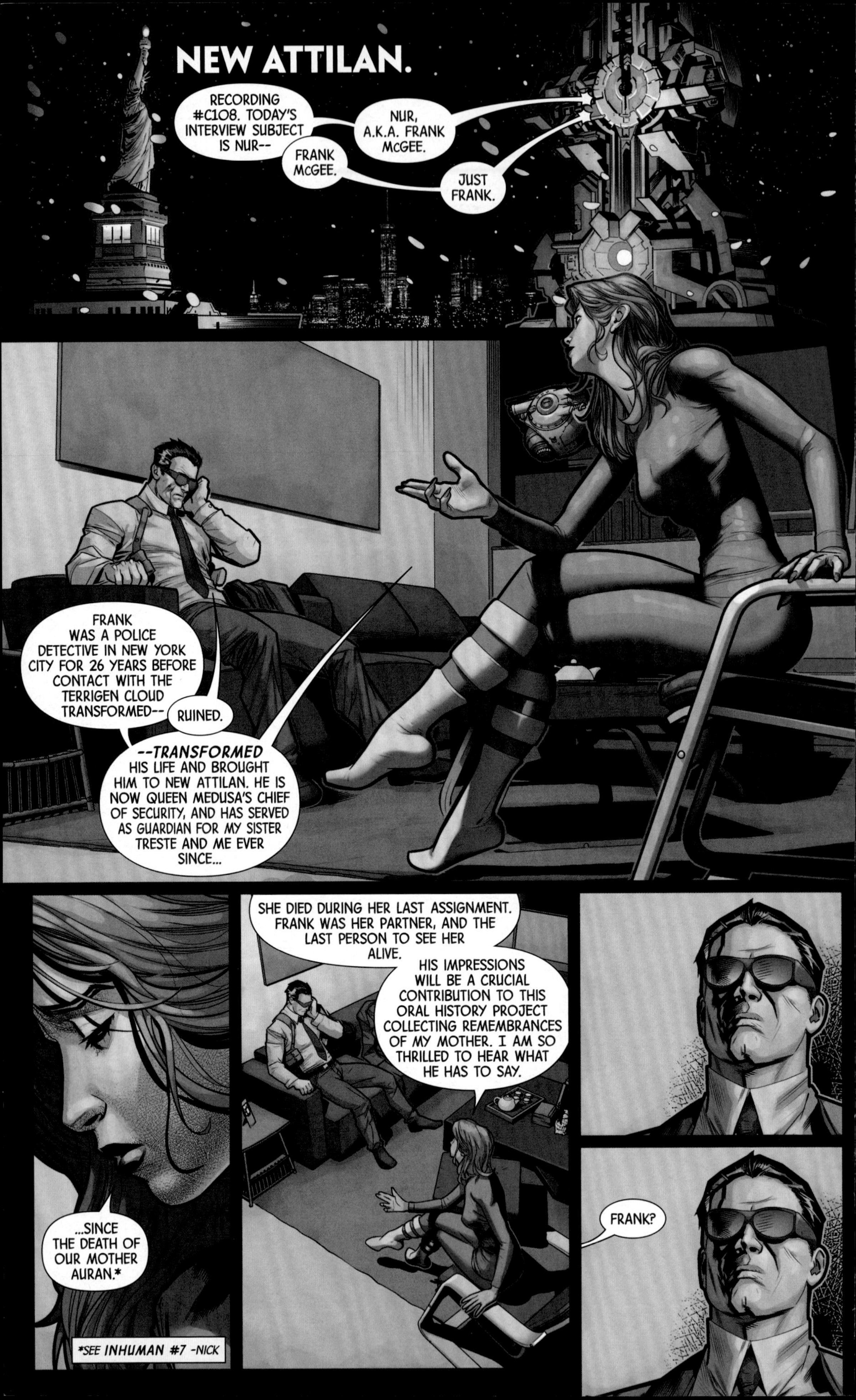

NEW ATTILAN.
RECORDING #C108. TODAY'S INTERVIEW SUBJECT IS NUR--
NUR, A.K.A. FRANK McGEE.
FRANK McGEE.
JUST FRANK.
FRANK WAS A POLICE DETECTIVE IN NEW YORK CITY FOR 26 YEARS BEFORE CONTACT WITH THE TERRIGEN CLOUD TRANSFORMED--
RUINED.
--TRANSFORMED HIS LIFE AND BROUGHT HIM TO NEW ATTILAN. HE IS NOW QUEEN MEDUSA'S CHIEF OF SECURITY, AND HAS SERVED AS GUARDIAN FOR MY SISTER TRESTE AND ME EVER SINCE...
...SINCE THE DEATH OF OUR MOTHER AURAN.*
*SEE INHUMAN #7 -NICK
SHE DIED DURING HER LAST ASSIGNMENT. FRANK WAS HER PARTNER, AND THE LAST PERSON TO SEE HER ALIVE.
HIS IMPRESSIONS WILL BE A CRUCIAL CONTRIBUTION TO THIS ORAL HISTORY PROJECT COLLECTING REMEMBRANCES OF MY MOTHER. I AM SO THRILLED TO HEAR WHAT HE HAS TO SAY.
FRANK?

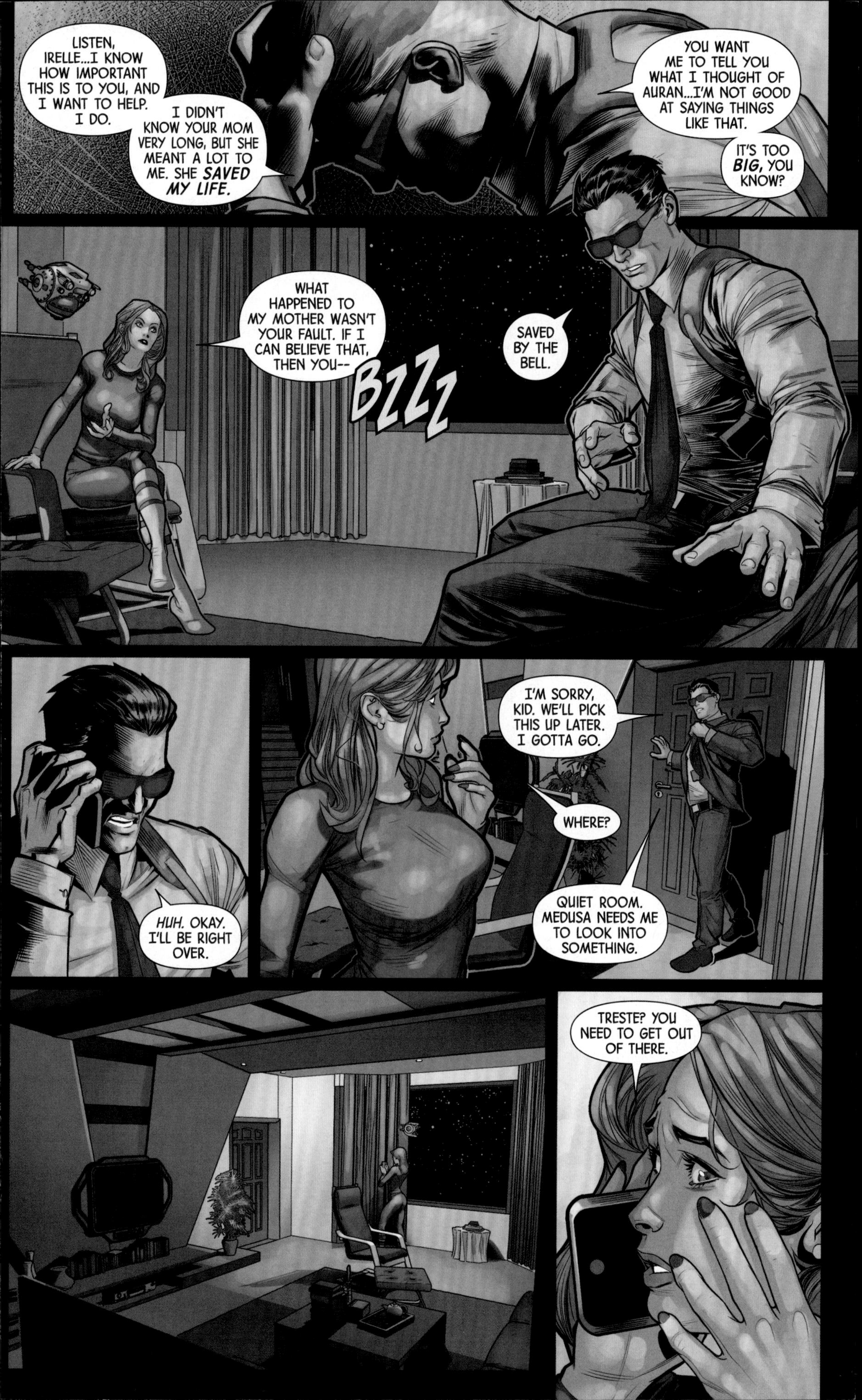
LISTEN, IRELLE...I KNOW HOW IMPORTANT THIS IS TO YOU, AND I WANT TO HELP. I DO.
I DIDN'T KNOW YOUR MOM VERY LONG, BUT SHE MEANT A LOT TO ME. SHE SAVED MY LIFE.
YOU WANT ME TO TELL YOU WHAT I THOUGHT OF AURAN...I'M NOT GOOD AT SAYING THINGS LIKE THAT.
IT'S TOO BIG, YOU KNOW?
WHAT HAPPENED TO MY MOTHER WASN'T YOUR FAULT. IF I CAN BELIEVE THAT, THEN YOU--
BZZZ
SAVED BY THE BELL.
HUH. OKAY. I'LL BE RIGHT OVER.
I'M SORRY, KID. WE'LL PICK THIS UP LATER. I GOTTA GO.
WHERE?
QUIET ROOM. MEDUSA NEEDS ME TO LOOK INTO SOMETHING.
TRESTE? YOU NEED TO GET OUT OF THERE.

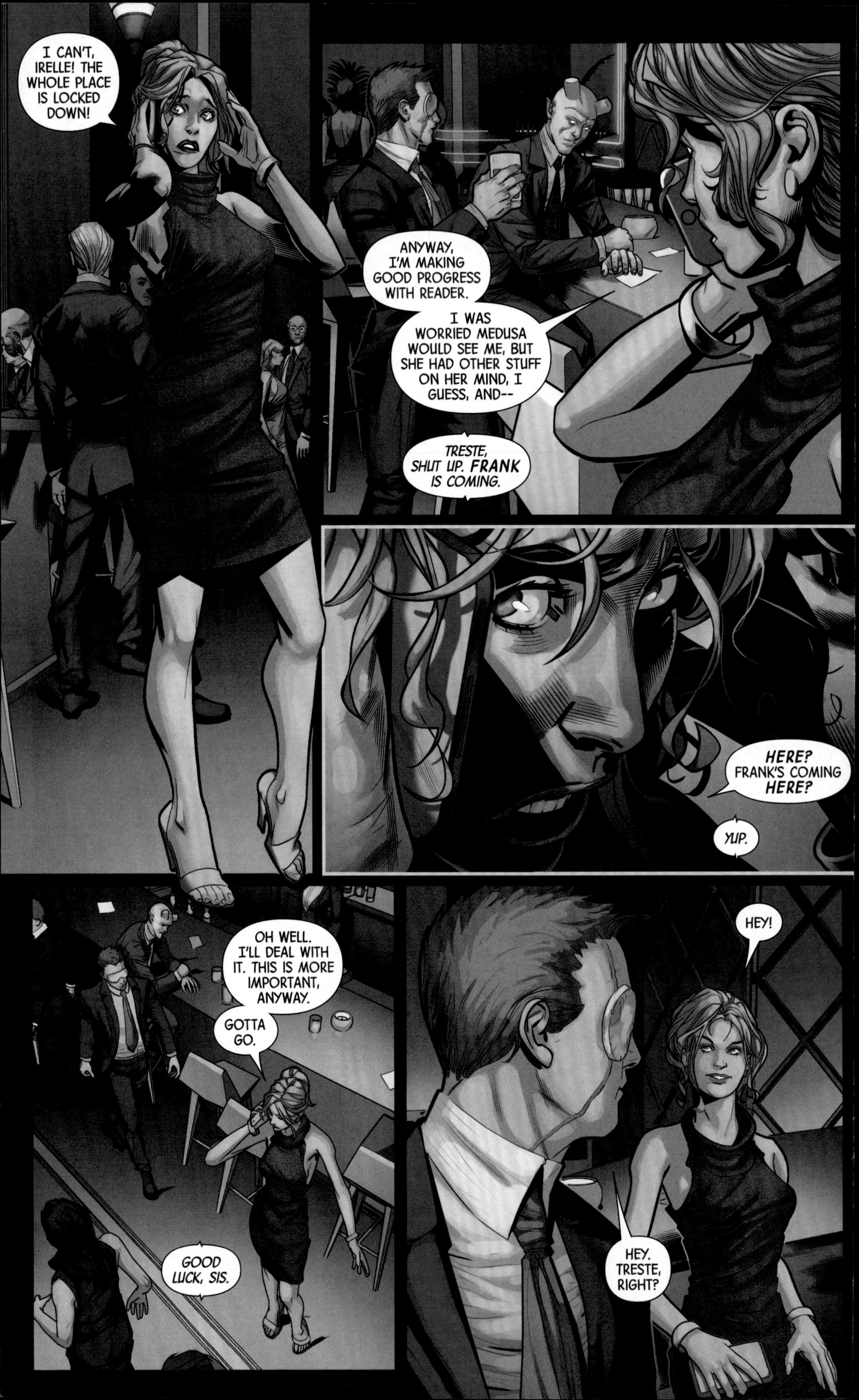
I CAN'T, IRELLE! THE WHOLE PLACE IS LOCKED DOWN!
ANYWAY, I'M MAKING GOOD PROGRESS WITH READER.
I WAS WORRIED MEDUSA WOULD SEE ME, BUT SHE HAD OTHER STUFF ON HER MIND, I GUESS, AND--
TRESTE, SHUT UP. FRANK IS COMING.
HERE? FRANK'S COMING HERE?
YUP.
OH WELL. I'LL DEAL WITH IT. THIS IS MORE IMPORTANT, ANYWAY.
GOTTA GO.
GOOD LUCK, SIS.
HEY!
HEY. TRESTE, RIGHT?

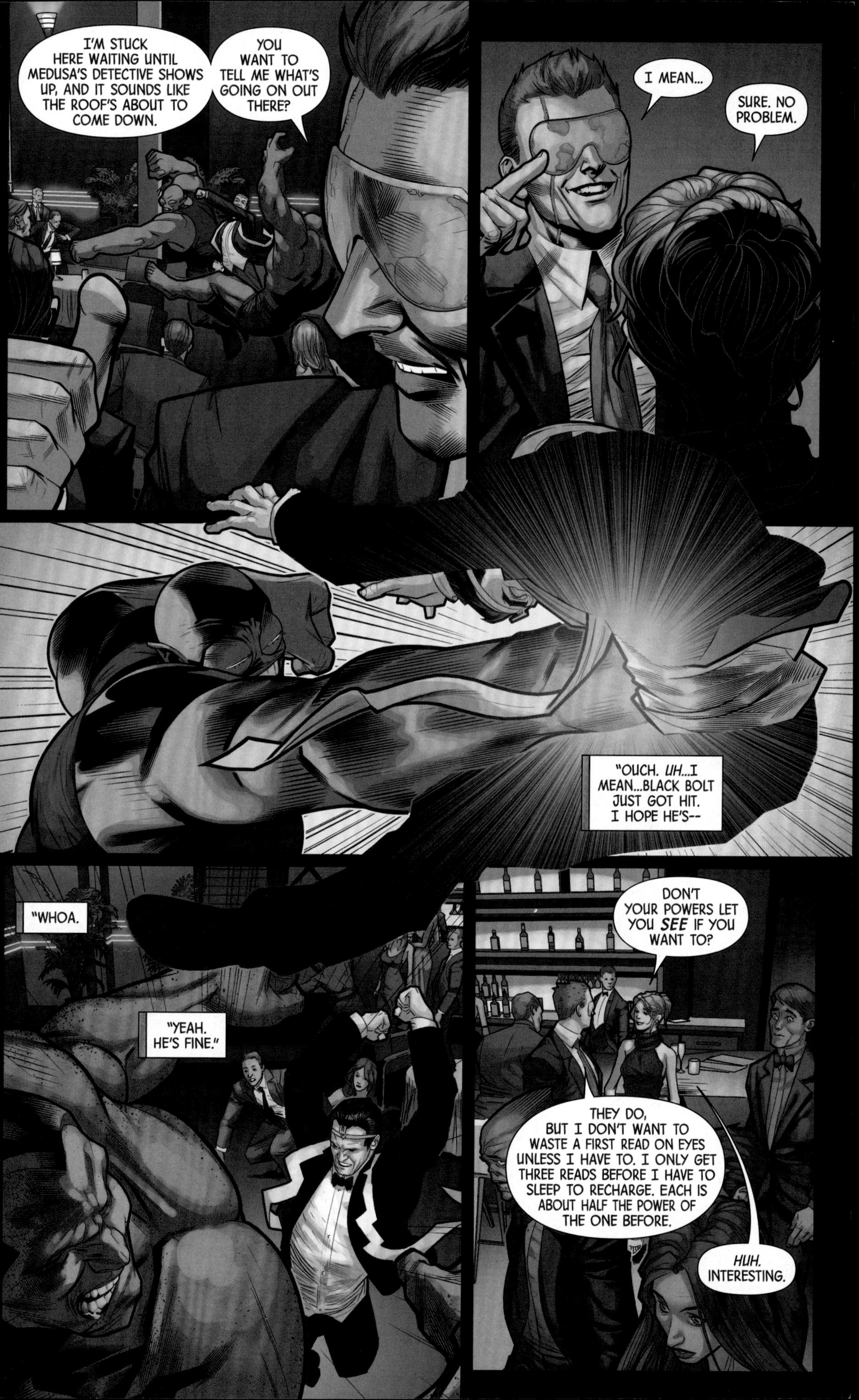
I'M STUCK HERE WAITING UNTIL MEDUSA'S DETECTIVE SHOWS UP, AND IT SOUNDS LIKE THE ROOF'S ABOUT TO COME DOWN.
YOU WANT TO TELL ME WHAT'S GOING ON OUT THERE?
I MEAN...
SURE. NO PROBLEM.
"OUCH. *UH*...I MEAN...BLACK BOLT JUST GOT HIT. I HOPE HE'S--
"WHOA.
"YEAH. HE'S FINE."
DON'T YOUR POWERS LET YOU ***SEE*** IF YOU WANT TO?
THEY DO, BUT I DON'T WANT TO WASTE A FIRST READ ON EYES UNLESS I HAVE TO. I ONLY GET THREE READS BEFORE I HAVE TO SLEEP TO RECHARGE. EACH IS ABOUT HALF THE POWER OF THE ONE BEFORE.
HUH. INTERESTING.

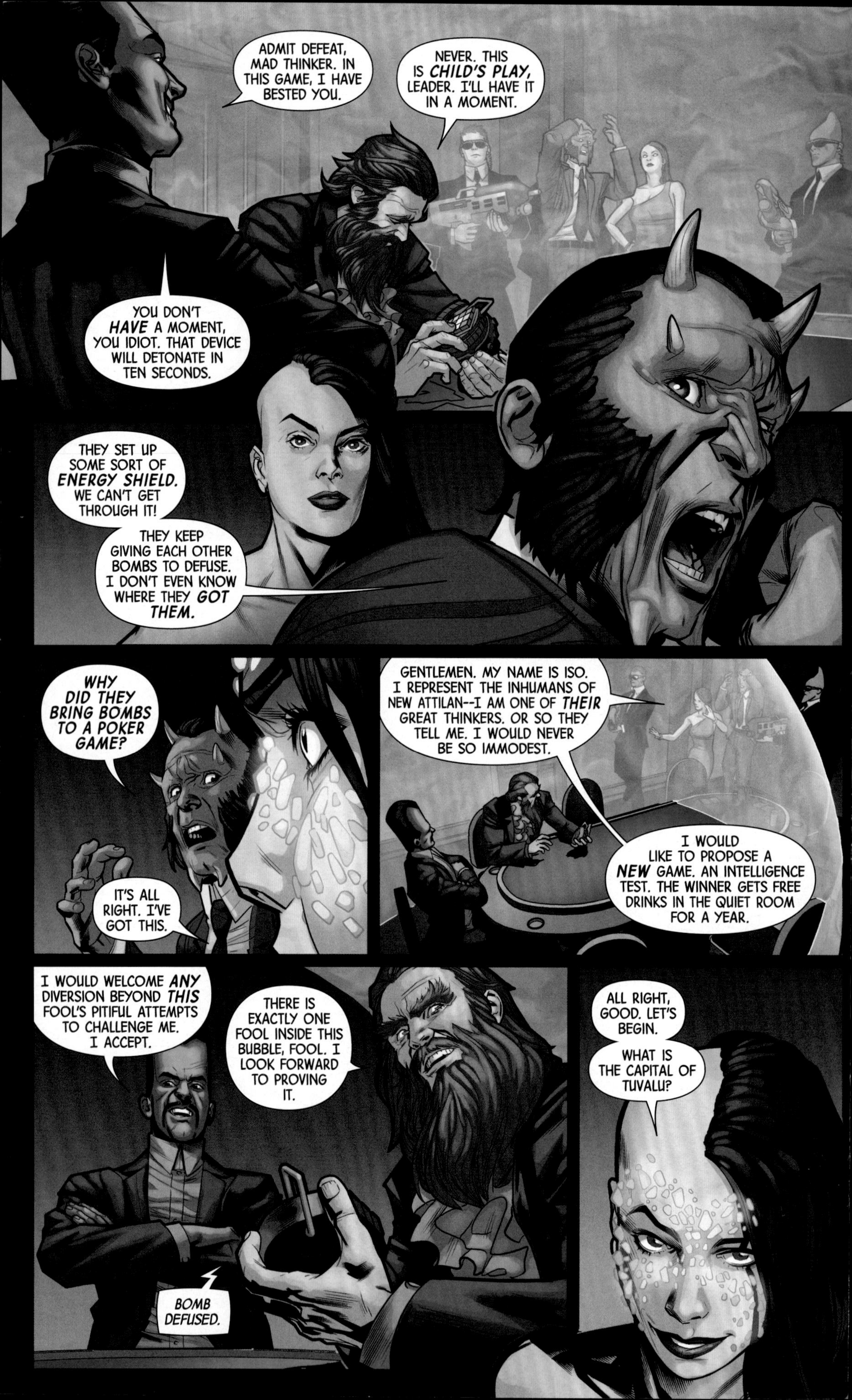
ADMIT DEFEAT, MAD THINKER. IN THIS GAME, I HAVE BESTED YOU.
NEVER. THIS IS CHILD'S PLAY, LEADER. I'LL HAVE IT IN A MOMENT.
YOU DON'T HAVE A MOMENT, YOU IDIOT. THAT DEVICE WILL DETONATE IN TEN SECONDS.
THEY SET UP SOME SORT OF ENERGY SHIELD. WE CAN'T GET THROUGH IT!
THEY KEEP GIVING EACH OTHER BOMBS TO DEFUSE. I DON'T EVEN KNOW WHERE THEY GOT THEM.
WHY DID THEY BRING BOMBS TO A POKER GAME?
IT'S ALL RIGHT. I'VE GOT THIS.
GENTLEMEN. MY NAME IS ISO. I REPRESENT THE INHUMANS OF NEW ATTILAN--I AM ONE OF THEIR GREAT THINKERS. OR SO THEY TELL ME. I WOULD NEVER BE SO IMMODEST.
I WOULD LIKE TO PROPOSE A NEW GAME. AN INTELLIGENCE TEST. THE WINNER GETS FREE DRINKS IN THE QUIET ROOM FOR A YEAR.
I WOULD WELCOME ANY DIVERSION BEYOND THIS FOOL'S PITIFUL ATTEMPTS TO CHALLENGE ME. I ACCEPT.
THERE IS EXACTLY ONE FOOL INSIDE THIS BUBBLE, FOOL. I LOOK FORWARD TO PROVING IT.
BOMB DEFUSED.
ALL RIGHT, GOOD. LET'S BEGIN.
WHAT IS THE CAPITAL OF TUVALU?

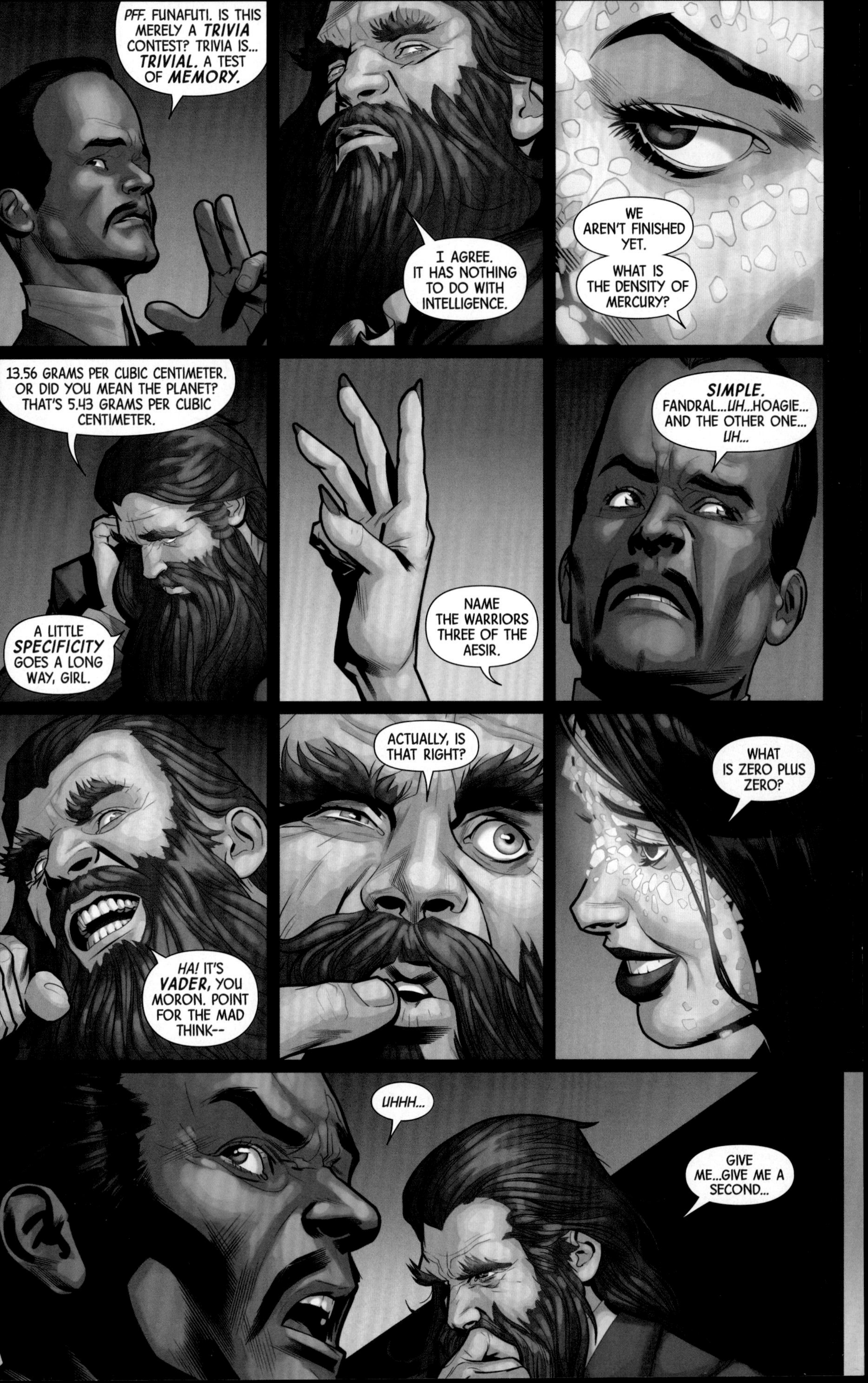
PFF. FUNAFUTI. IS THIS MERELY A TRIVIA CONTEST? TRIVIA IS... TRIVIAL. A TEST OF MEMORY.
I AGREE. IT HAS NOTHING TO DO WITH INTELLIGENCE.
WE AREN'T FINISHED YET.
WHAT IS THE DENSITY OF MERCURY?
13.56 GRAMS PER CUBIC CENTIMETER. OR DID YOU MEAN THE PLANET? THAT'S 5.43 GRAMS PER CUBIC CENTIMETER.
A LITTLE SPECIFICITY GOES A LONG WAY, GIRL.
NAME THE WARRIORS THREE OF THE AESIR.
SIMPLE. FANDRAL...UH...HOAGIE... AND THE OTHER ONE... UH...
HA! IT'S VADER, YOU MORON. POINT FOR THE MAD THINK--
ACTUALLY, IS THAT RIGHT?
WHAT IS ZERO PLUS ZERO?
UHHH...
GIVE ME...GIVE ME A SECOND...

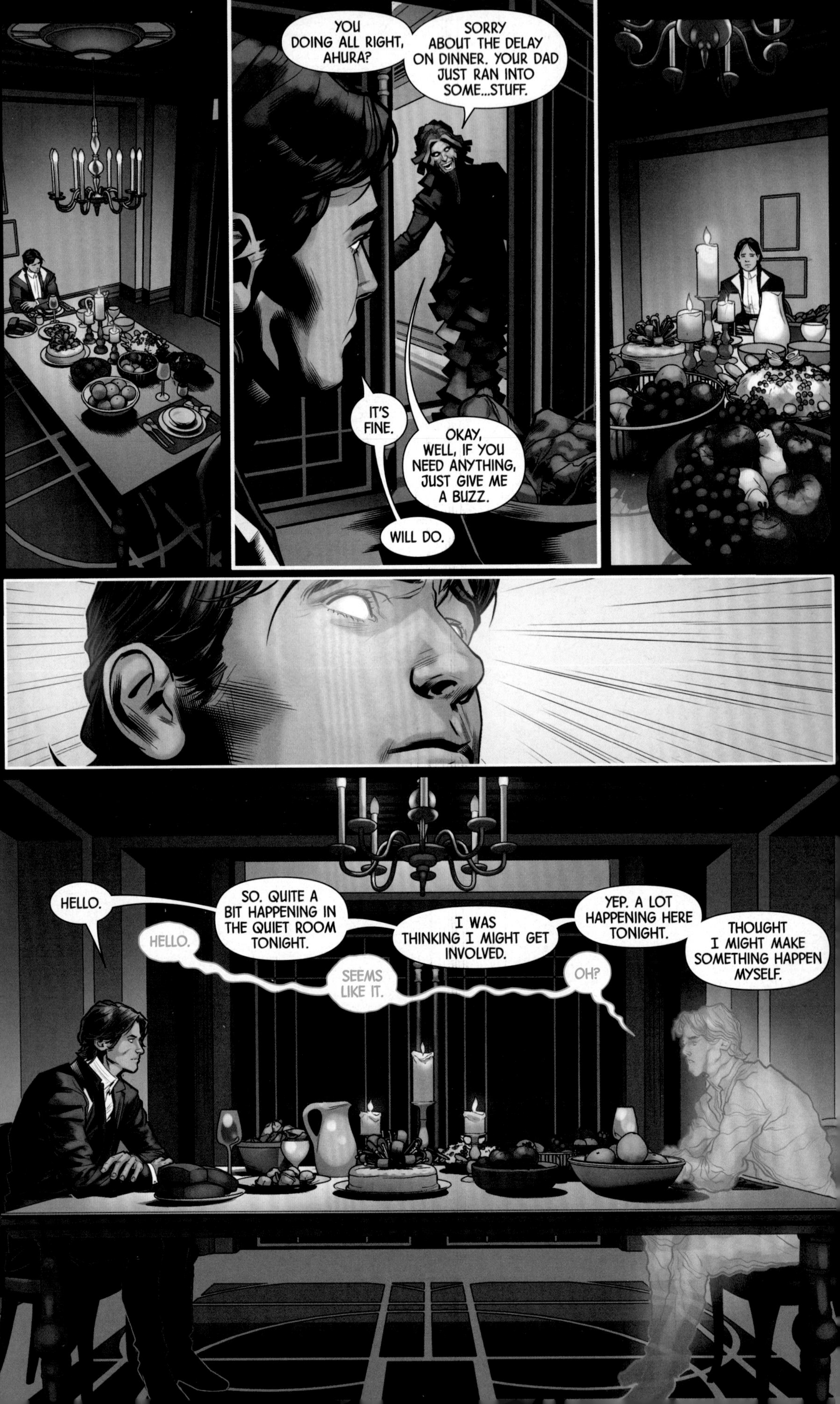
YOU DOING ALL RIGHT, AHURA?
SORRY ABOUT THE DELAY ON DINNER. YOUR DAD JUST RAN INTO SOME...STUFF.
IT'S FINE.
OKAY, WELL, IF YOU NEED ANYTHING, JUST GIVE ME A BUZZ.
WILL DO.
HELLO.
HELLO.
SO. QUITE A BIT HAPPENING IN THE QUIET ROOM TONIGHT.
SEEMS LIKE IT.
I WAS THINKING I MIGHT GET INVOLVED.
OH?
YEP. A LOT HAPPENING HERE TONIGHT.
THOUGHT I MIGHT MAKE SOMETHING HAPPEN MYSELF.

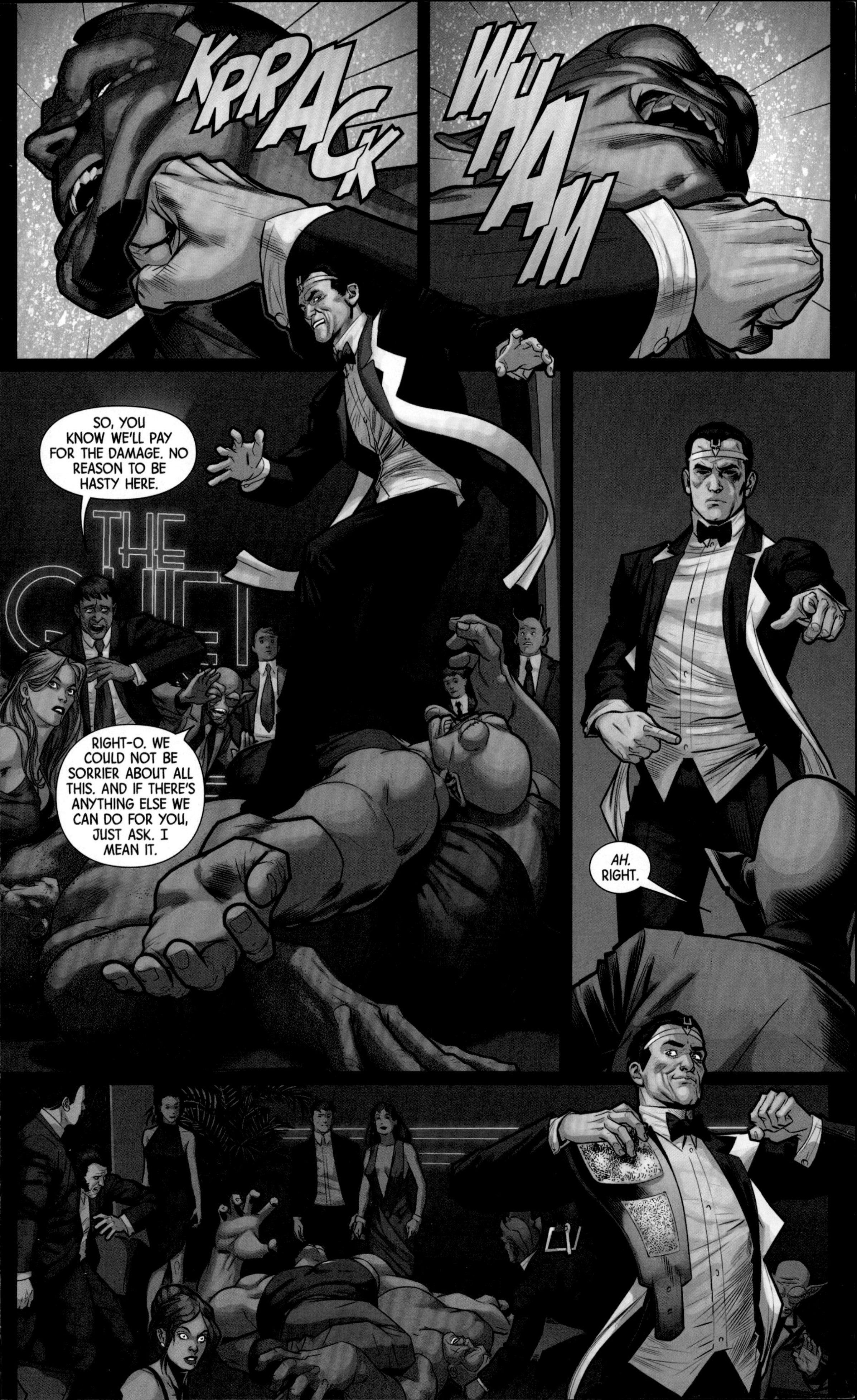
KRRACK
WHAM
SO, YOU KNOW WE'LL PAY FOR THE DAMAGE. NO REASON TO BE HASTY HERE.
RIGHT-O. WE COULD NOT BE SORRIER ABOUT ALL THIS. AND IF THERE'S ANYTHING ELSE WE CAN DO FOR YOU, JUST ASK. I MEAN IT.
AH. RIGHT.

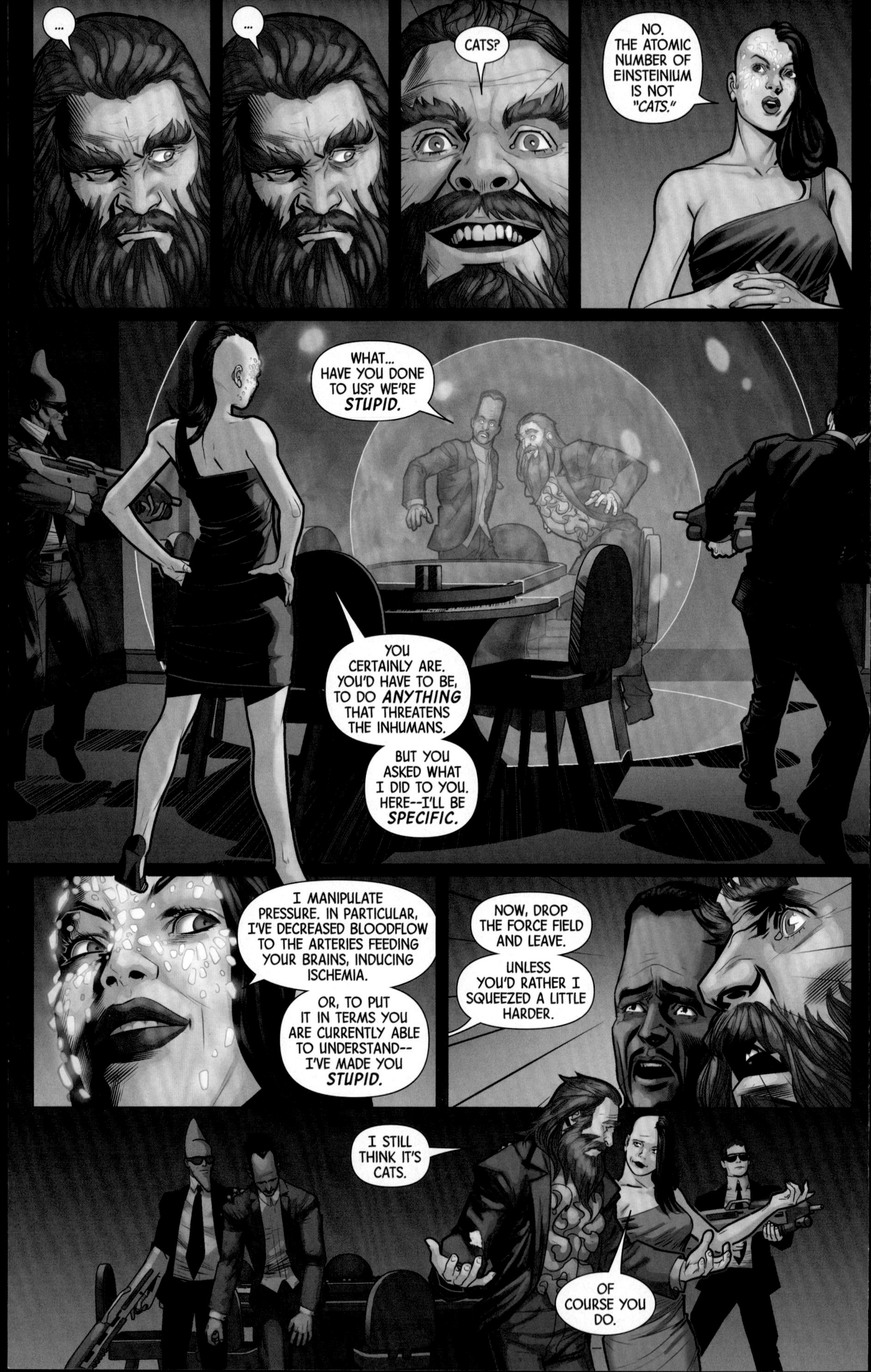
...
...
CATS?
NO. THE ATOMIC NUMBER OF EINSTEINIUM IS NOT "CATS."
WHAT... HAVE YOU DONE TO US? WE'RE STUPID.
YOU CERTAINLY ARE. YOU'D HAVE TO BE, TO DO ANYTHING THAT THREATENS THE INHUMANS.
BUT YOU ASKED WHAT I DID TO YOU. HERE--I'LL BE SPECIFIC.
I MANIPULATE PRESSURE. IN PARTICULAR, I'VE DECREASED BLOODFLOW TO THE ARTERIES FEEDING YOUR BRAINS, INDUCING ISCHEMIA.
OR, TO PUT IT IN TERMS YOU ARE CURRENTLY ABLE TO UNDERSTAND-- I'VE MADE YOU STUPID.
NOW, DROP THE FORCE FIELD AND LEAVE.
UNLESS YOU'D RATHER I SQUEEZED A LITTLE HARDER.
I STILL THINK IT'S CATS.
OF COURSE YOU DO.

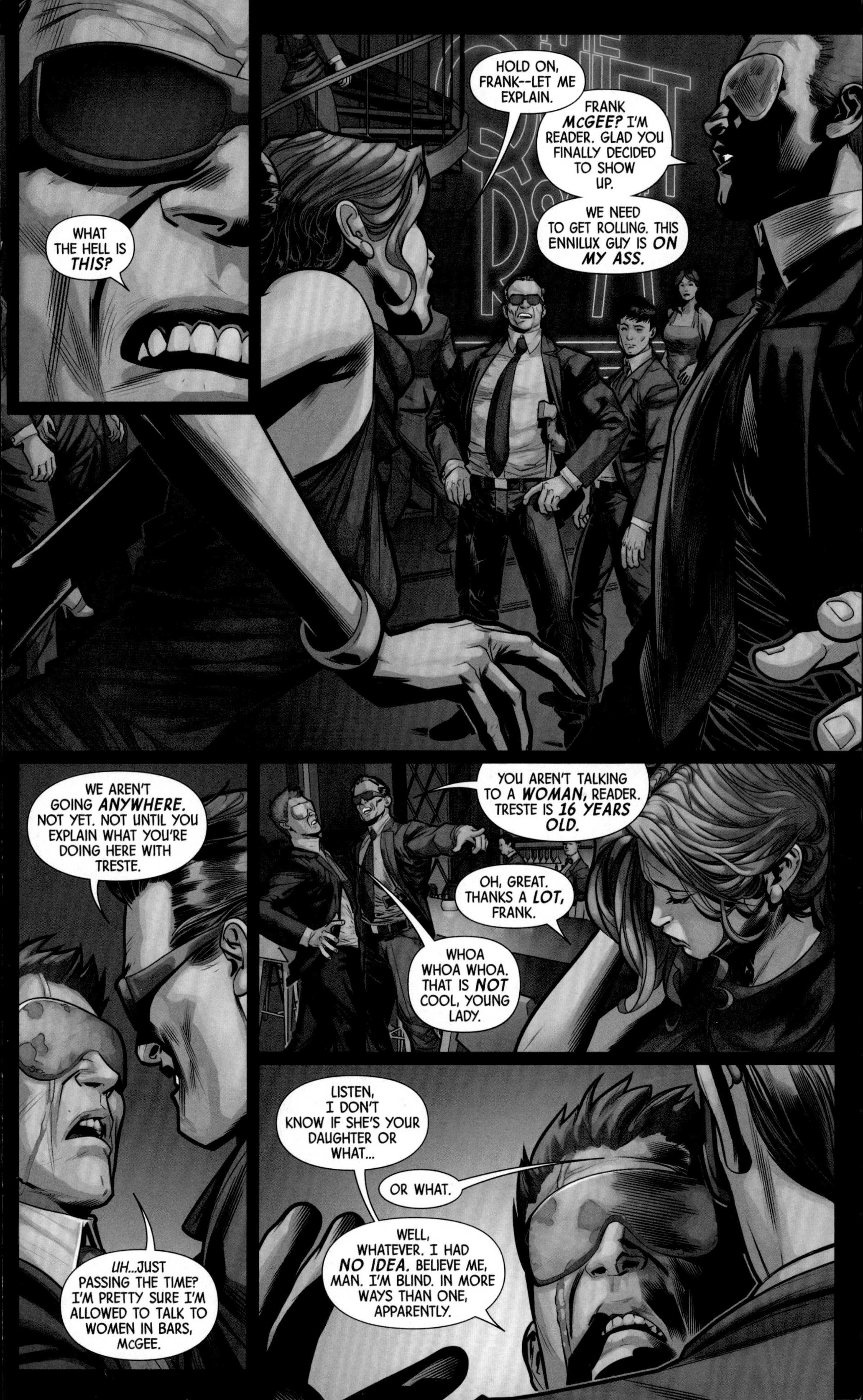
WHAT THE HELL IS *THIS?*
HOLD ON, FRANK--LET ME EXPLAIN.
FRANK *McGEE?* I'M READER. GLAD YOU FINALLY DECIDED TO SHOW UP.
WE NEED TO GET ROLLING. THIS ENNILUX GUY IS **ON MY ASS.**
WE AREN'T GOING ***ANYWHERE.*** NOT YET. NOT UNTIL YOU EXPLAIN WHAT YOU'RE DOING HERE WITH TRESTE.
UH...JUST PASSING THE TIME? I'M PRETTY SURE I'M ALLOWED TO TALK TO WOMEN IN BARS, McGEE.
YOU AREN'T TALKING TO A ***WOMAN,*** READER. TRESTE IS ***16 YEARS OLD.***
OH, GREAT. THANKS A *LOT,* FRANK.
WHOA WHOA WHOA. THAT IS *NOT* COOL, YOUNG LADY.
LISTEN, I DON'T KNOW IF SHE'S YOUR DAUGHTER OR WHAT...
OR WHAT.
WELL, WHATEVER. I HAD ***NO IDEA.*** BELIEVE ME, MAN. I'M BLIND. IN MORE WAYS THAN ONE, APPARENTLY.

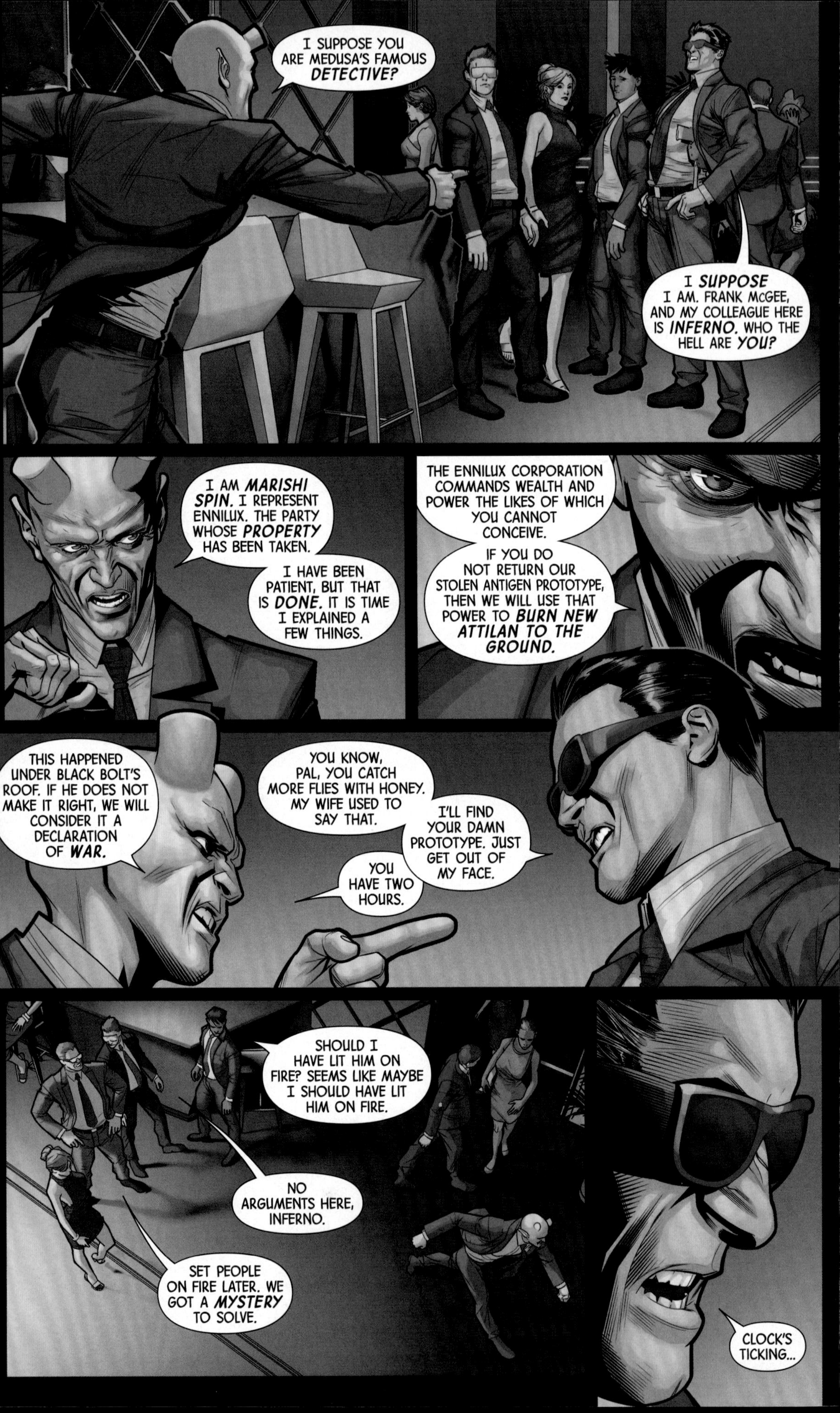

I SUPPOSE YOU ARE MEDUSA'S FAMOUS DETECTIVE?
I SUPPOSE I AM. FRANK McGEE, AND MY COLLEAGUE HERE IS INFERNO. WHO THE HELL ARE YOU?
I AM MARISHI SPIN. I REPRESENT ENNILUX. THE PARTY WHOSE PROPERTY HAS BEEN TAKEN.
I HAVE BEEN PATIENT, BUT THAT IS DONE. IT IS TIME I EXPLAINED A FEW THINGS.
THE ENNILUX CORPORATION COMMANDS WEALTH AND POWER THE LIKES OF WHICH YOU CANNOT CONCEIVE.
IF YOU DO NOT RETURN OUR STOLEN ANTIGEN PROTOTYPE, THEN WE WILL USE THAT POWER TO BURN NEW ATTILAN TO THE GROUND.
THIS HAPPENED UNDER BLACK BOLT'S ROOF. IF HE DOES NOT MAKE IT RIGHT, WE WILL CONSIDER IT A DECLARATION OF WAR.
YOU KNOW, PAL, YOU CATCH MORE FLIES WITH HONEY. MY WIFE USED TO SAY THAT.
I'LL FIND YOUR DAMN PROTOTYPE. JUST GET OUT OF MY FACE.
YOU HAVE TWO HOURS.
SHOULD I HAVE LIT HIM ON FIRE? SEEMS LIKE MAYBE I SHOULD HAVE LIT HIM ON FIRE.
NO ARGUMENTS HERE, INFERNO.
SET PEOPLE ON FIRE LATER. WE GOT A MYSTERY TO SOLVE.
CLOCK'S TICKING...

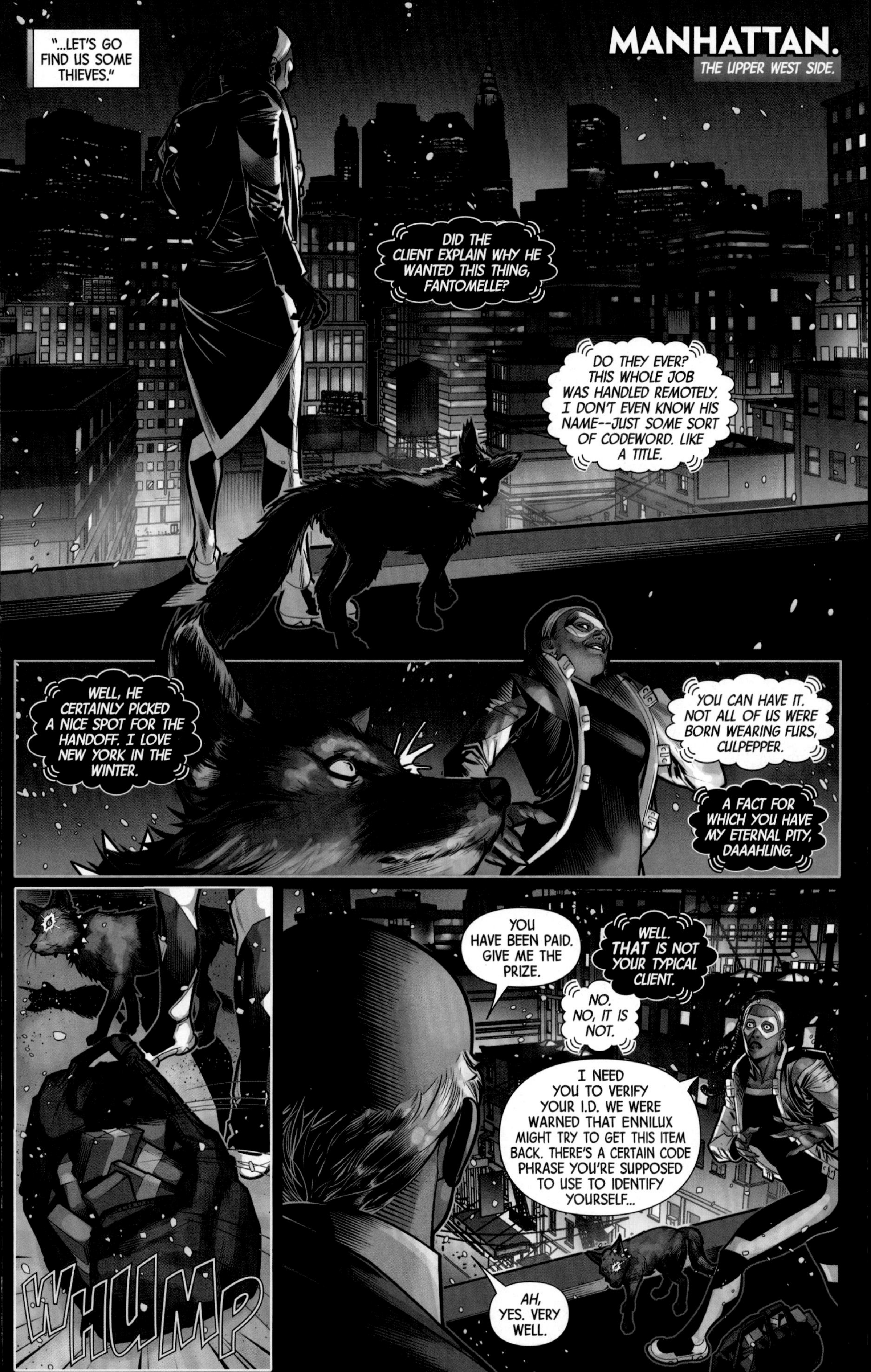

"...LET'S GO FIND US SOME THIEVES."
MANHATTAN.
THE UPPER WEST SIDE.
DID THE CLIENT EXPLAIN WHY HE WANTED THIS THING, FANTOMELLE?
DO THEY EVER? THIS WHOLE JOB WAS HANDLED REMOTELY. I DON'T EVEN KNOW HIS NAME--JUST SOME SORT OF CODEWORD. LIKE A TITLE.
WELL, HE CERTAINLY PICKED A NICE SPOT FOR THE HANDOFF. I LOVE NEW YORK IN THE WINTER.
YOU CAN HAVE IT. NOT ALL OF US WERE BORN WEARING FURS, CULPEPPER.
A FACT FOR WHICH YOU HAVE MY ETERNAL PITY, DAAAHLING.
WHUMP
YOU HAVE BEEN PAID. GIVE ME THE PRIZE.
WELL. THAT IS NOT YOUR TYPICAL CLIENT.
NO. NO, IT IS NOT.
I NEED YOU TO VERIFY YOUR I.D. WE WERE WARNED THAT ENNILUX MIGHT TRY TO GET THIS ITEM BACK. THERE'S A CERTAIN CODE PHRASE YOU'RE SUPPOSED TO USE TO IDENTIFY YOURSELF...
AH, YES. VERY WELL.

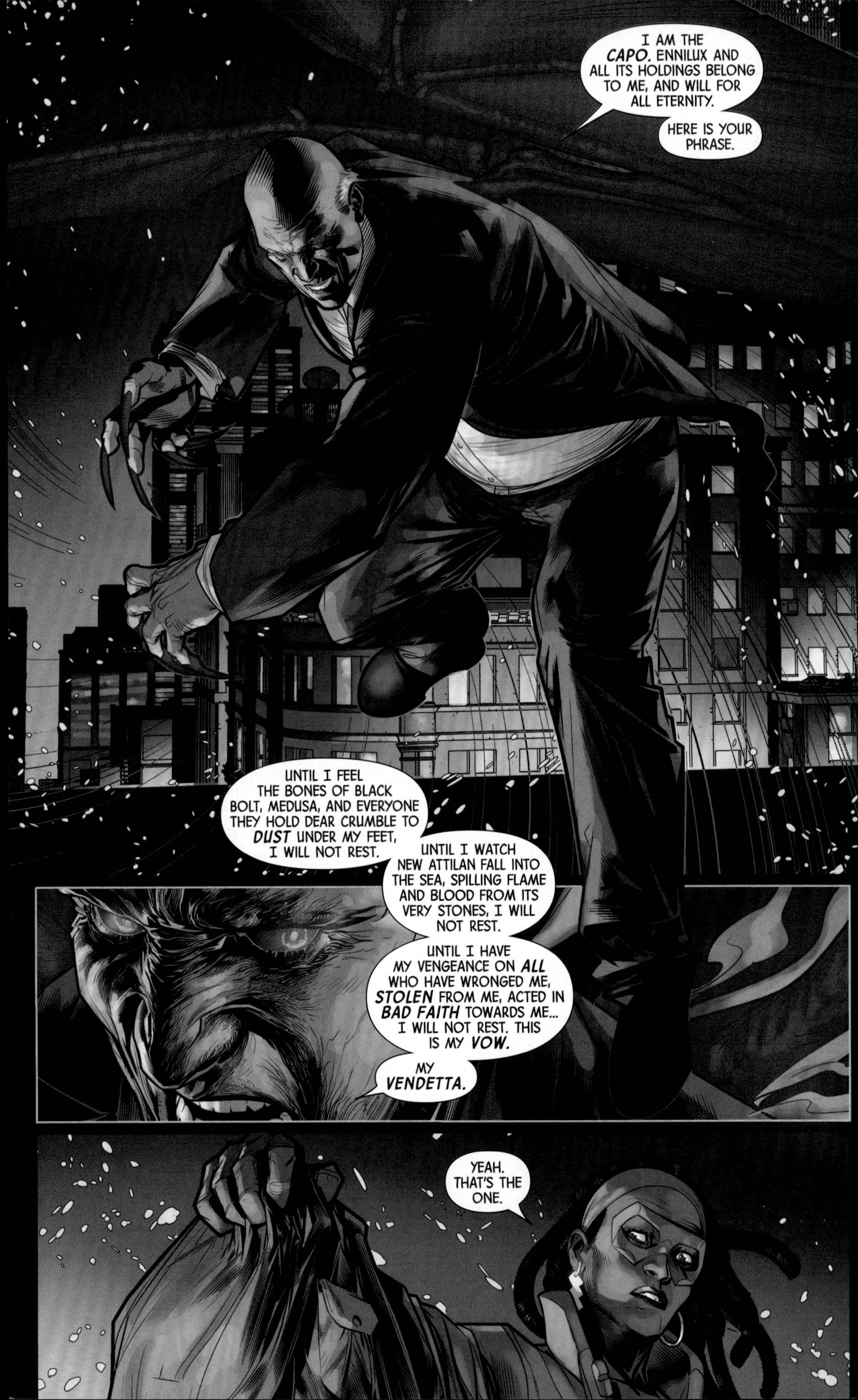
I AM THE CAPO. ENNILUX AND ALL ITS HOLDINGS BELONG TO ME, AND WILL FOR ALL ETERNITY.
HERE IS YOUR PHRASE.
UNTIL I FEEL THE BONES OF BLACK BOLT, MEDUSA, AND EVERYONE THEY HOLD DEAR CRUMBLE TO DUST UNDER MY FEET, I WILL NOT REST.
UNTIL I WATCH NEW ATTILAN FALL INTO THE SEA, SPILLING FLAME AND BLOOD FROM ITS VERY STONES, I WILL NOT REST.
UNTIL I HAVE MY VENGEANCE ON ALL WHO HAVE WRONGED ME, STOLEN FROM ME, ACTED IN BAD FAITH TOWARDS ME... I WILL NOT REST. THIS IS MY VOW.
MY VENDETTA.
YEAH. THAT'S THE ONE.

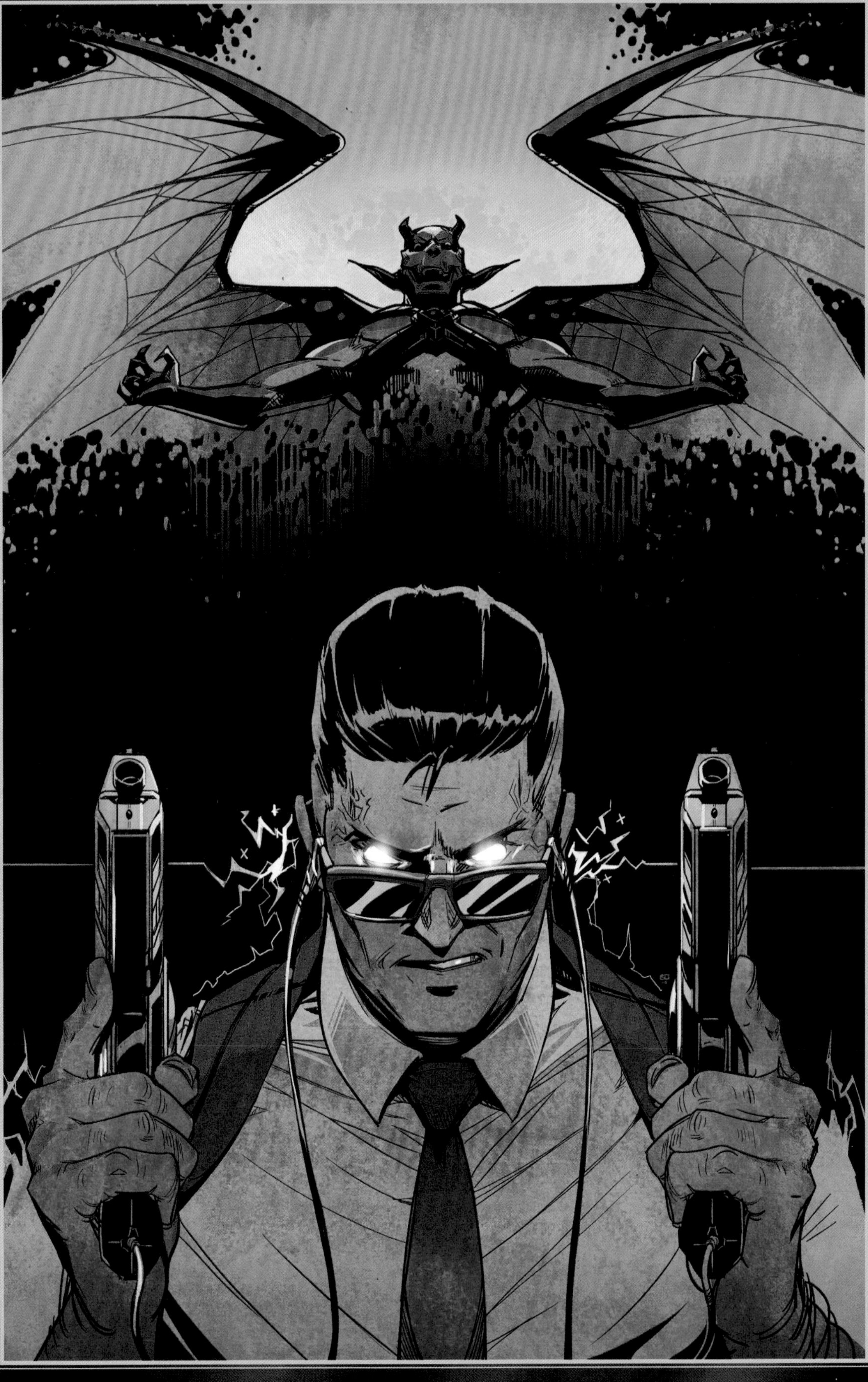

7

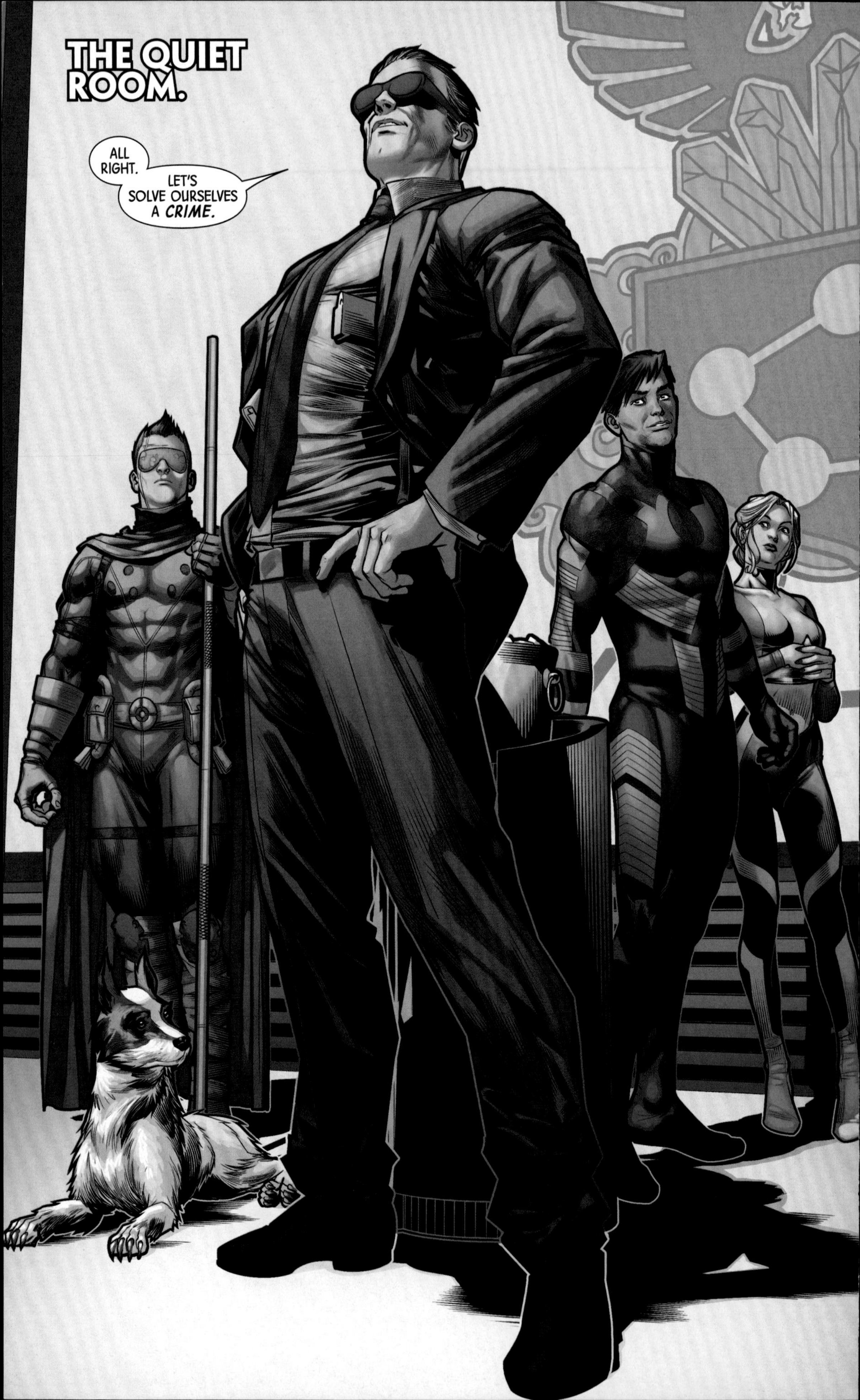
THE QUIET ROOM.
ALL RIGHT.
LET'S SOLVE OURSELVES A CRIME.

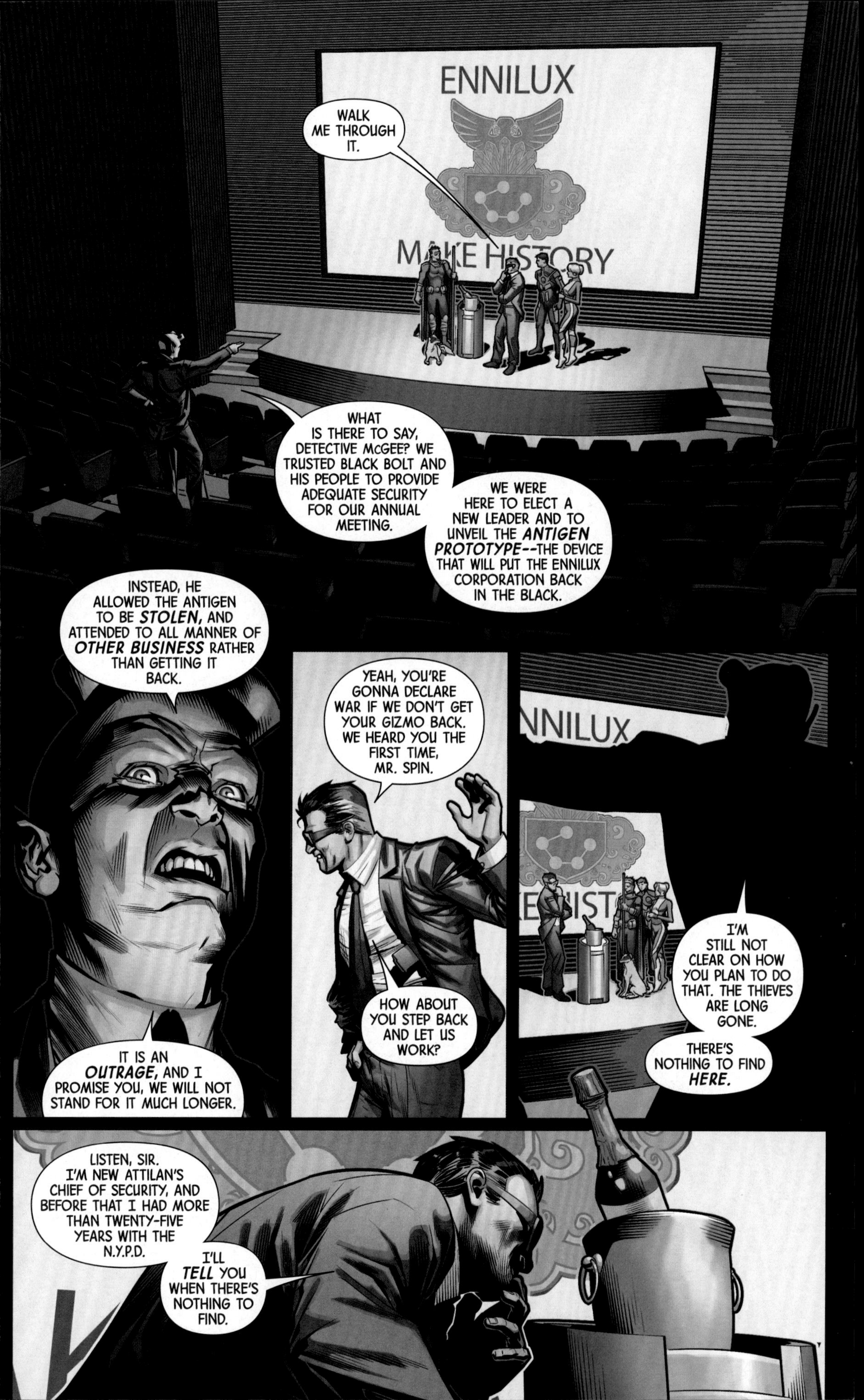
ENNILUX
MAKE HISTORY
WALK ME THROUGH IT.
WHAT IS THERE TO SAY, DETECTIVE McGEE? WE TRUSTED BLACK BOLT AND HIS PEOPLE TO PROVIDE ADEQUATE SECURITY FOR OUR ANNUAL MEETING.
WE WERE HERE TO ELECT A NEW LEADER AND TO UNVEIL THE ANTIGEN PROTOTYPE--THE DEVICE THAT WILL PUT THE ENNILUX CORPORATION BACK IN THE BLACK.
INSTEAD, HE ALLOWED THE ANTIGEN TO BE STOLEN, AND ATTENDED TO ALL MANNER OF OTHER BUSINESS RATHER THAN GETTING IT BACK.
IT IS AN OUTRAGE, AND I PROMISE YOU, WE WILL NOT STAND FOR IT MUCH LONGER.
YEAH, YOU'RE GONNA DECLARE WAR IF WE DON'T GET YOUR GIZMO BACK. WE HEARD YOU THE FIRST TIME, MR. SPIN.
HOW ABOUT YOU STEP BACK AND LET US WORK?
NNILUX
I'M STILL NOT CLEAR ON HOW YOU PLAN TO DO THAT. THE THIEVES ARE LONG GONE.
THERE'S NOTHING TO FIND HERE.
LISTEN, SIR. I'M NEW ATTILAN'S CHIEF OF SECURITY, AND BEFORE THAT I HAD MORE THAN TWENTY-FIVE YEARS WITH THE N.Y.P.D.
I'LL TELL YOU WHEN THERE'S NOTHING TO FIND.

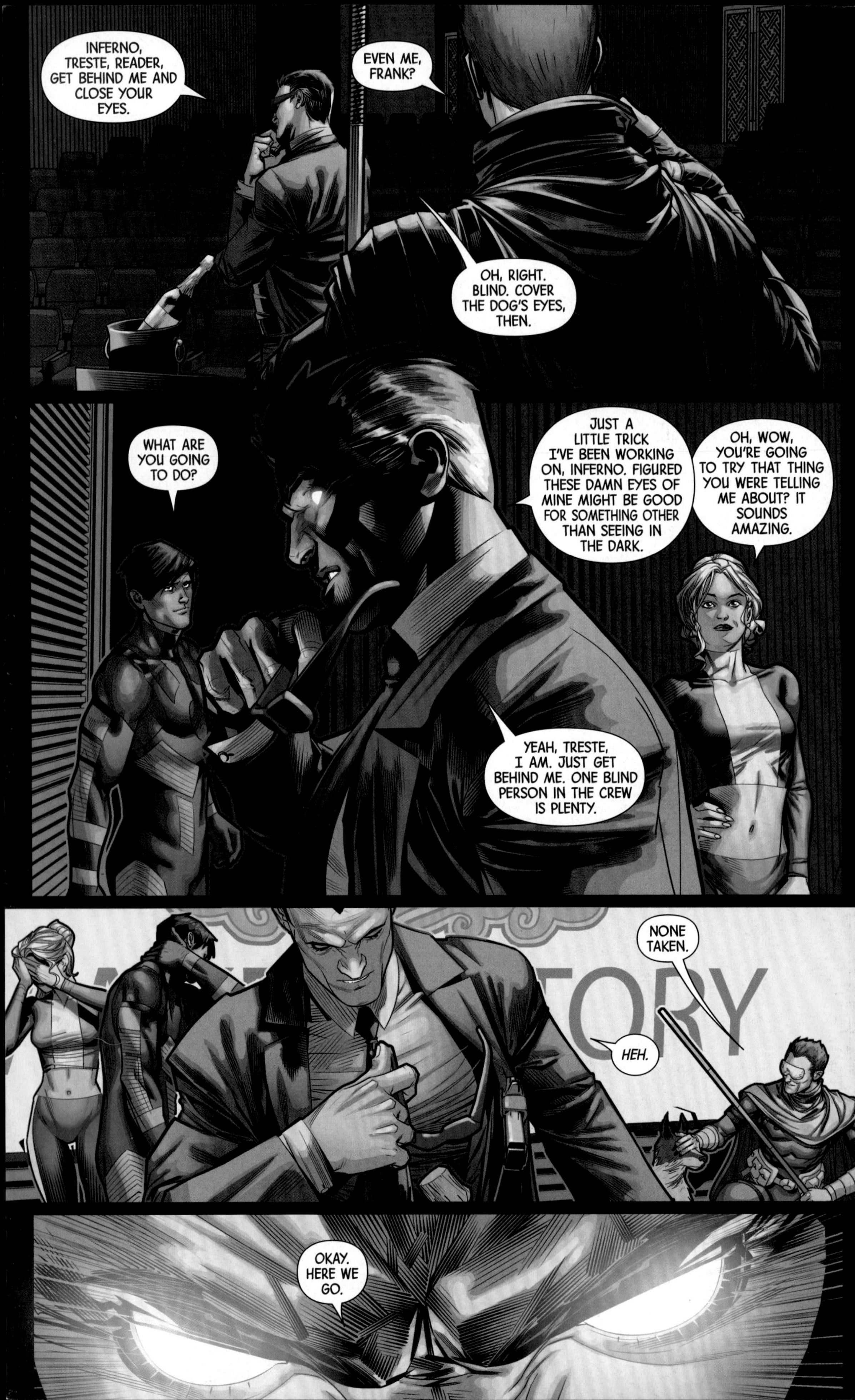
INFERNO, TRESTE, READER, GET BEHIND ME AND CLOSE YOUR EYES.
EVEN ME, FRANK?
OH, RIGHT. BLIND. COVER THE DOG'S EYES, THEN.
WHAT ARE YOU GOING TO DO?
JUST A LITTLE TRICK I'VE BEEN WORKING ON, INFERNO. FIGURED THESE DAMN EYES OF MINE MIGHT BE GOOD FOR SOMETHING OTHER THAN SEEING IN THE DARK.
OH, WOW, YOU'RE GOING TO TRY THAT THING YOU WERE TELLING ME ABOUT? IT SOUNDS AMAZING.
YEAH, TRESTE, I AM. JUST GET BEHIND ME. ONE BLIND PERSON IN THE CREW IS PLENTY.
NONE TAKEN.
HEH.
OKAY. HERE WE GO.

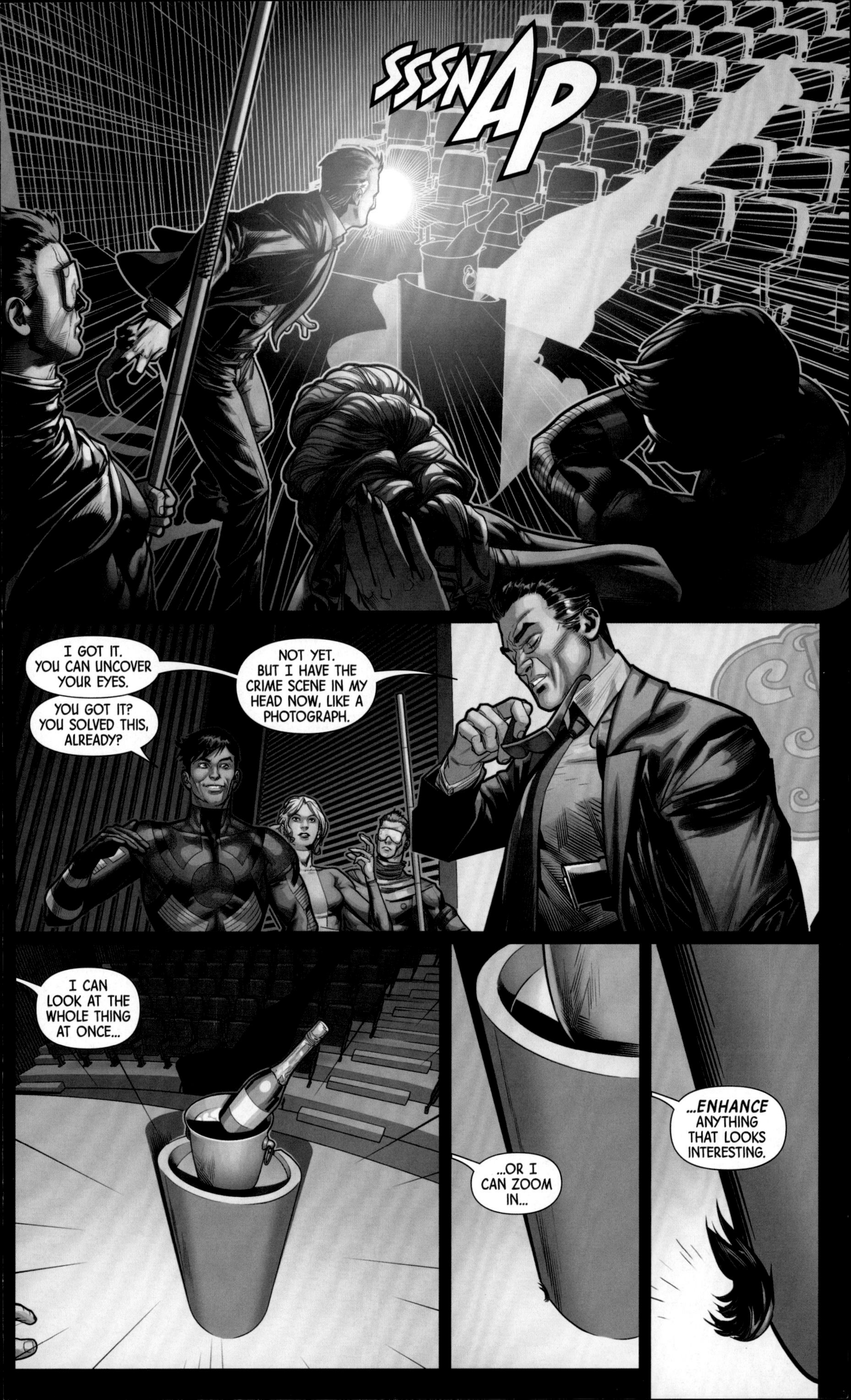
SSSNAP
I GOT IT. YOU CAN UNCOVER YOUR EYES.
YOU GOT IT? YOU SOLVED THIS, ALREADY?
NOT YET. BUT I HAVE THE CRIME SCENE IN MY HEAD NOW, LIKE A PHOTOGRAPH.
I CAN LOOK AT THE WHOLE THING AT ONCE...
...OR I CAN ZOOM IN...
...ENHANCE ANYTHING THAT LOOKS INTERESTING.

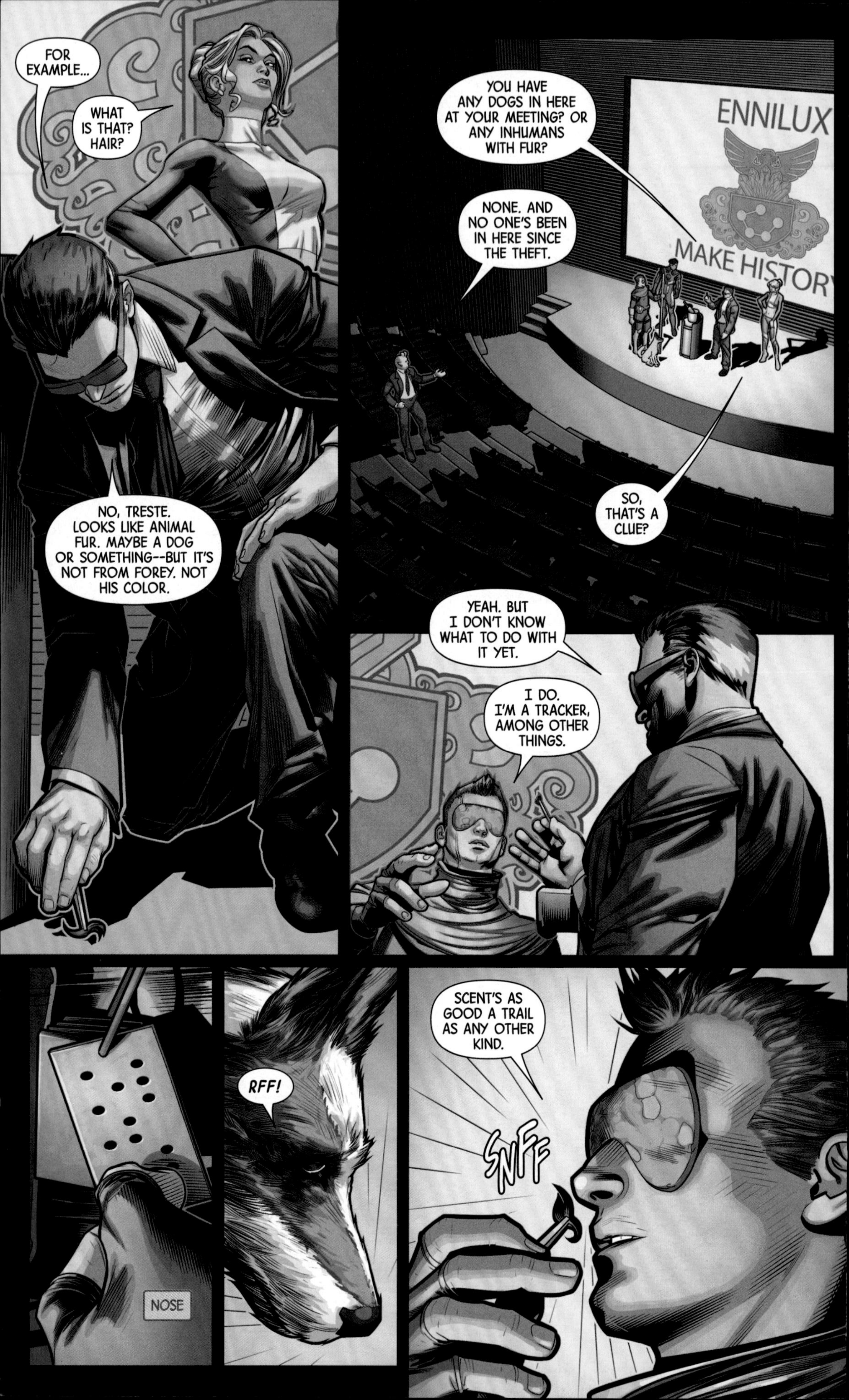
FOR EXAMPLE...
WHAT IS THAT? HAIR?
NO, TRESTE. LOOKS LIKE ANIMAL FUR. MAYBE A DOG OR SOMETHING--BUT IT'S NOT FROM FOREY. NOT HIS COLOR.
YOU HAVE ANY DOGS IN HERE AT YOUR MEETING? OR ANY INHUMANS WITH FUR?
NONE. AND NO ONE'S BEEN IN HERE SINCE THE THEFT.
ENNILUX
MAKE HISTORY
SO, THAT'S A CLUE?
YEAH. BUT I DON'T KNOW WHAT TO DO WITH IT YET.
I DO. I'M A TRACKER, AMONG OTHER THINGS.
NOSE
RFF!
SCENT'S AS GOOD A TRAIL AS ANY OTHER KIND.
SNIFF

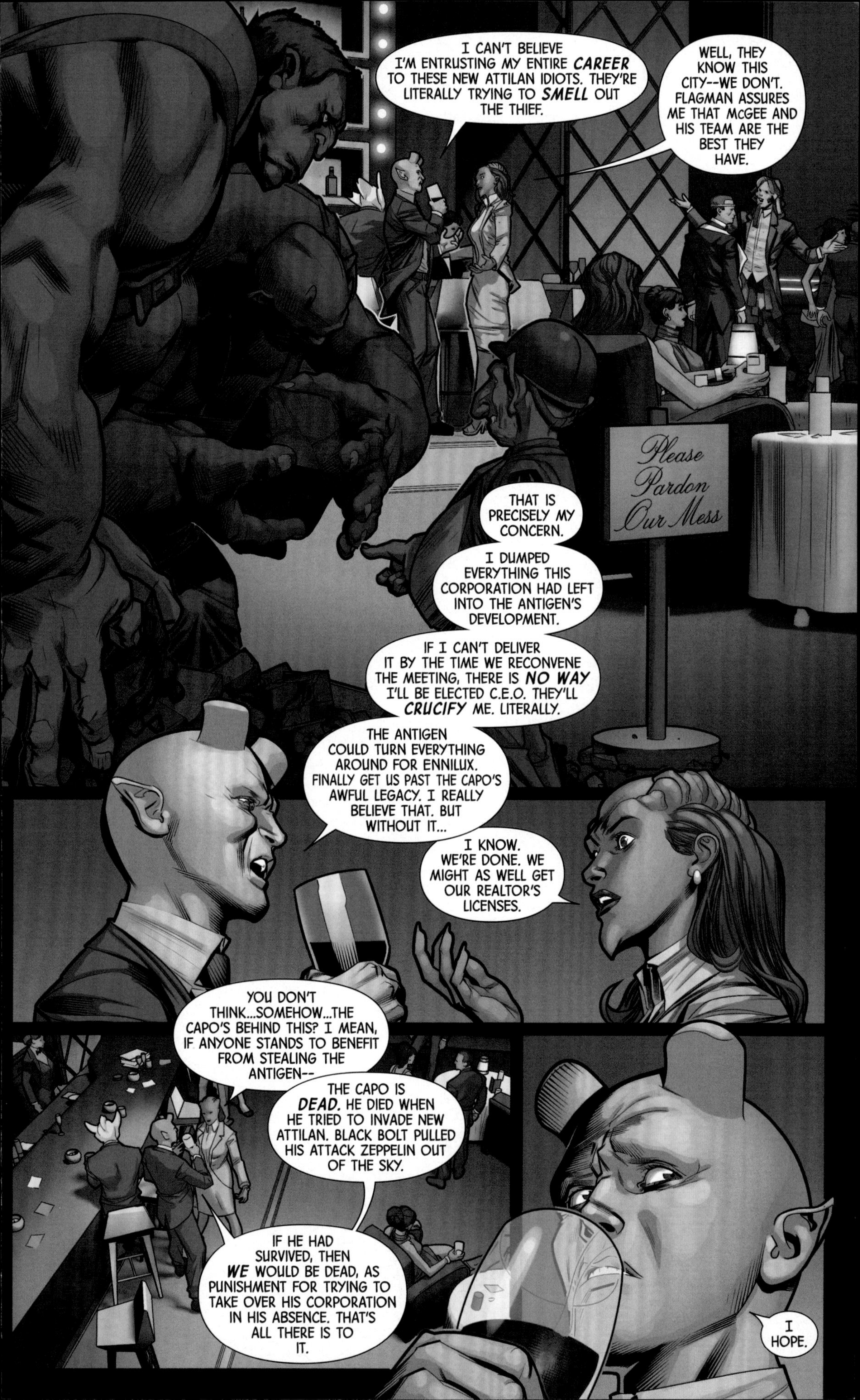
I CAN'T BELIEVE I'M ENTRUSTING MY ENTIRE CAREER TO THESE NEW ATTILAN IDIOTS. THEY'RE LITERALLY TRYING TO SMELL OUT THE THIEF.
WELL, THEY KNOW THIS CITY--WE DON'T. FLAGMAN ASSURES ME THAT McGEE AND HIS TEAM ARE THE BEST THEY HAVE.
Please Pardon Our Mess
THAT IS PRECISELY MY CONCERN.
I DUMPED EVERYTHING THIS CORPORATION HAD LEFT INTO THE ANTIGEN'S DEVELOPMENT.
IF I CAN'T DELIVER IT BY THE TIME WE RECONVENE THE MEETING, THERE IS NO WAY I'LL BE ELECTED C.E.O. THEY'LL CRUCIFY ME. LITERALLY.
THE ANTIGEN COULD TURN EVERYTHING AROUND FOR ENNILUX. FINALLY GET US PAST THE CAPO'S AWFUL LEGACY. I REALLY BELIEVE THAT. BUT WITHOUT IT...
I KNOW. WE'RE DONE. WE MIGHT AS WELL GET OUR REALTOR'S LICENSES.
YOU DON'T THINK...SOMEHOW...THE CAPO'S BEHIND THIS? I MEAN, IF ANYONE STANDS TO BENEFIT FROM STEALING THE ANTIGEN--
THE CAPO IS DEAD. HE DIED WHEN HE TRIED TO INVADE NEW ATTILAN. BLACK BOLT PULLED HIS ATTACK ZEPPELIN OUT OF THE SKY.
IF HE HAD SURVIVED, THEN WE WOULD BE DEAD, AS PUNISHMENT FOR TRYING TO TAKE OVER HIS CORPORATION IN HIS ABSENCE. THAT'S ALL THERE IS TO IT.
I HOPE.

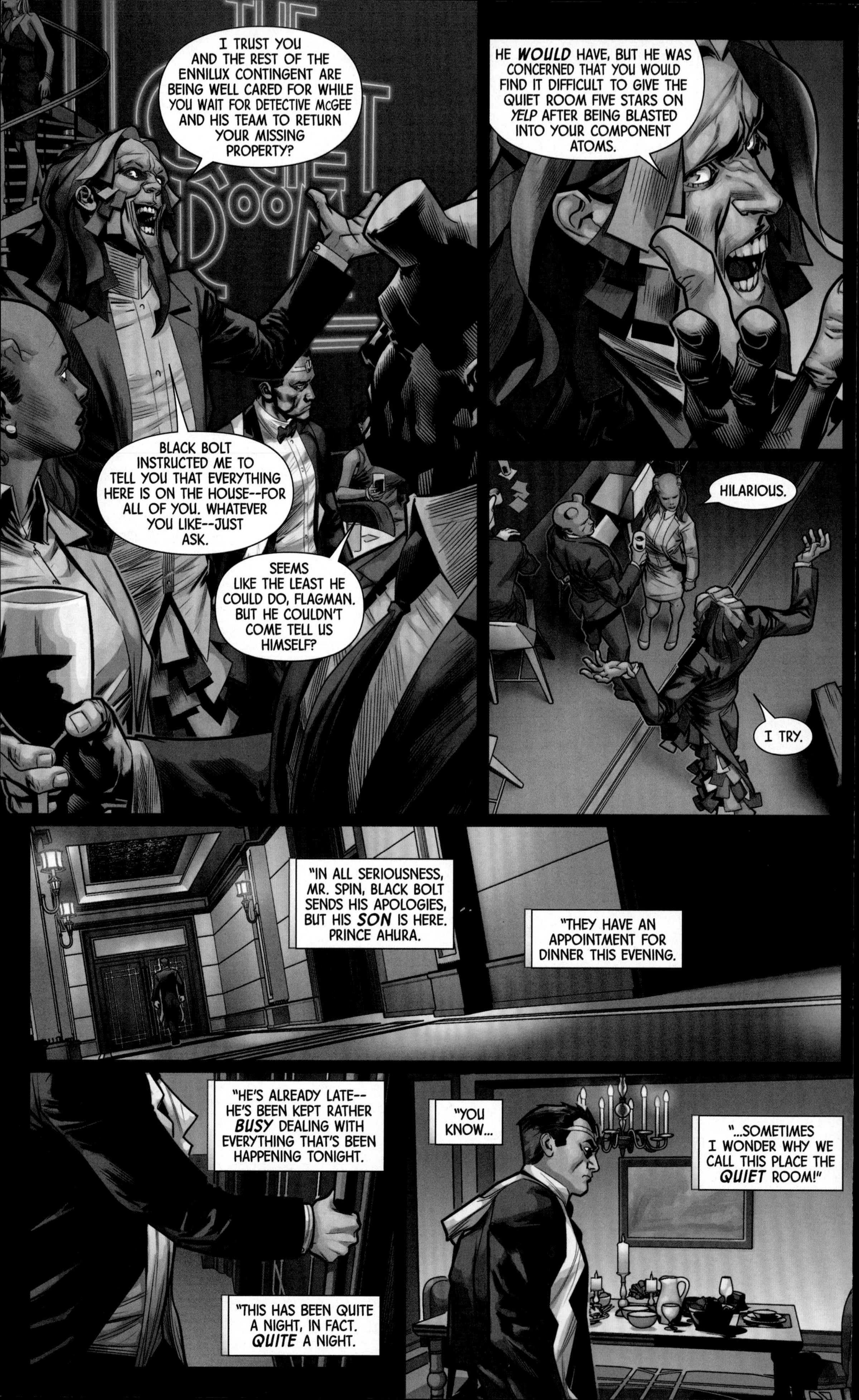
I TRUST YOU AND THE REST OF THE ENNILUX CONTINGENT ARE BEING WELL CARED FOR WHILE YOU WAIT FOR DETECTIVE McGEE AND HIS TEAM TO RETURN YOUR MISSING PROPERTY?
BLACK BOLT INSTRUCTED ME TO TELL YOU THAT EVERYTHING HERE IS ON THE HOUSE--FOR ALL OF YOU. WHATEVER YOU LIKE--JUST ASK.
SEEMS LIKE THE LEAST HE COULD DO, FLAGMAN. BUT HE COULDN'T COME TELL US HIMSELF?
HE WOULD HAVE, BUT HE WAS CONCERNED THAT YOU WOULD FIND IT DIFFICULT TO GIVE THE QUIET ROOM FIVE STARS ON YELP AFTER BEING BLASTED INTO YOUR COMPONENT ATOMS.
HILARIOUS.
I TRY.
"IN ALL SERIOUSNESS, MR. SPIN, BLACK BOLT SENDS HIS APOLOGIES, BUT HIS SON IS HERE. PRINCE AHURA.
"THEY HAVE AN APPOINTMENT FOR DINNER THIS EVENING.
"HE'S ALREADY LATE-- HE'S BEEN KEPT RATHER BUSY DEALING WITH EVERYTHING THAT'S BEEN HAPPENING TONIGHT.
"THIS HAS BEEN QUITE A NIGHT, IN FACT. QUITE A NIGHT.
"YOU KNOW...
"...SOMETIMES I WONDER WHY WE CALL THIS PLACE THE QUIET ROOM!"

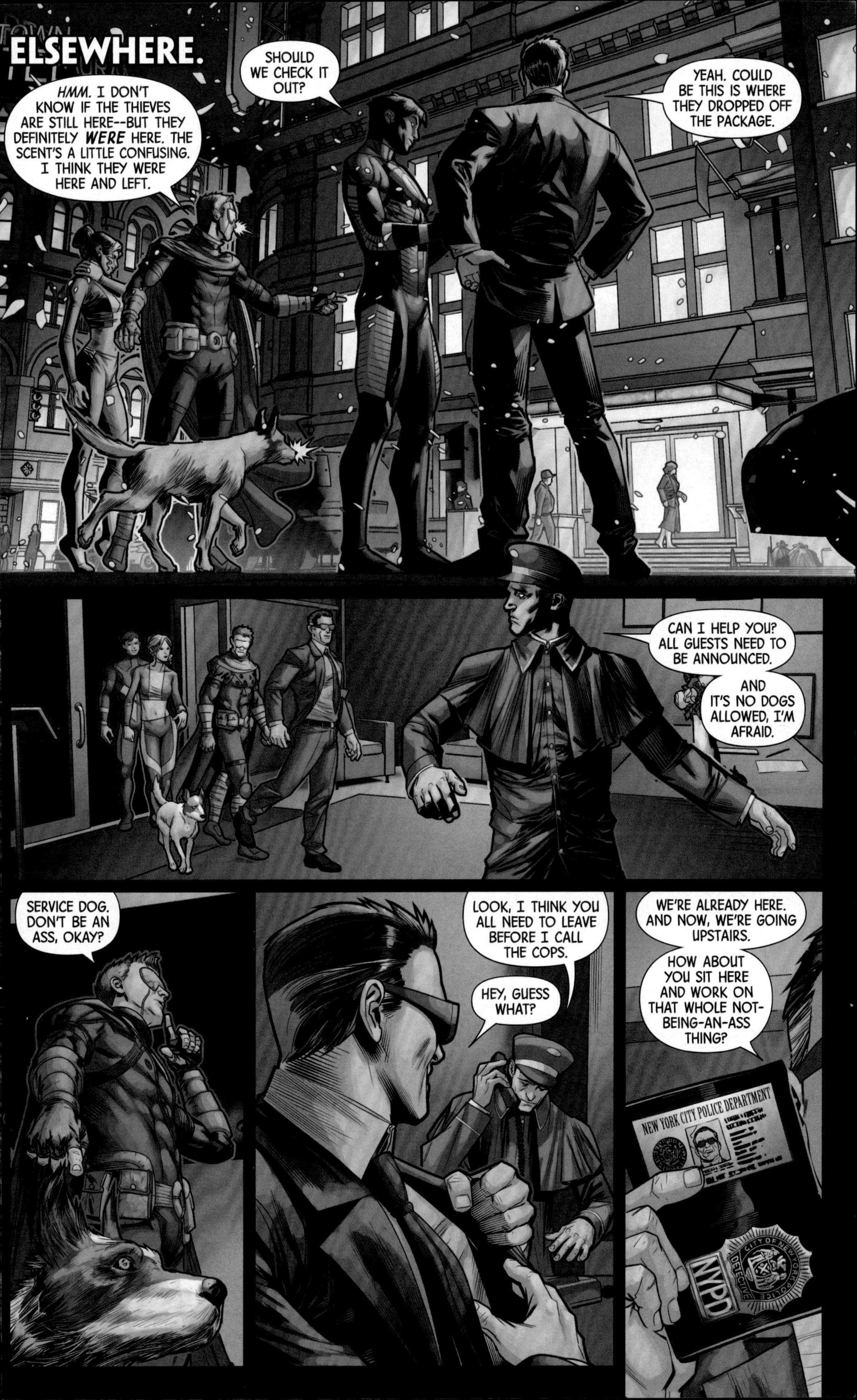
ELSEWHERE.
HMM. I DON'T KNOW IF THE THIEVES ARE STILL HERE--BUT THEY DEFINITELY WERE HERE. THE SCENT'S A LITTLE CONFUSING. I THINK THEY WERE HERE AND LEFT.
SHOULD WE CHECK IT OUT?
YEAH. COULD BE THIS IS WHERE THEY DROPPED OFF THE PACKAGE.
CAN I HELP YOU? ALL GUESTS NEED TO BE ANNOUNCED.
AND IT'S NO DOGS ALLOWED, I'M AFRAID.
SERVICE DOG. DON'T BE AN ASS, OKAY?
LOOK, I THINK YOU ALL NEED TO LEAVE BEFORE I CALL THE COPS.
HEY, GUESS WHAT?
WE'RE ALREADY HERE. AND NOW, WE'RE GOING UPSTAIRS.
HOW ABOUT YOU SIT HERE AND WORK ON THAT WHOLE NOT-BEING-AN-ASS THING?
NEW YORK CITY POLICE DEPARTMENT
NYPD

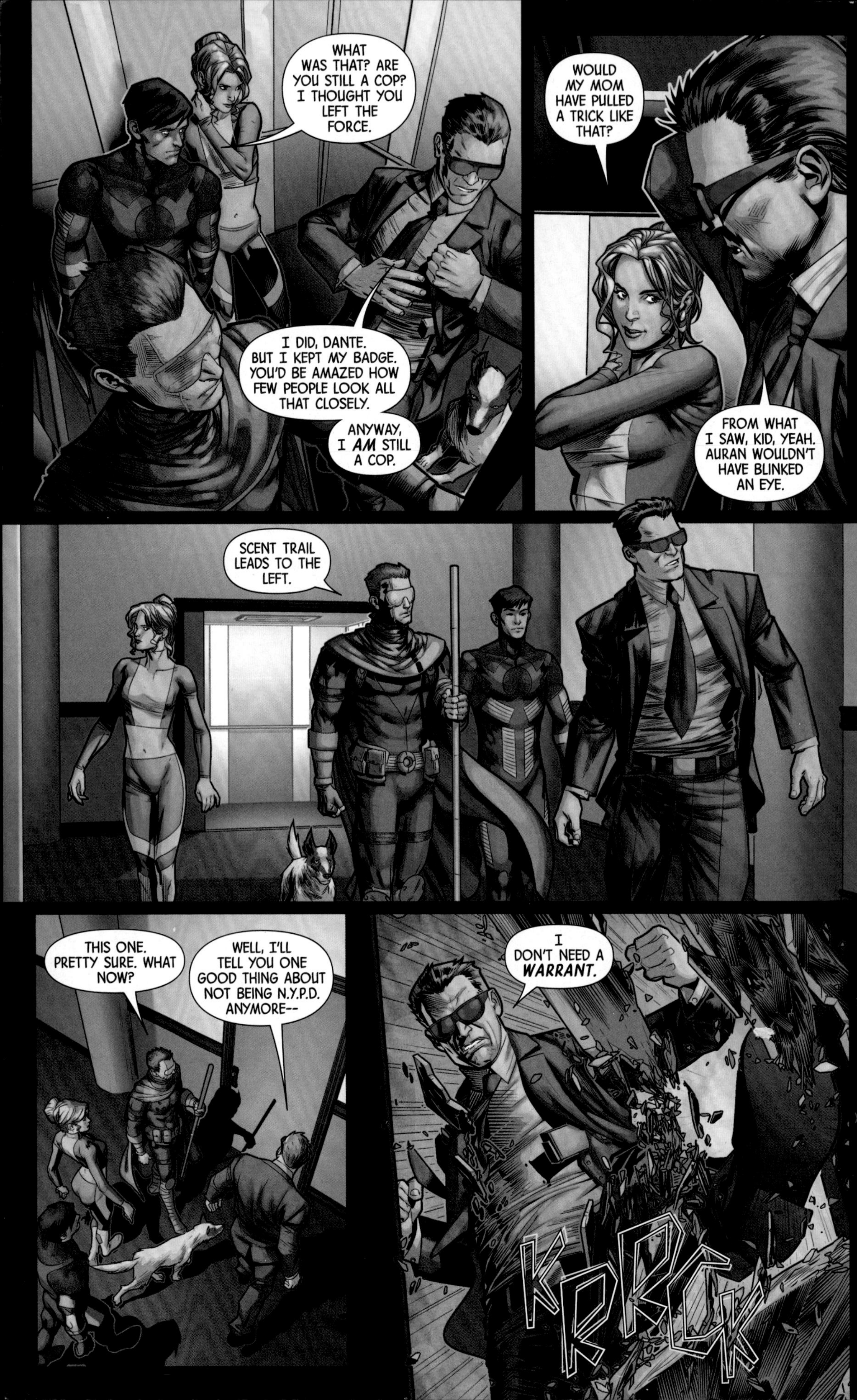
WHAT WAS THAT? ARE YOU STILL A COP? I THOUGHT YOU LEFT THE FORCE.
I DID, DANTE. BUT I KEPT MY BADGE. YOU'D BE AMAZED HOW FEW PEOPLE LOOK ALL THAT CLOSELY.
ANYWAY, I *AM* STILL A COP.
WOULD MY MOM HAVE PULLED A TRICK LIKE THAT?
FROM WHAT I SAW, KID, YEAH. AURAN WOULDN'T HAVE BLINKED AN EYE.
SCENT TRAIL LEADS TO THE LEFT.
THIS ONE. PRETTY SURE. WHAT NOW?
WELL, I'LL TELL YOU ONE GOOD THING ABOUT NOT BEING N.Y.P.D. ANYMORE--
I DON'T NEED A *WARRANT.*
KRRCK

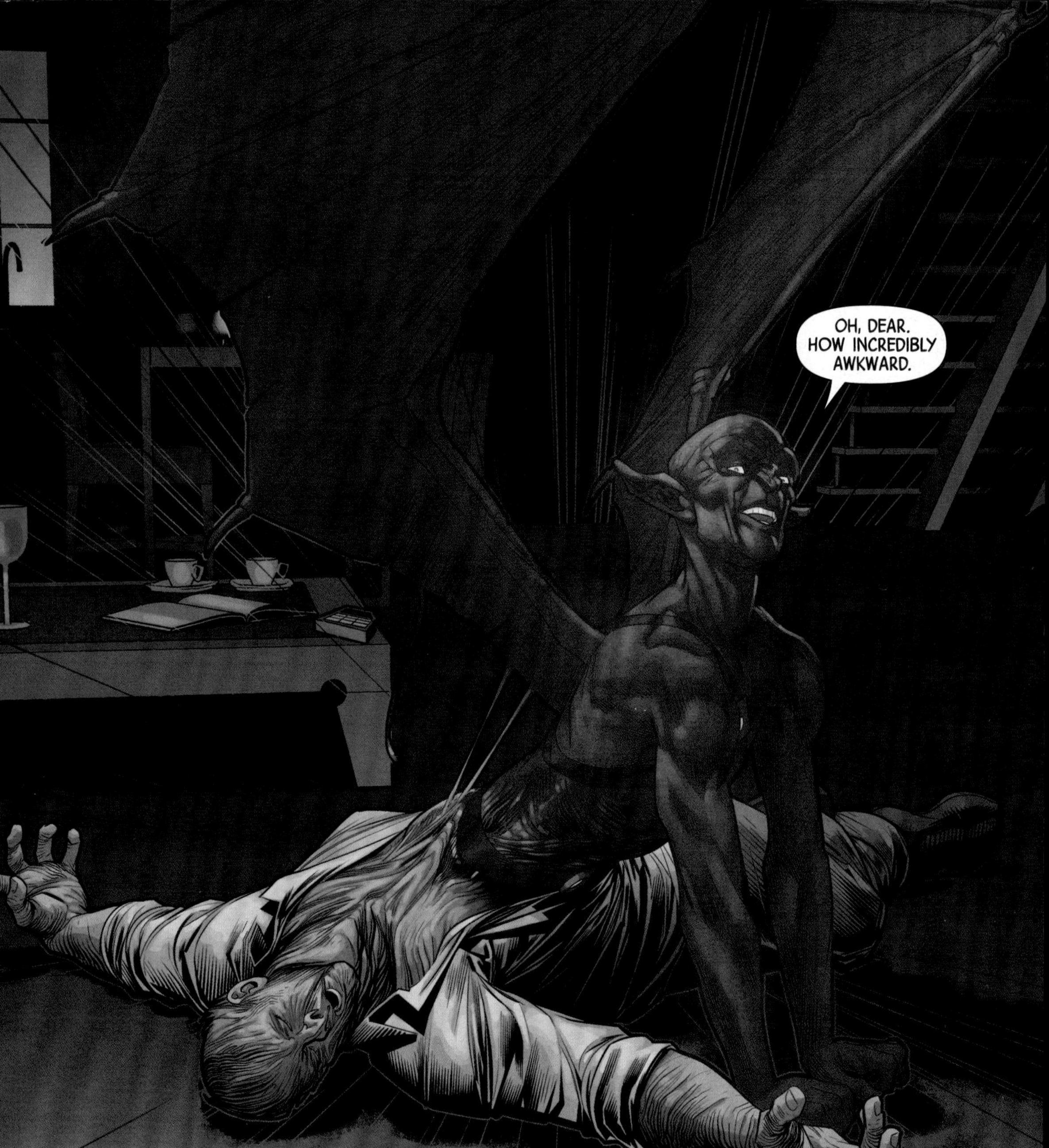
OH, DEAR. HOW INCREDIBLY AWKWARD.

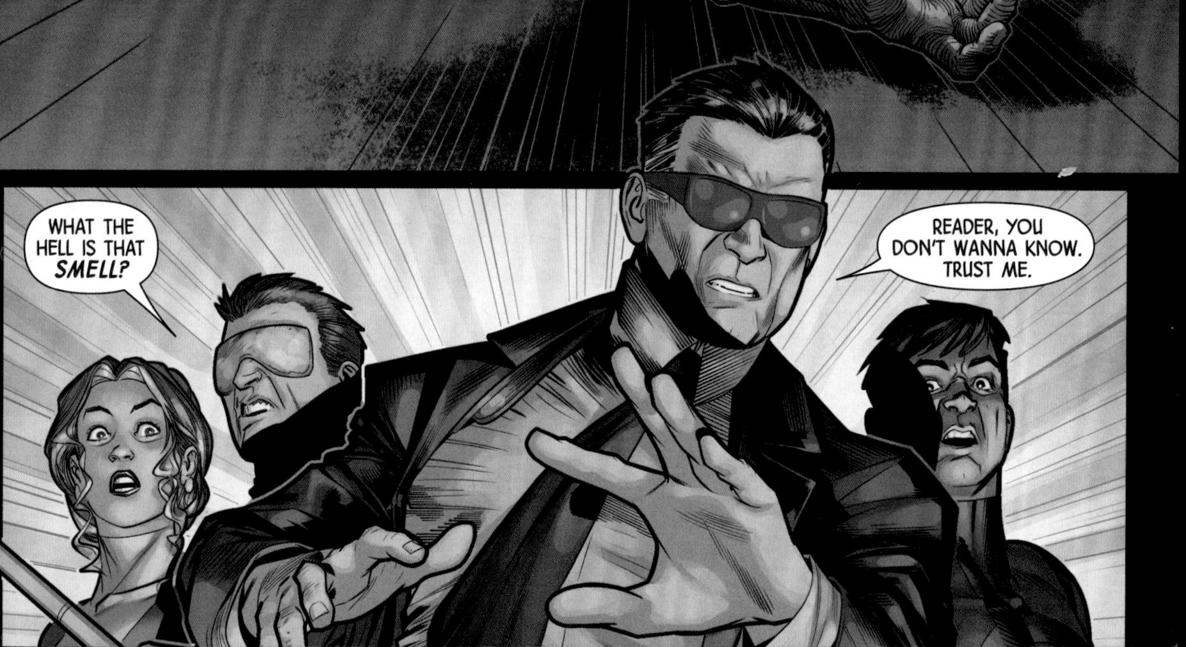
WHAT THE HELL IS THAT *SMELL?*
READER, YOU DON'T WANNA KNOW. TRUST ME.

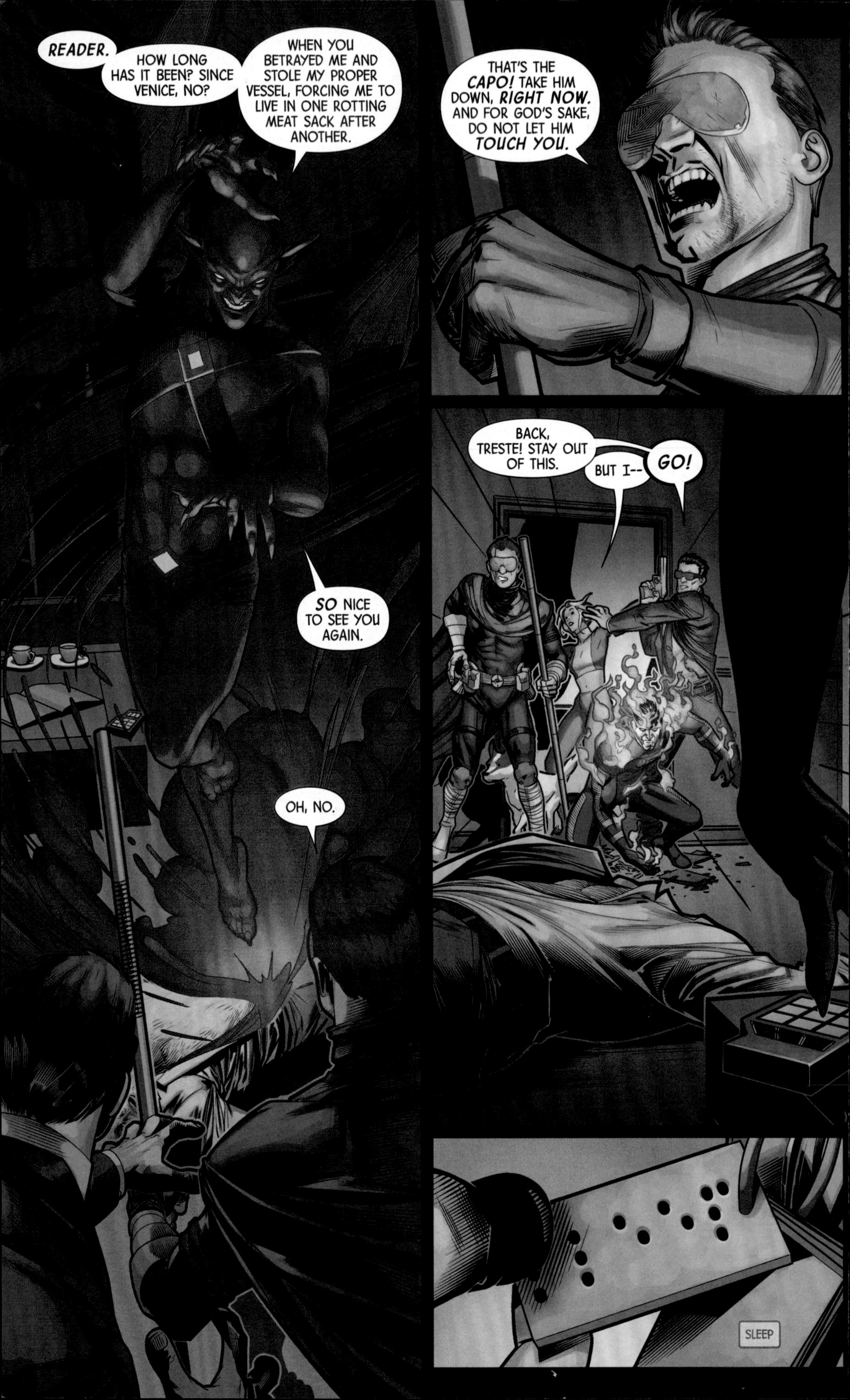
READER.
HOW LONG HAS IT BEEN? SINCE VENICE, NO?
WHEN YOU BETRAYED ME AND STOLE MY PROPER VESSEL, FORCING ME TO LIVE IN ONE ROTTING MEAT SACK AFTER ANOTHER.
SO NICE TO SEE YOU AGAIN.
OH, NO.
THAT'S THE CAPO! TAKE HIM DOWN, RIGHT NOW. AND FOR GOD'S SAKE, DO NOT LET HIM TOUCH YOU.
BACK, TRESTE! STAY OUT OF THIS.
BUT I--
GO!
SLEEP

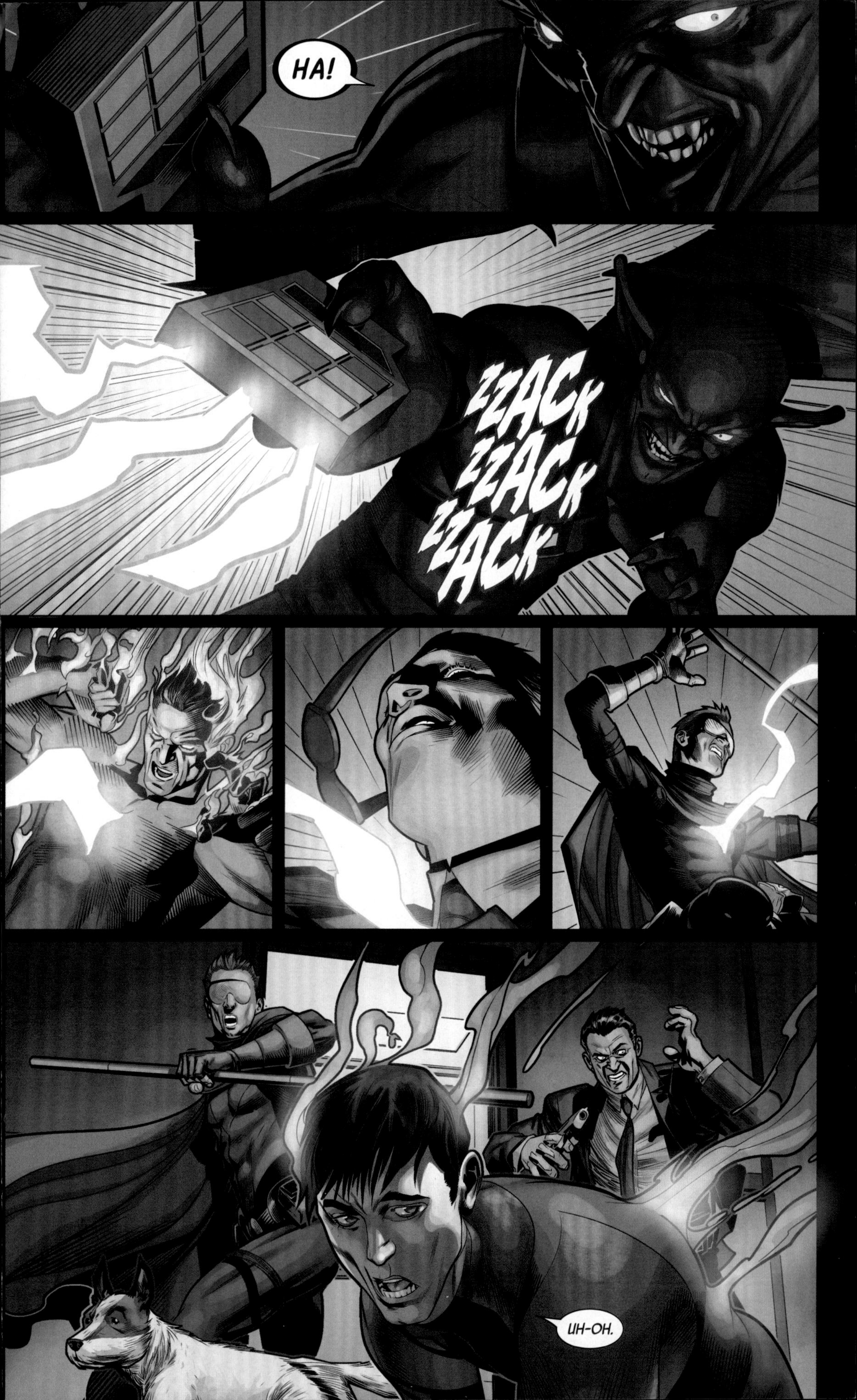
HA!
ZZACK
ZZACK
ZZACK
UH-OH.

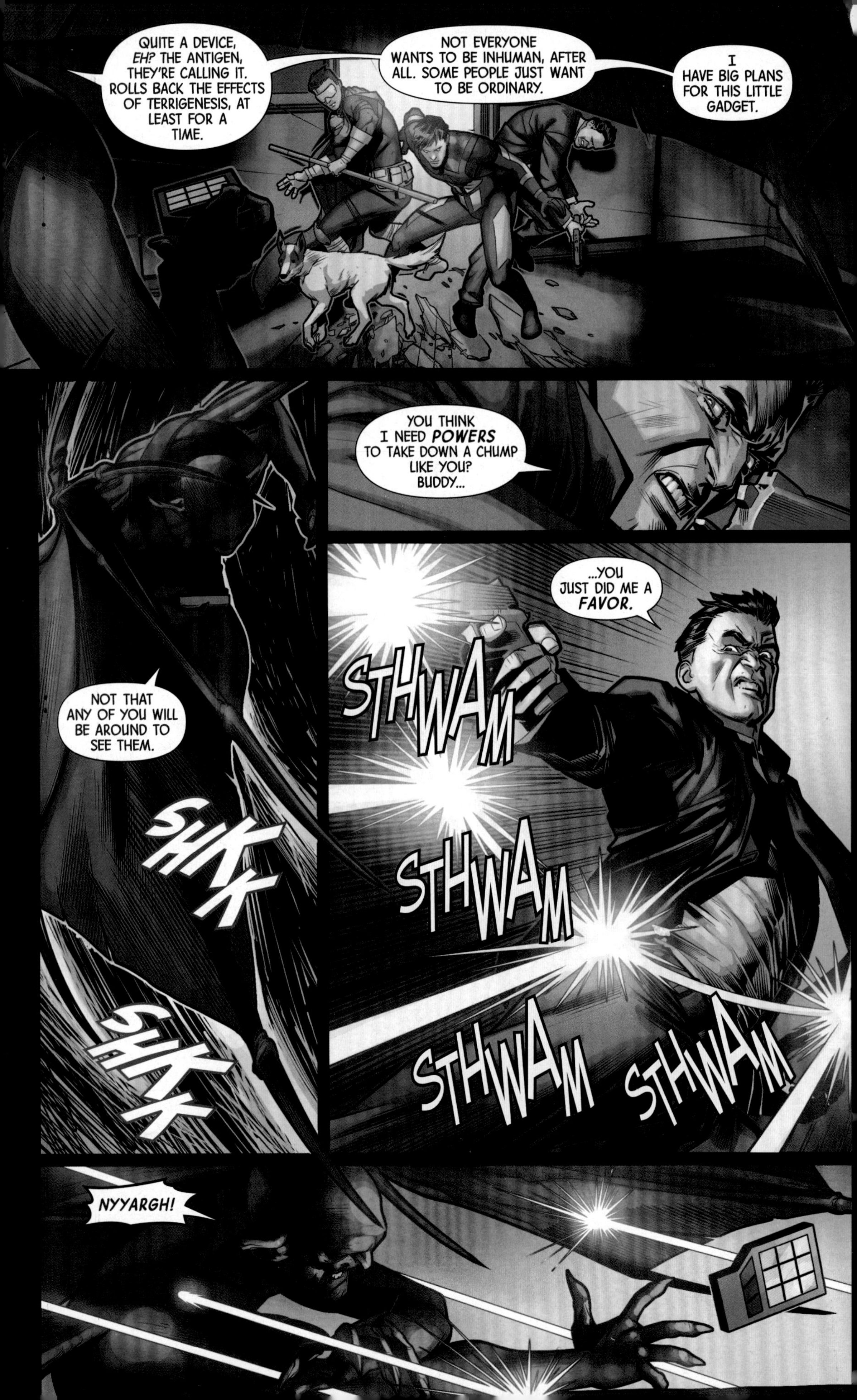
QUITE A DEVICE, EH? THE ANTIGEN, THEY'RE CALLING IT. ROLLS BACK THE EFFECTS OF TERRIGENESIS, AT LEAST FOR A TIME.
NOT EVERYONE WANTS TO BE INHUMAN, AFTER ALL. SOME PEOPLE JUST WANT TO BE ORDINARY.
I HAVE BIG PLANS FOR THIS LITTLE GADGET.
YOU THINK I NEED POWERS TO TAKE DOWN A CHUMP LIKE YOU? BUDDY...
NOT THAT ANY OF YOU WILL BE AROUND TO SEE THEM.
...YOU JUST DID ME A FAVOR.
STHWAM
SHKK
STHWAM
SHKK
STHWAM
STHWAM
NYYARGH!

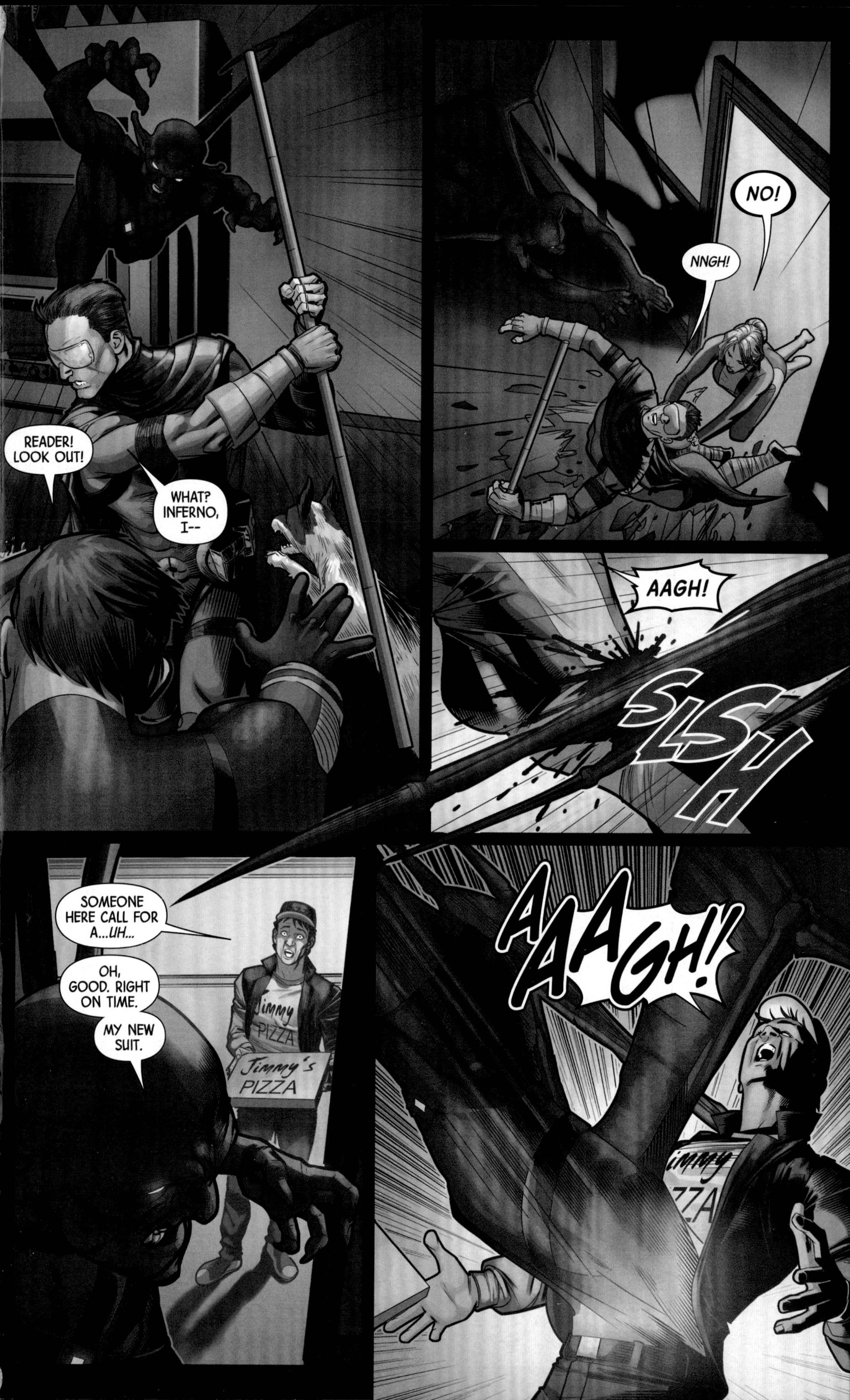
READER! LOOK OUT!
WHAT? INFERNO, I--
NO!
NNGH!
AAGH!
SLSH
SOMEONE HERE CALL FOR A...UH...
OH, GOOD. RIGHT ON TIME.
MY NEW SUIT.
Jimmy's PIZZA
AAAGH!

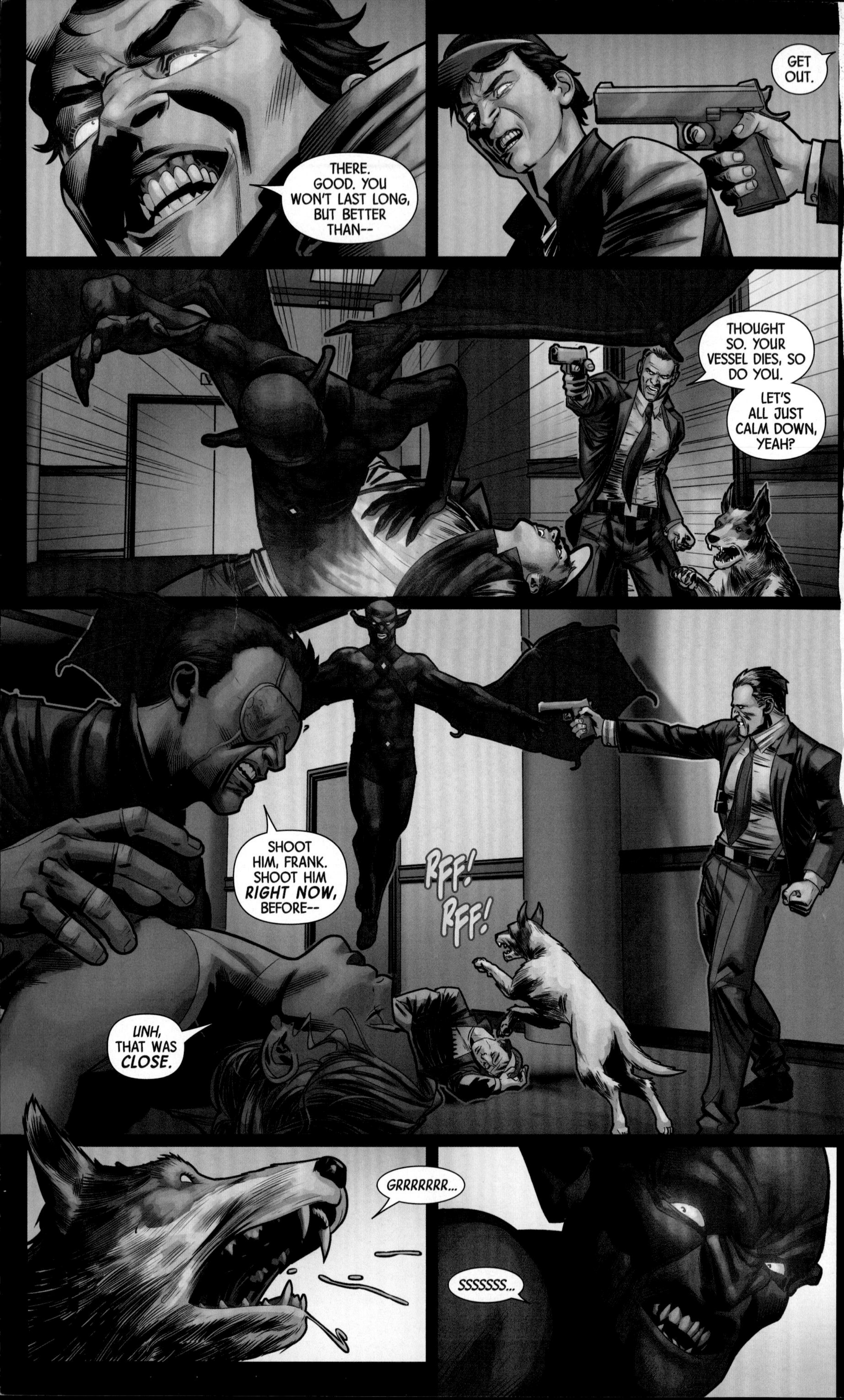
THERE. GOOD. YOU WON'T LAST LONG, BUT BETTER THAN--
GET OUT.
THOUGHT SO. YOUR VESSEL DIES, SO DO YOU.
LET'S ALL JUST CALM DOWN, YEAH?
SHOOT HIM, FRANK. SHOOT HIM RIGHT NOW, BEFORE--
RFF! RFF!
UNH, THAT WAS CLOSE.
GRRRRRRR...
SSSSSSS...

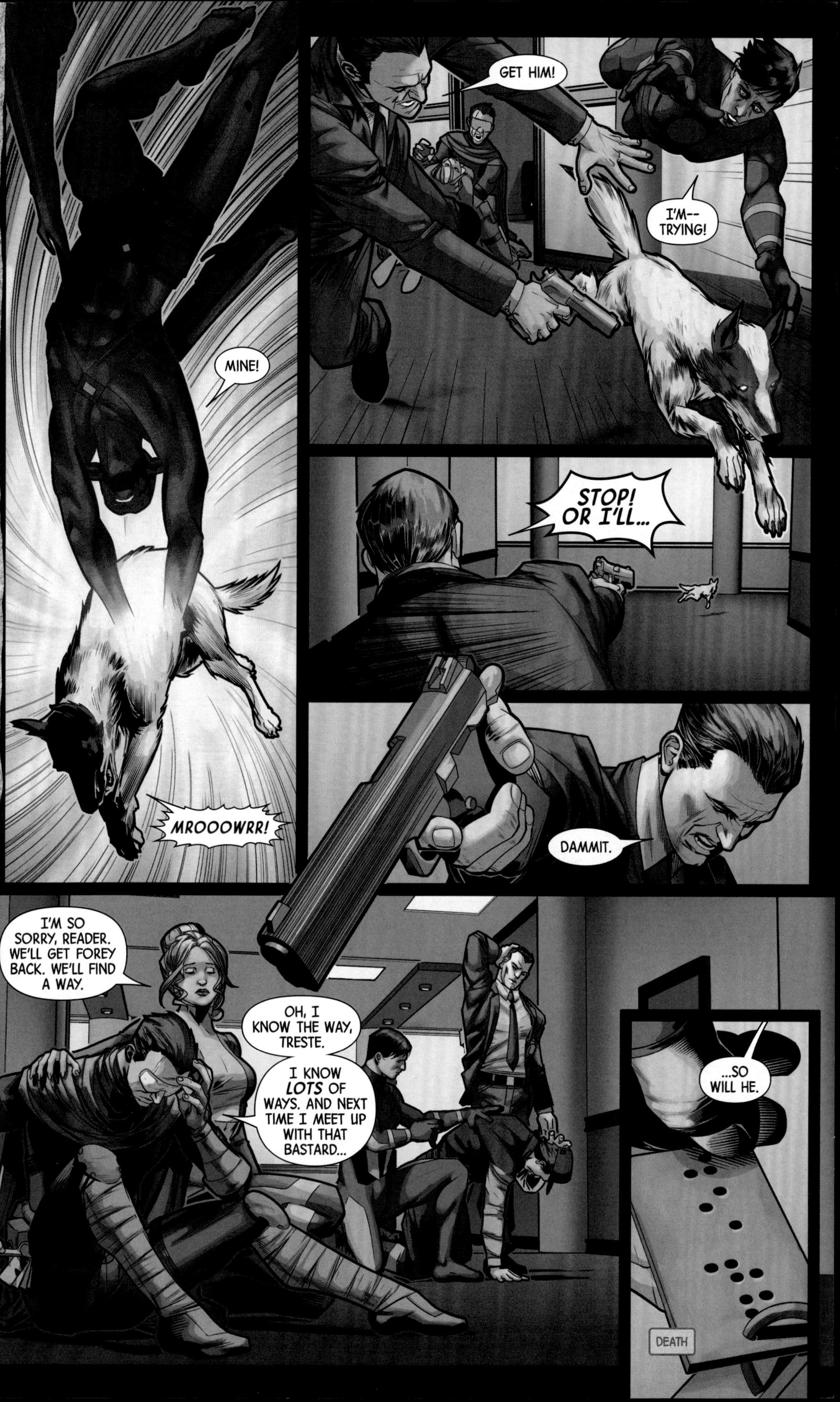
MINE!
MROOOWRR!
GET HIM!
I'M-- TRYING!
STOP! OR I'LL...
DAMMIT.
I'M SO SORRY, READER. WE'LL GET FOREY BACK. WE'LL FIND A WAY.
OH, I KNOW THE WAY, TRESTE.
I KNOW LOTS OF WAYS. AND NEXT TIME I MEET UP WITH THAT BASTARD...
...SO WILL HE.
DEATH

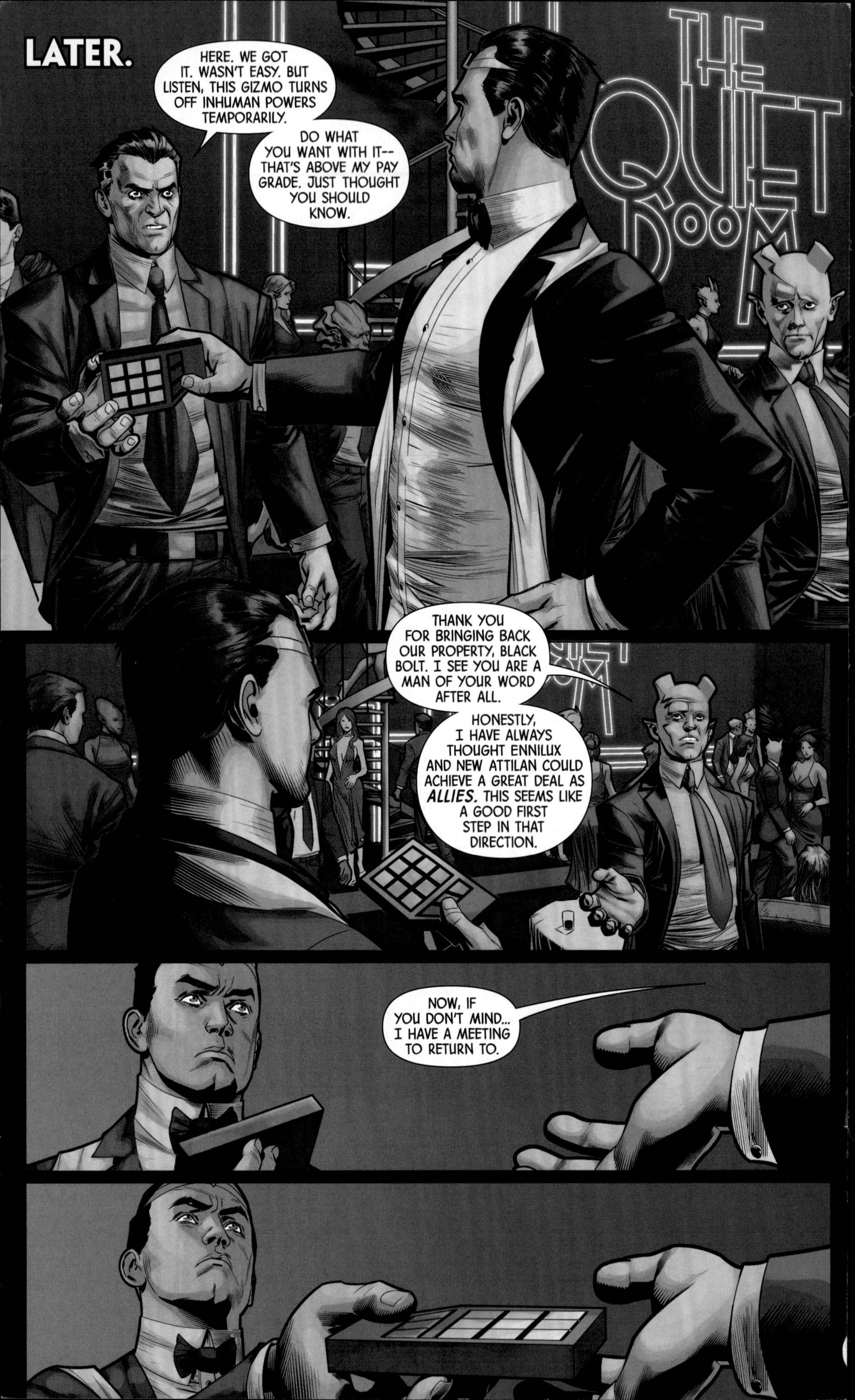
LATER.
HERE. WE GOT IT. WASN'T EASY. BUT LISTEN, THIS GIZMO TURNS OFF INHUMAN POWERS TEMPORARILY.
DO WHAT YOU WANT WITH IT-- THAT'S ABOVE MY PAY GRADE. JUST THOUGHT YOU SHOULD KNOW.
THE QUIET ROOM
THANK YOU FOR BRINGING BACK OUR PROPERTY, BLACK BOLT. I SEE YOU ARE A MAN OF YOUR WORD AFTER ALL.
HONESTLY, I HAVE ALWAYS THOUGHT ENNILUX AND NEW ATTILAN COULD ACHIEVE A GREAT DEAL AS *ALLIES.* THIS SEEMS LIKE A GOOD FIRST STEP IN THAT DIRECTION.
NOW, IF YOU DON'T MIND... I HAVE A MEETING TO RETURN TO.

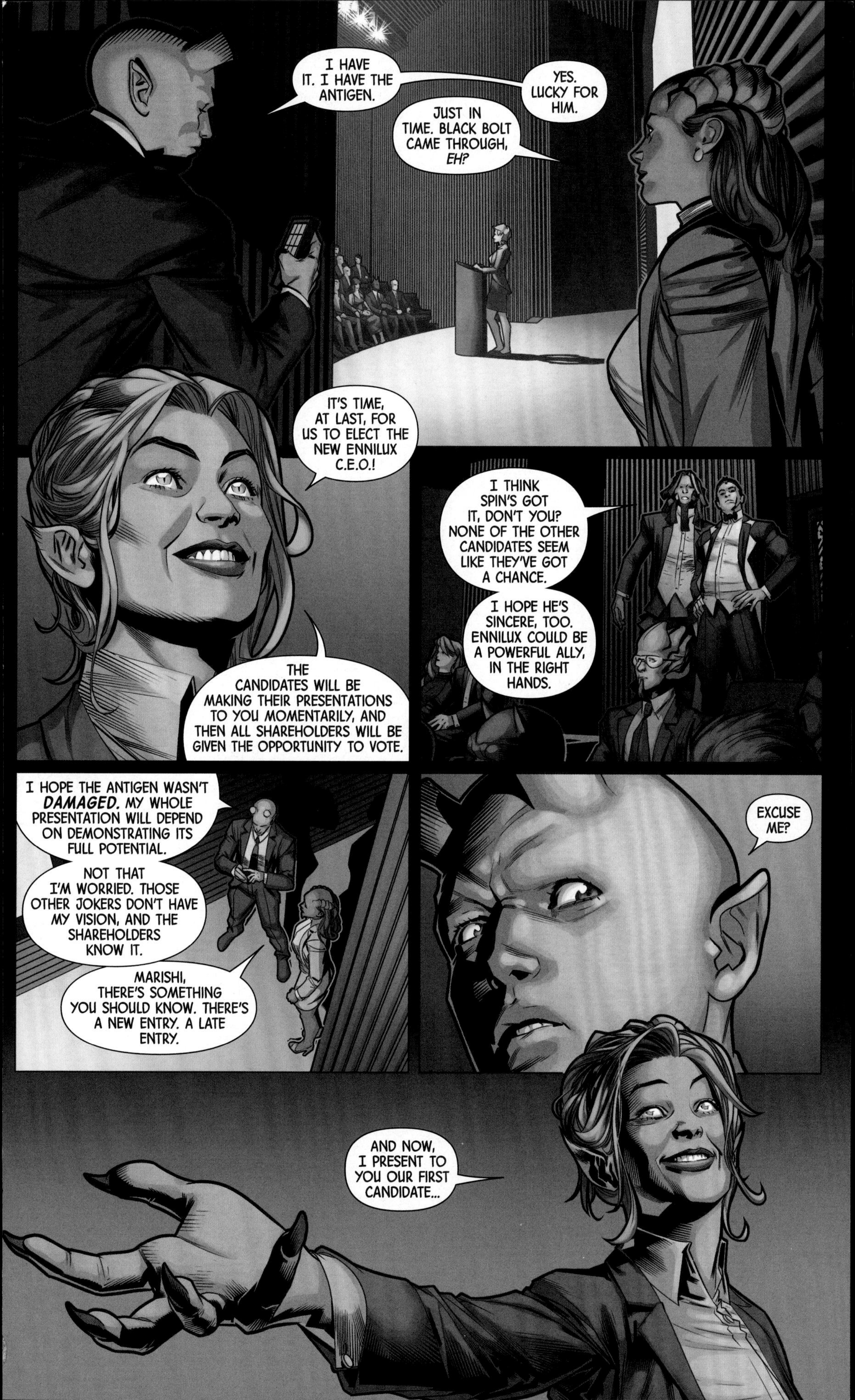
I HAVE IT. I HAVE THE ANTIGEN.
YES. LUCKY FOR HIM.
JUST IN TIME. BLACK BOLT CAME THROUGH, *EH?*
IT'S TIME, AT LAST, FOR US TO ELECT THE NEW ENNILUX C.E.O.!
THE CANDIDATES WILL BE MAKING THEIR PRESENTATIONS TO YOU MOMENTARILY, AND THEN ALL SHAREHOLDERS WILL BE GIVEN THE OPPORTUNITY TO VOTE.
I THINK SPIN'S GOT IT, DON'T YOU? NONE OF THE OTHER CANDIDATES SEEM LIKE THEY'VE GOT A CHANCE.
I HOPE HE'S SINCERE, TOO. ENNILUX COULD BE A POWERFUL ALLY, IN THE RIGHT HANDS.
I HOPE THE ANTIGEN WASN'T ***DAMAGED.*** MY WHOLE PRESENTATION WILL DEPEND ON DEMONSTRATING ITS FULL POTENTIAL.
NOT THAT I'M WORRIED. THOSE OTHER JOKERS DON'T HAVE MY VISION, AND THE SHAREHOLDERS KNOW IT.
MARISHI, THERE'S SOMETHING YOU SHOULD KNOW. THERE'S A NEW ENTRY. A LATE ENTRY.
EXCUSE ME?
AND NOW, I PRESENT TO YOU OUR FIRST CANDIDATE...

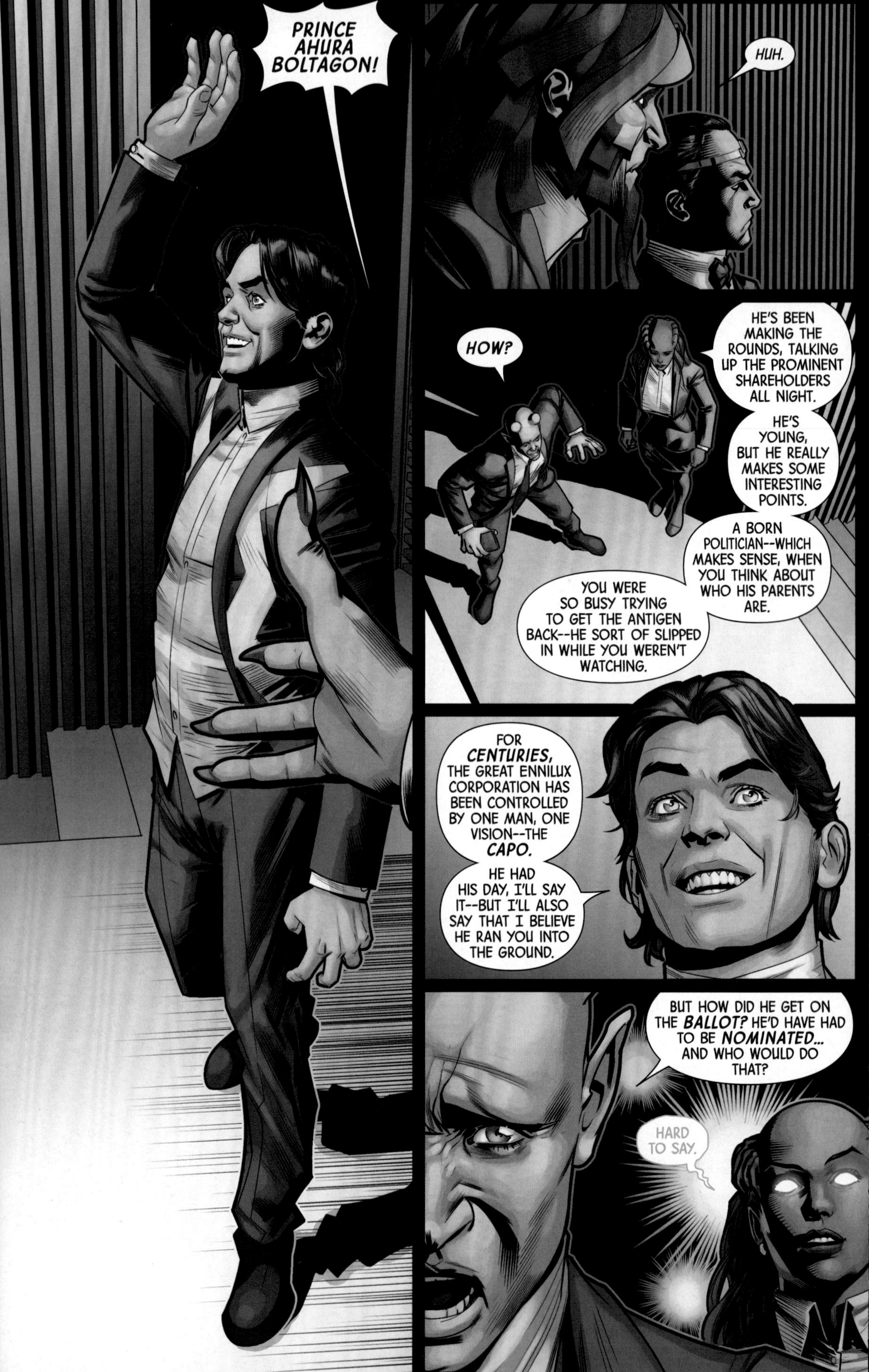
PRINCE AHURA BOLTAGON!
HUH.
HOW?
HE'S BEEN MAKING THE ROUNDS, TALKING UP THE PROMINENT SHAREHOLDERS ALL NIGHT.
HE'S YOUNG, BUT HE REALLY MAKES SOME INTERESTING POINTS.
A BORN POLITICIAN--WHICH MAKES SENSE, WHEN YOU THINK ABOUT WHO HIS PARENTS ARE.
YOU WERE SO BUSY TRYING TO GET THE ANTIGEN BACK--HE SORT OF SLIPPED IN WHILE YOU WEREN'T WATCHING.
FOR CENTURIES, THE GREAT ENNILUX CORPORATION HAS BEEN CONTROLLED BY ONE MAN, ONE VISION--THE CAPO.
HE HAD HIS DAY, I'LL SAY IT--BUT I'LL ALSO SAY THAT I BELIEVE HE RAN YOU INTO THE GROUND.
BUT HOW DID HE GET ON THE BALLOT? HE'D HAVE HAD TO BE NOMINATED... AND WHO WOULD DO THAT?
HARD TO SAY.

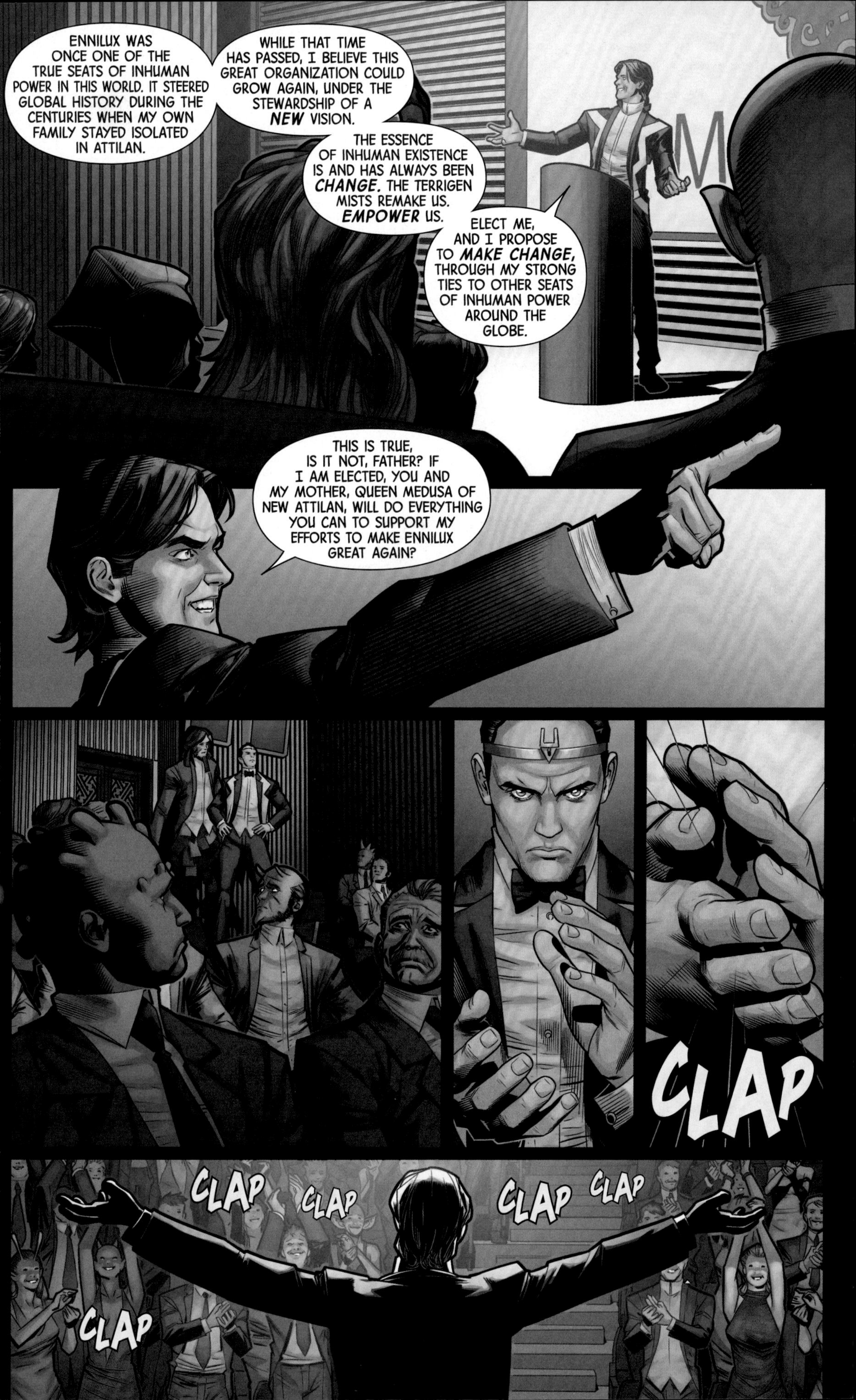
ENNILUX WAS ONCE ONE OF THE TRUE SEATS OF INHUMAN POWER IN THIS WORLD. IT STEERED GLOBAL HISTORY DURING THE CENTURIES WHEN MY OWN FAMILY STAYED ISOLATED IN ATTILAN.
WHILE THAT TIME HAS PASSED, I BELIEVE THIS GREAT ORGANIZATION COULD GROW AGAIN, UNDER THE STEWARDSHIP OF A *NEW* VISION.
THE ESSENCE OF INHUMAN EXISTENCE IS AND HAS ALWAYS BEEN *CHANGE.* THE TERRIGEN MISTS REMAKE US. *EMPOWER* US.
ELECT ME, AND I PROPOSE TO *MAKE CHANGE,* THROUGH MY STRONG TIES TO OTHER SEATS OF INHUMAN POWER AROUND THE GLOBE.
THIS IS TRUE, IS IT NOT, FATHER? IF I AM ELECTED, YOU AND MY MOTHER, QUEEN MEDUSA OF NEW ATTILAN, WILL DO EVERYTHING YOU CAN TO SUPPORT MY EFFORTS TO MAKE ENNILUX GREAT AGAIN?
CLAP
CLAP
CLAP
CLAP
CLAP
CLAP

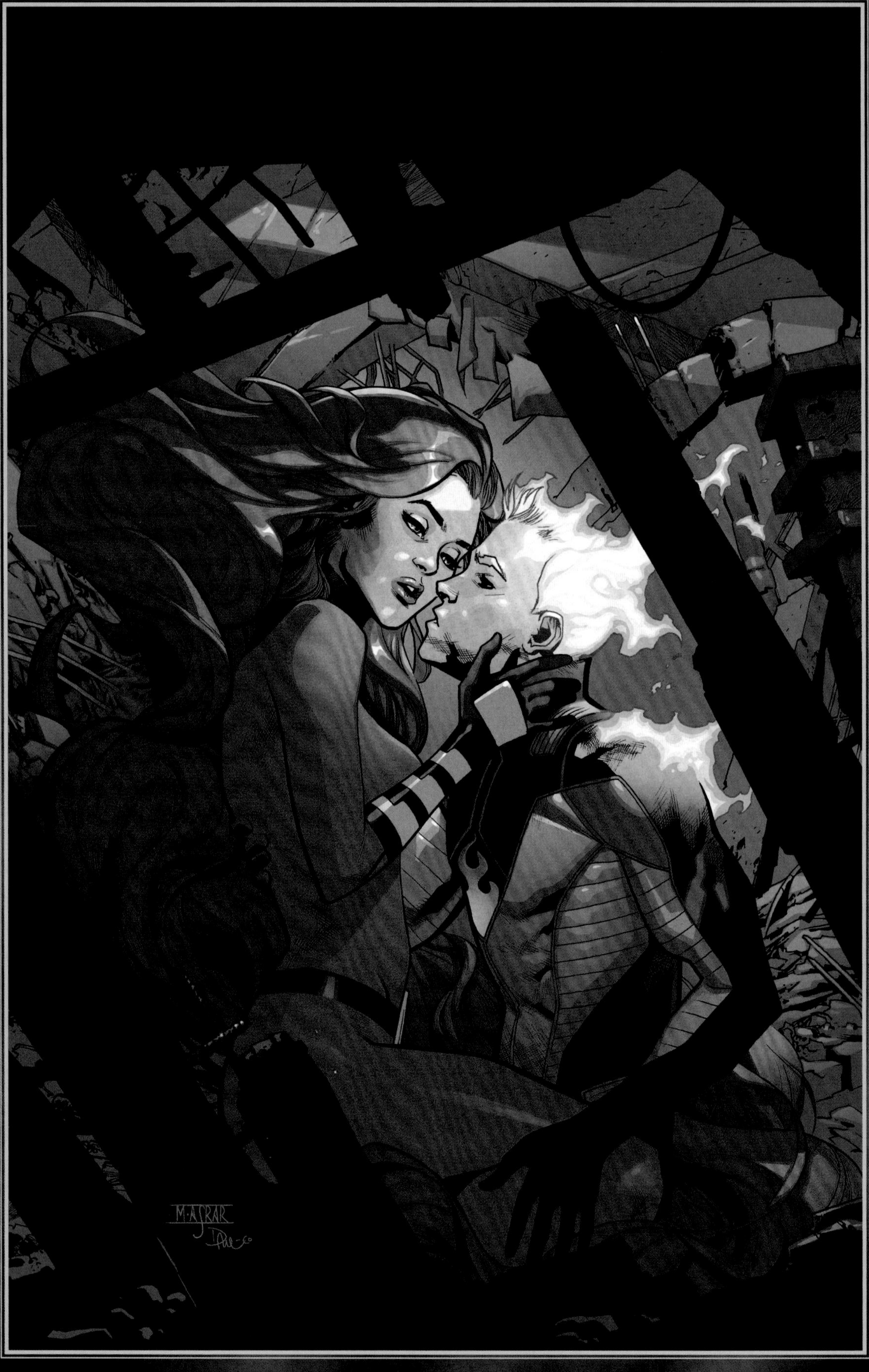
M·ASRAR

8

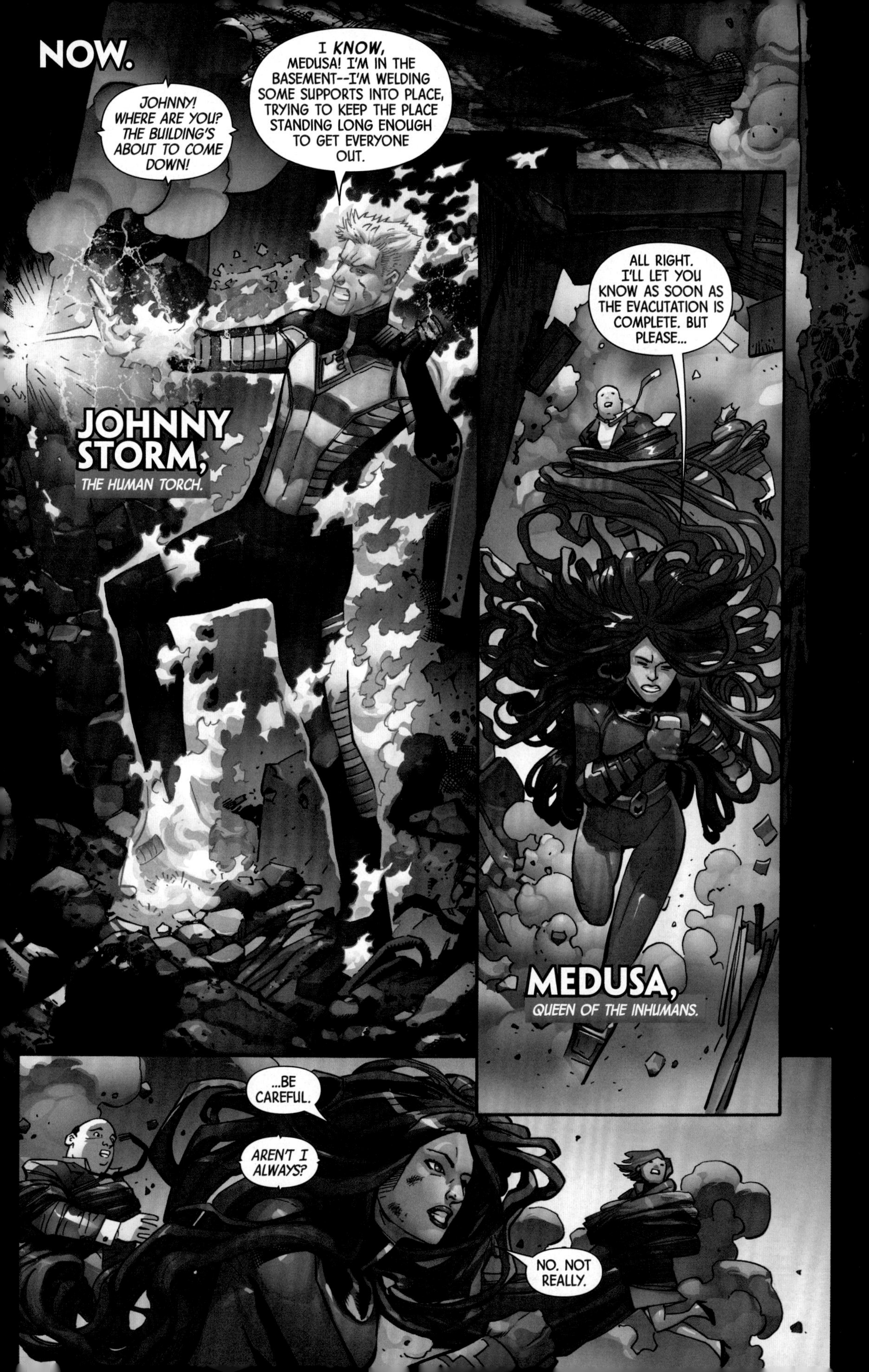
NOW.
JOHNNY! WHERE ARE YOU? THE BUILDING'S ABOUT TO COME DOWN!
I KNOW, MEDUSA! I'M IN THE BASEMENT--I'M WELDING SOME SUPPORTS INTO PLACE, TRYING TO KEEP THE PLACE STANDING LONG ENOUGH TO GET EVERYONE OUT.
JOHNNY STORM,
THE HUMAN TORCH.
ALL RIGHT. I'LL LET YOU KNOW AS SOON AS THE EVACUTATION IS COMPLETE. BUT PLEASE...
MEDUSA,
QUEEN OF THE INHUMANS.
...BE CAREFUL.
AREN'T I ALWAYS?
NO. NOT REALLY.

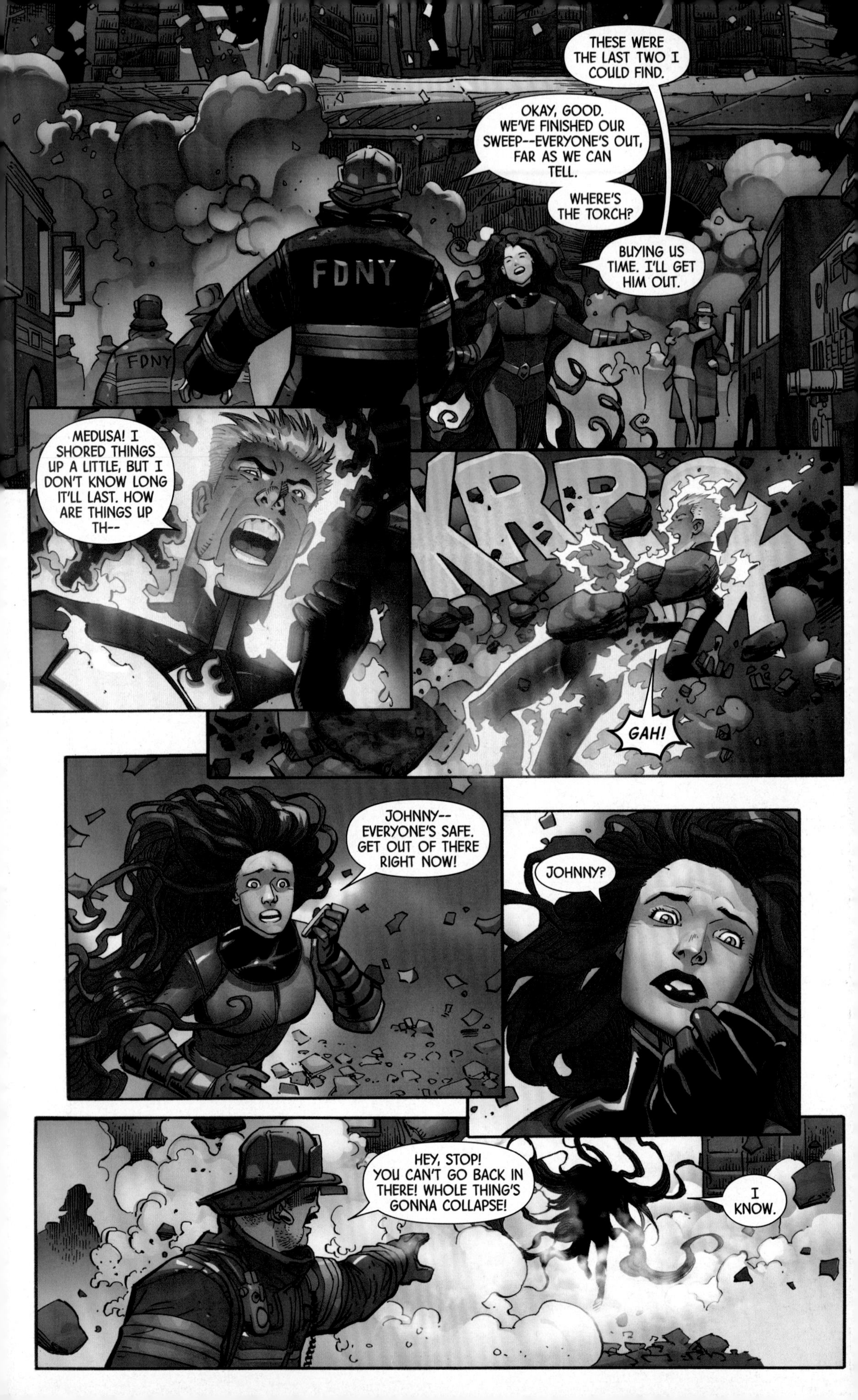

THESE WERE THE LAST TWO I COULD FIND.
OKAY, GOOD. WE'VE FINISHED OUR SWEEP--EVERYONE'S OUT, FAR AS WE CAN TELL.
WHERE'S THE TORCH?
BUYING US TIME. I'LL GET HIM OUT.
FDNY
FDNY
MEDUSA! I SHORED THINGS UP A LITTLE, BUT I DON'T KNOW LONG IT'LL LAST. HOW ARE THINGS UP TH--
KRRK
GAH!
JOHNNY-- EVERYONE'S SAFE. GET OUT OF THERE RIGHT NOW!
JOHNNY?
HEY, STOP! YOU CAN'T GO BACK IN THERE! WHOLE THING'S GONNA COLLAPSE!
I KNOW.

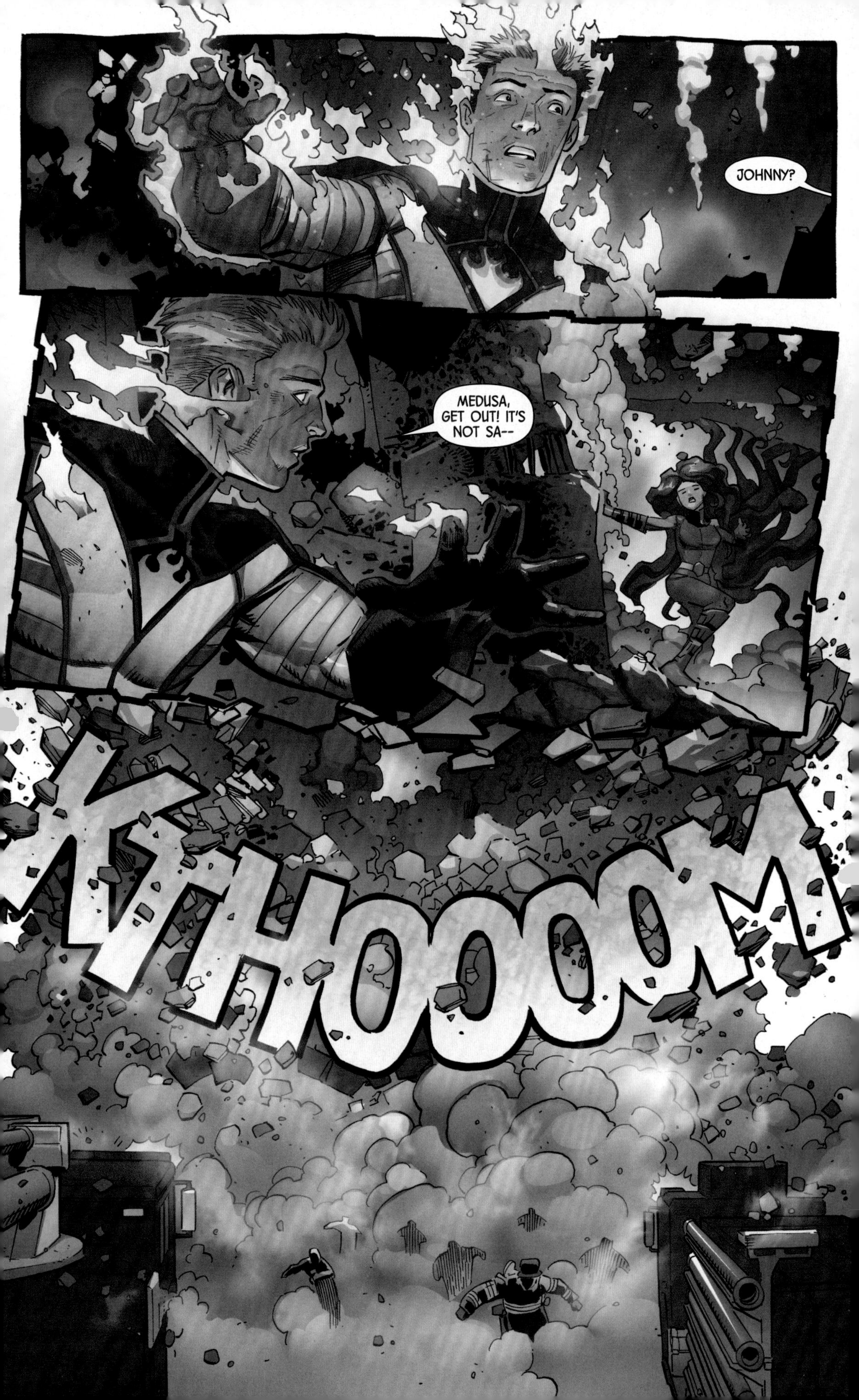
JOHNNY?
MEDUSA, GET OUT! IT'S NOT SA--
WHOOOOM!

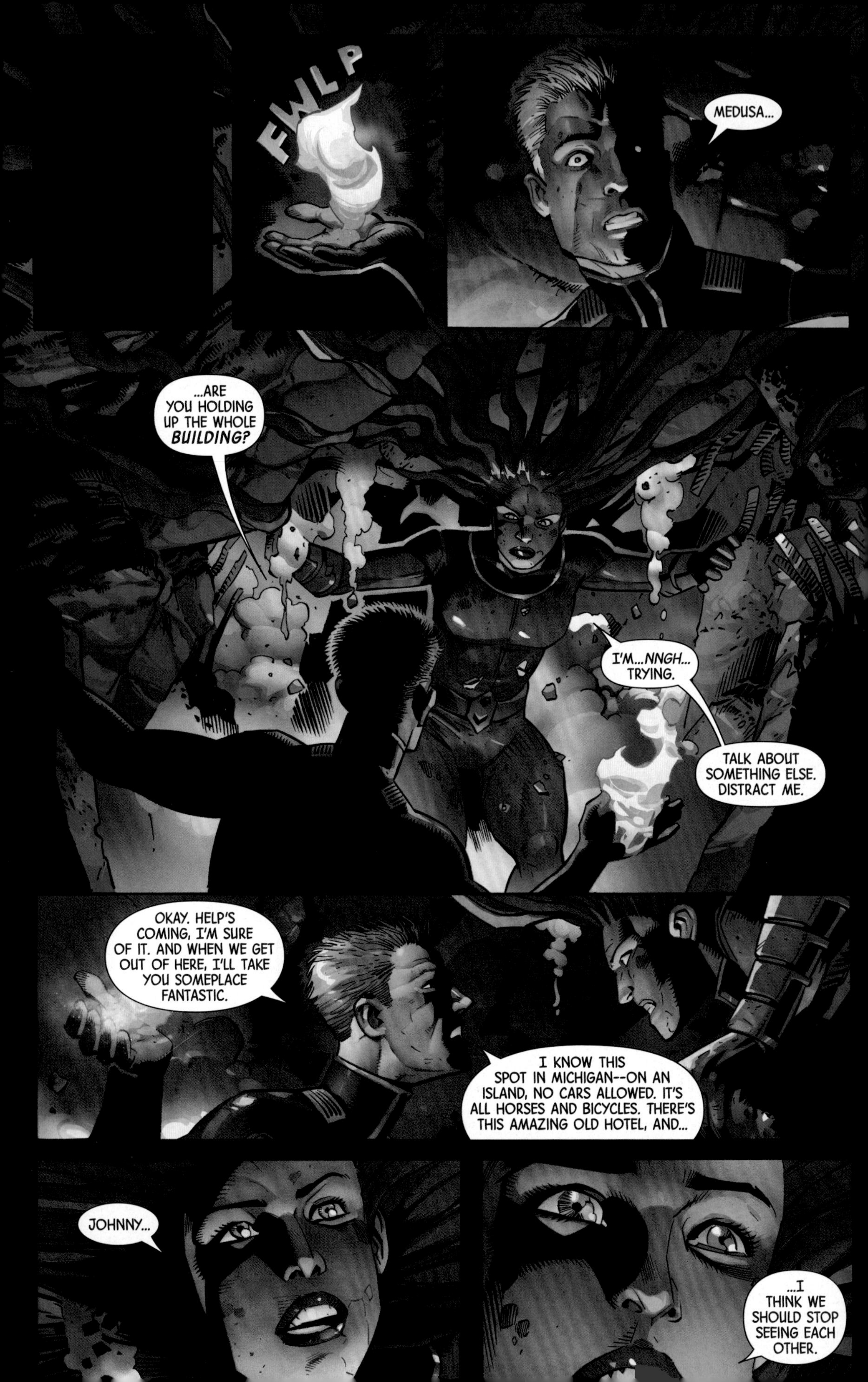
FWLP
MEDUSA...
...ARE YOU HOLDING UP THE WHOLE *BUILDING?*
I'M...*NNGH*... TRYING.
TALK ABOUT SOMETHING ELSE. DISTRACT ME.
OKAY. HELP'S COMING, I'M SURE OF IT. AND WHEN WE GET OUT OF HERE, I'LL TAKE YOU SOMEPLACE FANTASTIC.
I KNOW THIS SPOT IN MICHIGAN--ON AN ISLAND, NO CARS ALLOWED. IT'S ALL HORSES AND BICYCLES. THERE'S THIS AMAZING OLD HOTEL, AND...
JOHNNY...
...I THINK WE SHOULD STOP SEEING EACH OTHER.

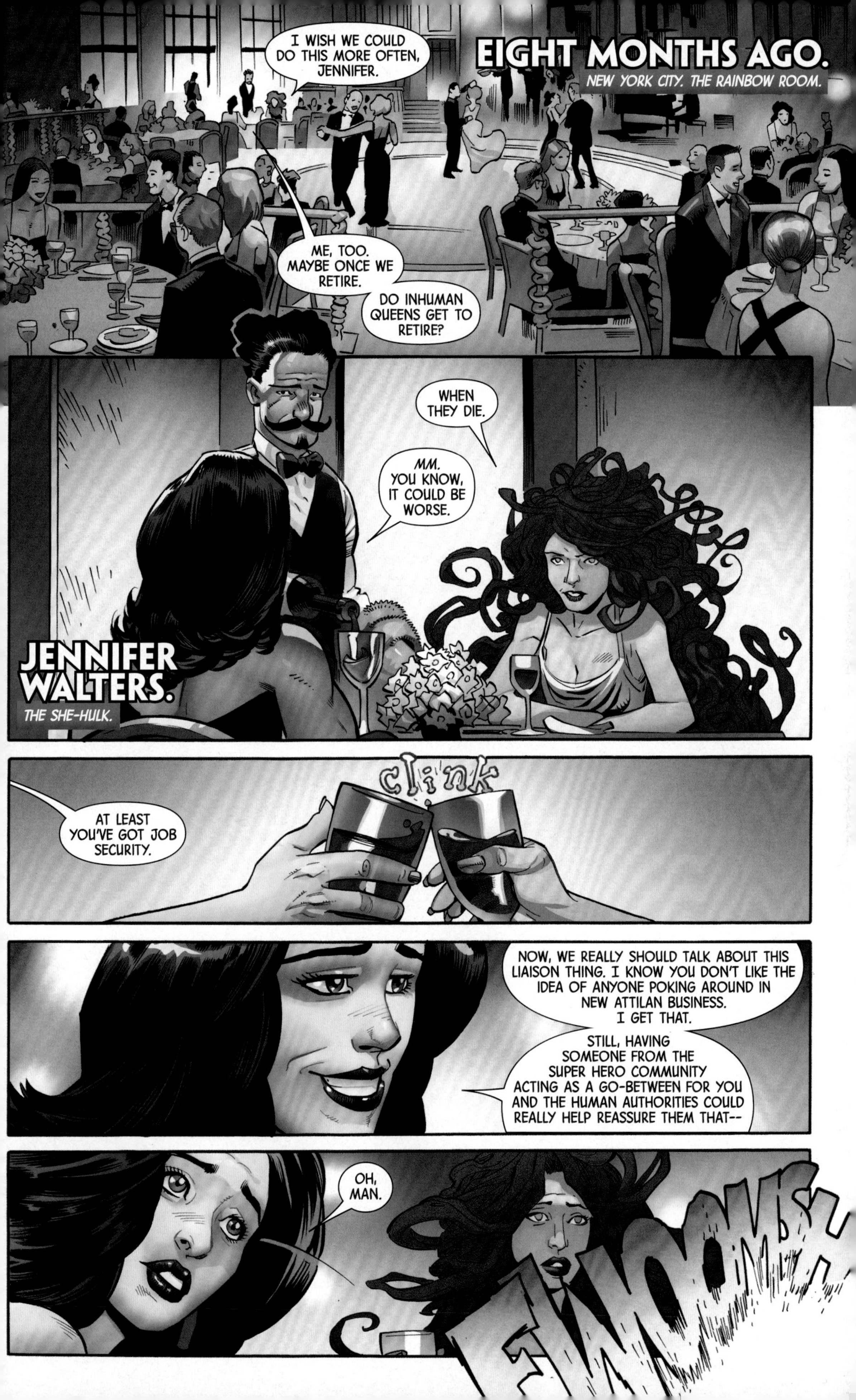
EIGHT MONTHS AGO.
NEW YORK CITY. THE RAINBOW ROOM.
I WISH WE COULD DO THIS MORE OFTEN, JENNIFER.
ME, TOO. MAYBE ONCE WE RETIRE.
DO INHUMAN QUEENS GET TO RETIRE?
WHEN THEY DIE.
MM. YOU KNOW, IT COULD BE WORSE.
JENNIFER WALTERS.
THE SHE-HULK.
clink
AT LEAST YOU'VE GOT JOB SECURITY.
NOW, WE REALLY SHOULD TALK ABOUT THIS LIAISON THING. I KNOW YOU DON'T LIKE THE IDEA OF ANYONE POKING AROUND IN NEW ATTILAN BUSINESS. I GET THAT.
STILL, HAVING SOMEONE FROM THE SUPER HERO COMMUNITY ACTING AS A GO-BETWEEN FOR YOU AND THE HUMAN AUTHORITIES COULD REALLY HELP REASSURE THEM THAT--
OH, MAN.

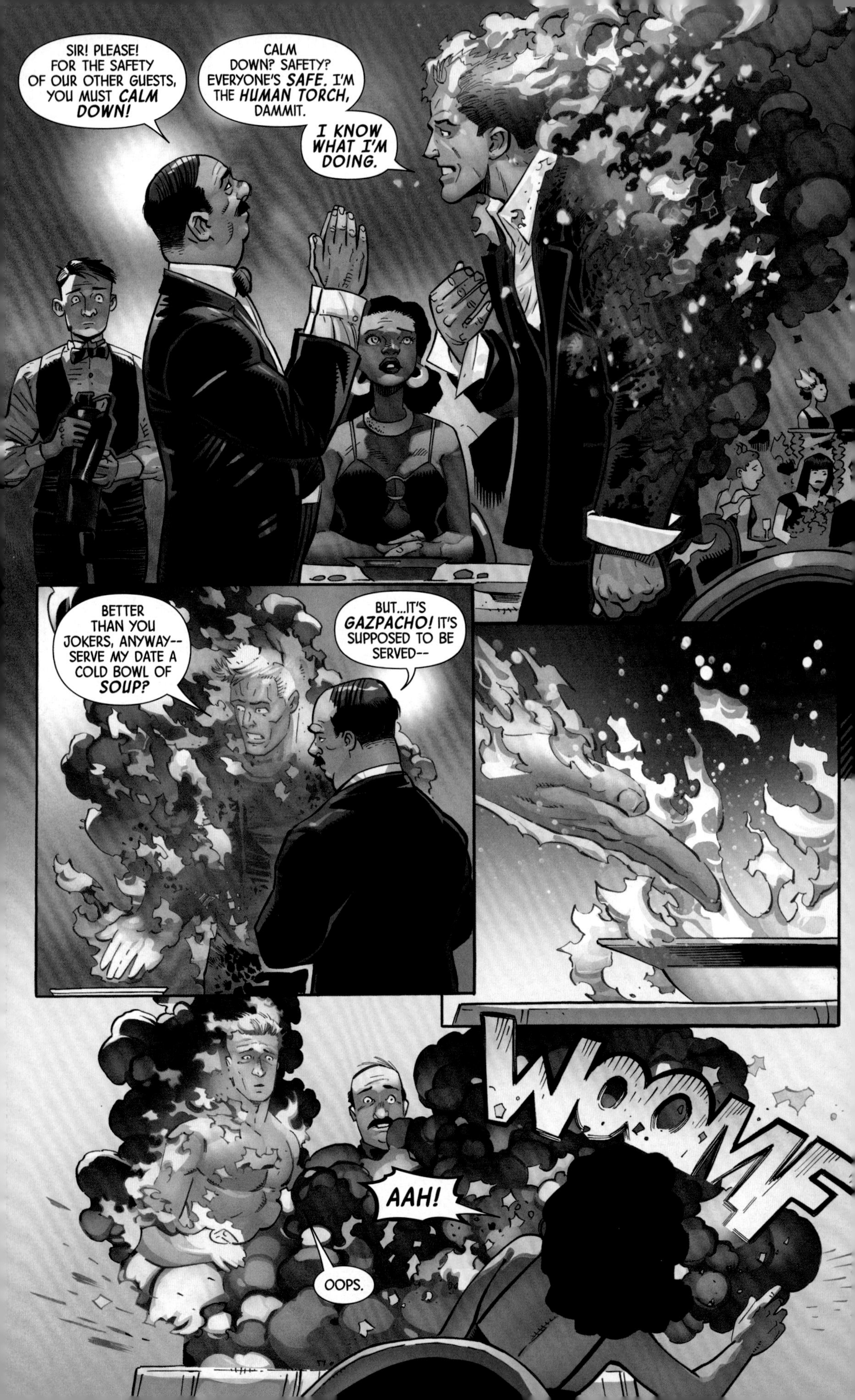

SIR! PLEASE! FOR THE SAFETY OF OUR OTHER GUESTS, YOU MUST CALM DOWN!
CALM DOWN? SAFETY? EVERYONE'S SAFE. I'M THE HUMAN TORCH, DAMMIT.
I KNOW WHAT I'M DOING.
BETTER THAN YOU JOKERS, ANYWAY-- SERVE MY DATE A COLD BOWL OF SOUP?
BUT...IT'S GAZPACHO! IT'S SUPPOSED TO BE SERVED--
WOOMF
AAH!
OOPS.

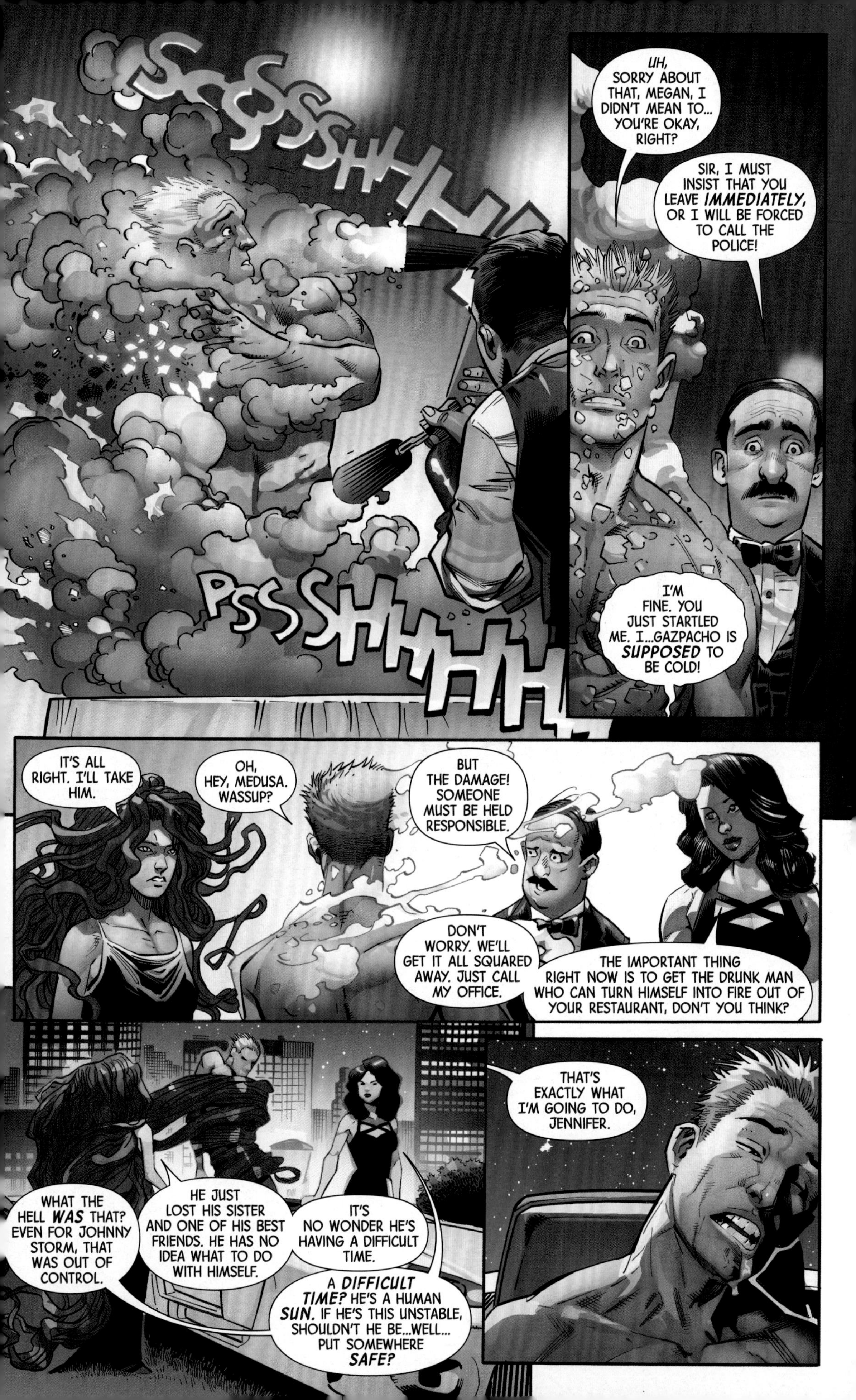
SSSSSHHHH
UH, SORRY ABOUT THAT, MEGAN, I DIDN'T MEAN TO... YOU'RE OKAY, RIGHT?
SIR, I MUST INSIST THAT YOU LEAVE *IMMEDIATELY*, OR I WILL BE FORCED TO CALL THE POLICE!
PSSSHHHHH
I'M FINE. YOU JUST STARTLED ME. I...GAZPACHO IS *SUPPOSED* TO BE COLD!
IT'S ALL RIGHT. I'LL TAKE HIM.
OH, HEY, MEDUSA. WASSUP?
BUT THE DAMAGE! SOMEONE MUST BE HELD RESPONSIBLE.
DON'T WORRY. WE'LL GET IT ALL SQUARED AWAY. JUST CALL MY OFFICE.
THE IMPORTANT THING RIGHT NOW IS TO GET THE DRUNK MAN WHO CAN TURN HIMSELF INTO FIRE OUT OF YOUR RESTAURANT, DON'T YOU THINK?
WHAT THE HELL *WAS* THAT? EVEN FOR JOHNNY STORM, THAT WAS OUT OF CONTROL.
HE JUST LOST HIS SISTER AND ONE OF HIS BEST FRIENDS. HE HAS NO IDEA WHAT TO DO WITH HIMSELF.
IT'S NO WONDER HE'S HAVING A DIFFICULT TIME.
A *DIFFICULT TIME?* HE'S A HUMAN *SUN*. IF HE'S THIS UNSTABLE, SHOULDN'T HE BE...WELL... PUT SOMEWHERE *SAFE?*
THAT'S EXACTLY WHAT I'M GOING TO DO, JENNIFER.

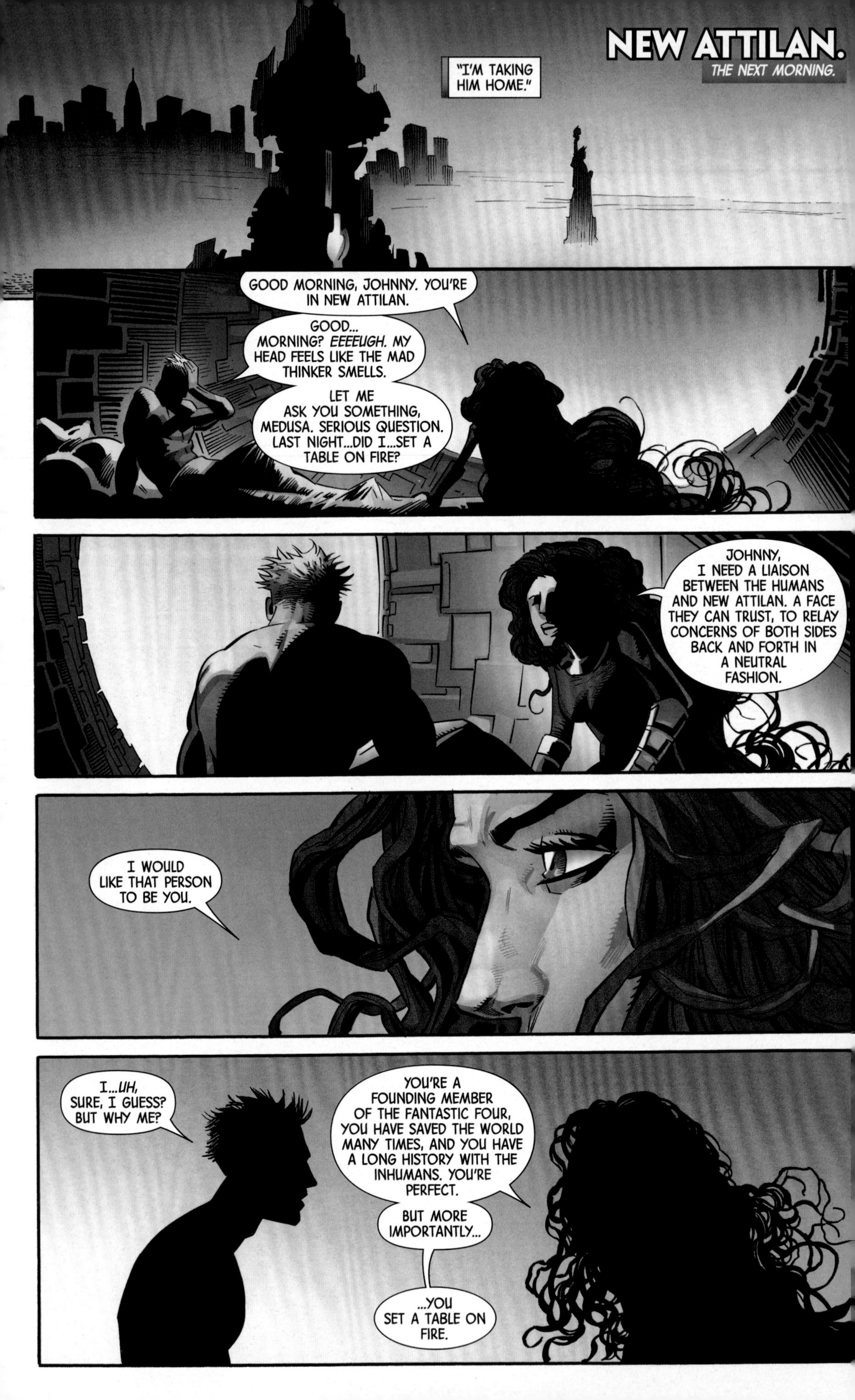
NEW ATTILAN.
THE NEXT MORNING.
"I'M TAKING HIM HOME."
GOOD MORNING, JOHNNY. YOU'RE IN NEW ATTILAN.
GOOD... MORNING? EEEEUGH. MY HEAD FEELS LIKE THE MAD THINKER SMELLS.
LET ME ASK YOU SOMETHING, MEDUSA. SERIOUS QUESTION. LAST NIGHT...DID I...SET A TABLE ON FIRE?
JOHNNY, I NEED A LIAISON BETWEEN THE HUMANS AND NEW ATTILAN. A FACE THEY CAN TRUST, TO RELAY CONCERNS OF BOTH SIDES BACK AND FORTH IN A NEUTRAL FASHION.
I WOULD LIKE THAT PERSON TO BE YOU.
I...UH, SURE, I GUESS? BUT WHY ME?
YOU'RE A FOUNDING MEMBER OF THE FANTASTIC FOUR, YOU HAVE SAVED THE WORLD MANY TIMES, AND YOU HAVE A LONG HISTORY WITH THE INHUMANS. YOU'RE PERFECT.
BUT MORE IMPORTANTLY...
...YOU SET A TABLE ON FIRE.

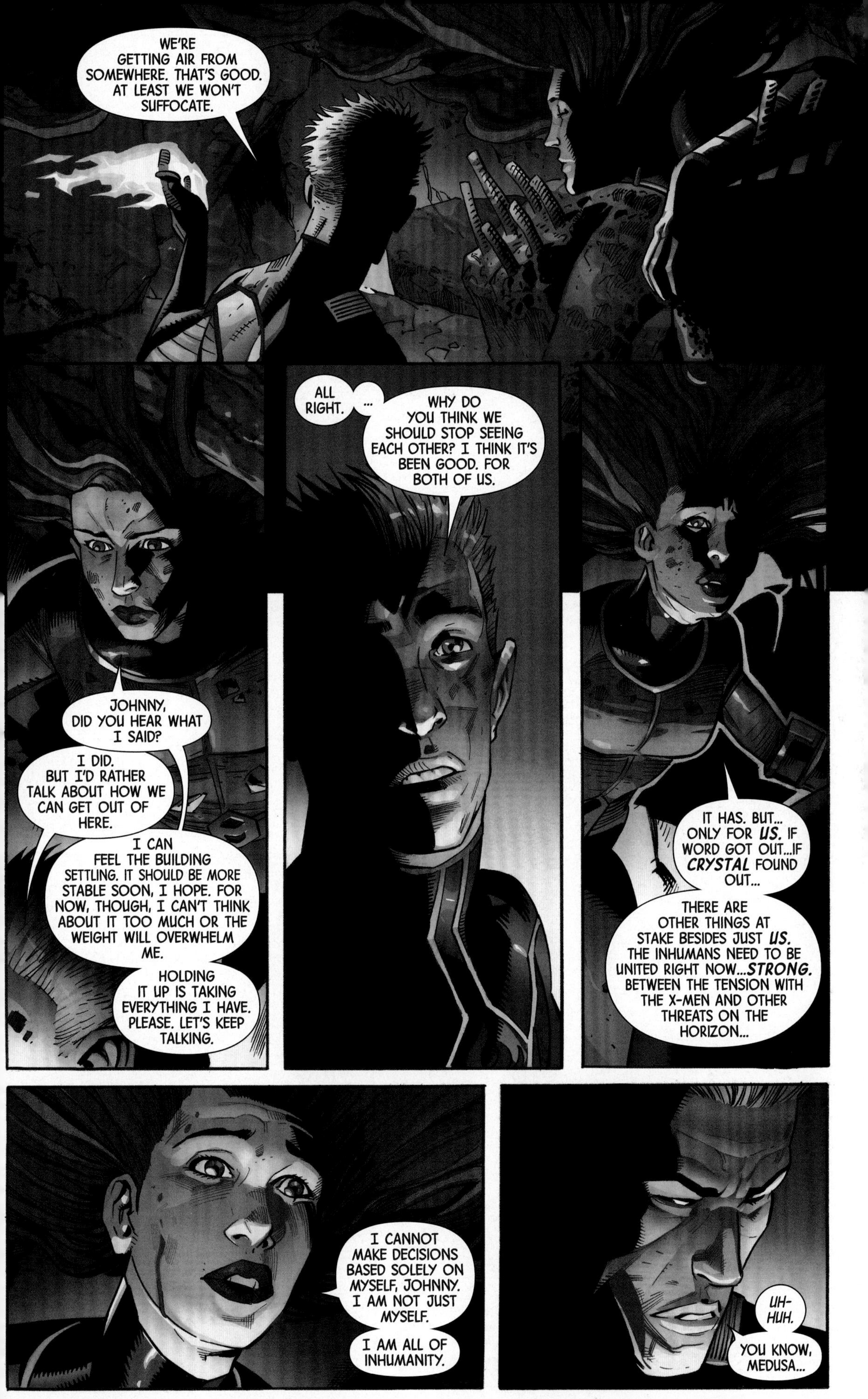
WE'RE GETTING AIR FROM SOMEWHERE. THAT'S GOOD. AT LEAST WE WON'T SUFFOCATE.
ALL RIGHT.
...
WHY DO YOU THINK WE SHOULD STOP SEEING EACH OTHER? I THINK IT'S BEEN GOOD. FOR BOTH OF US.
JOHNNY, DID YOU HEAR WHAT I SAID?
I DID. BUT I'D RATHER TALK ABOUT HOW WE CAN GET OUT OF HERE.
I CAN FEEL THE BUILDING SETTLING. IT SHOULD BE MORE STABLE SOON, I HOPE. FOR NOW, THOUGH, I CAN'T THINK ABOUT IT TOO MUCH OR THE WEIGHT WILL OVERWHELM ME.
HOLDING IT UP IS TAKING EVERYTHING I HAVE. PLEASE. LET'S KEEP TALKING.
IT HAS. BUT... ONLY FOR US. IF WORD GOT OUT...IF CRYSTAL FOUND OUT...
THERE ARE OTHER THINGS AT STAKE BESIDES JUST US. THE INHUMANS NEED TO BE UNITED RIGHT NOW...STRONG. BETWEEN THE TENSION WITH THE X-MEN AND OTHER THREATS ON THE HORIZON...
I CANNOT MAKE DECISIONS BASED SOLELY ON MYSELF, JOHNNY. I AM NOT JUST MYSELF.
I AM ALL OF INHUMANITY.
UH-HUH.
YOU KNOW, MEDUSA...

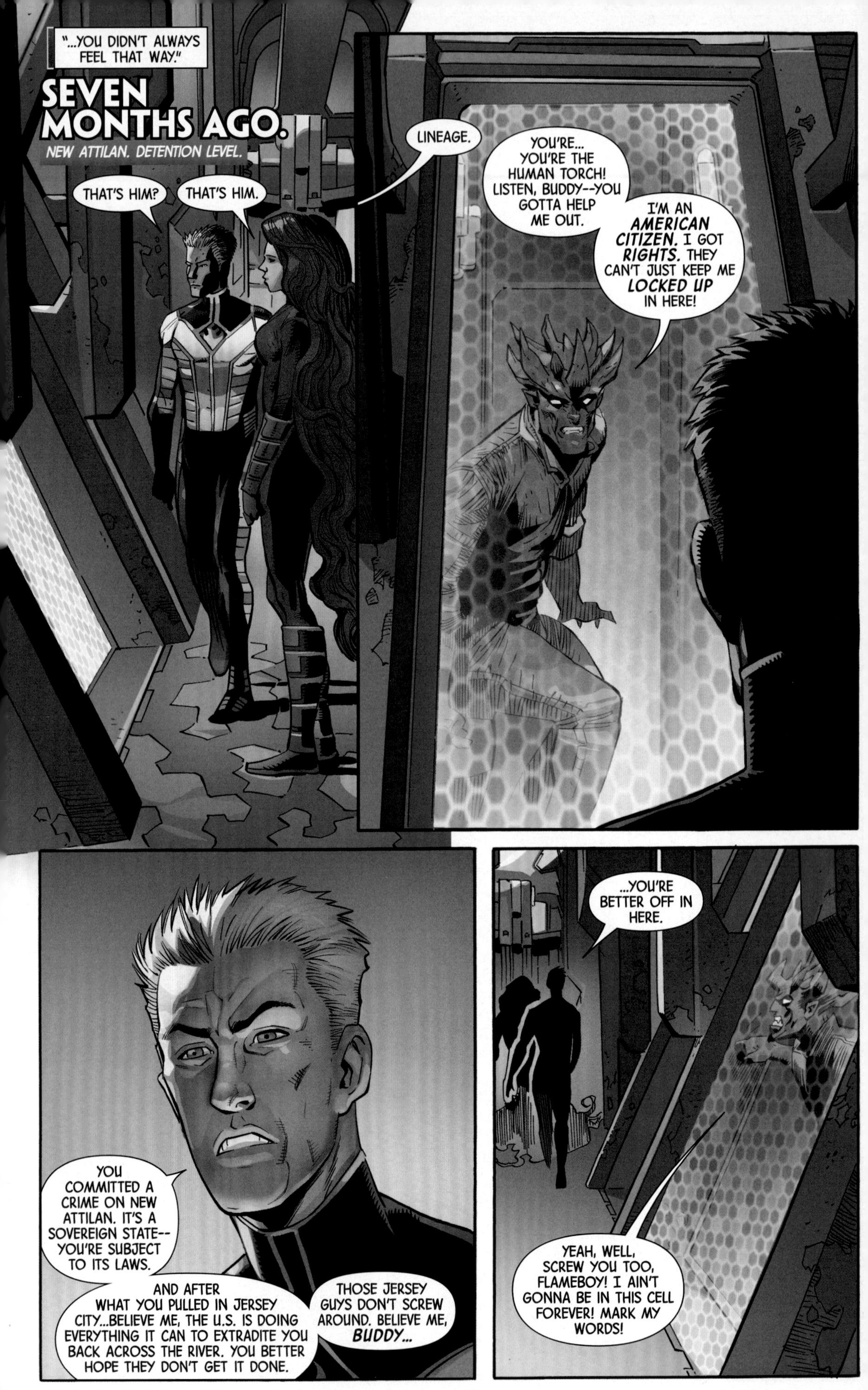
"...YOU DIDN'T ALWAYS FEEL THAT WAY."
SEVEN MONTHS AGO.
NEW ATTILAN. DETENTION LEVEL.
THAT'S HIM?
THAT'S HIM.
LINEAGE.
YOU'RE... YOU'RE THE HUMAN TORCH! LISTEN, BUDDY--YOU GOTTA HELP ME OUT.
I'M AN AMERICAN CITIZEN. I GOT RIGHTS. THEY CAN'T JUST KEEP ME LOCKED UP IN HERE!
YOU COMMITTED A CRIME ON NEW ATTILAN. IT'S A SOVEREIGN STATE--YOU'RE SUBJECT TO ITS LAWS.
AND AFTER WHAT YOU PULLED IN JERSEY CITY...BELIEVE ME, THE U.S. IS DOING EVERYTHING IT CAN TO EXTRADITE YOU BACK ACROSS THE RIVER. YOU BETTER HOPE THEY DON'T GET IT DONE.
THOSE JERSEY GUYS DON'T SCREW AROUND. BELIEVE ME, BUDDY...
...YOU'RE BETTER OFF IN HERE.
YEAH, WELL, SCREW YOU TOO, FLAMEBOY! I AIN'T GONNA BE IN THIS CELL FOREVER! MARK MY WORDS!

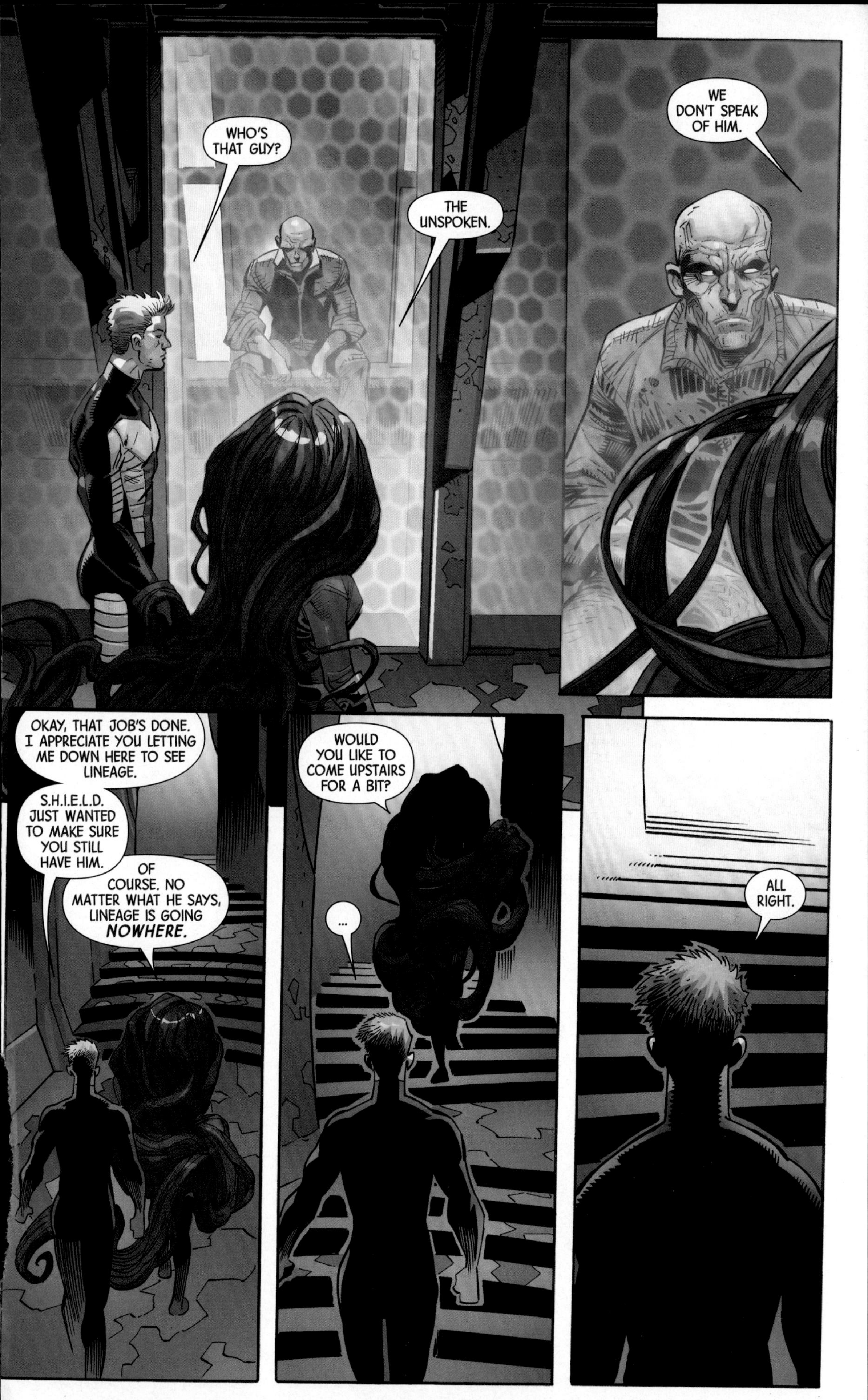
WHO'S THAT GUY?
THE UNSPOKEN.
WE DON'T SPEAK OF HIM.
OKAY, THAT JOB'S DONE. I APPRECIATE YOU LETTING ME DOWN HERE TO SEE LINEAGE.
S.H.I.E.L.D. JUST WANTED TO MAKE SURE YOU STILL HAVE HIM.
OF COURSE. NO MATTER WHAT HE SAYS, LINEAGE IS GOING *NOWHERE.*
WOULD YOU LIKE TO COME UPSTAIRS FOR A BIT?
...
ALL RIGHT.

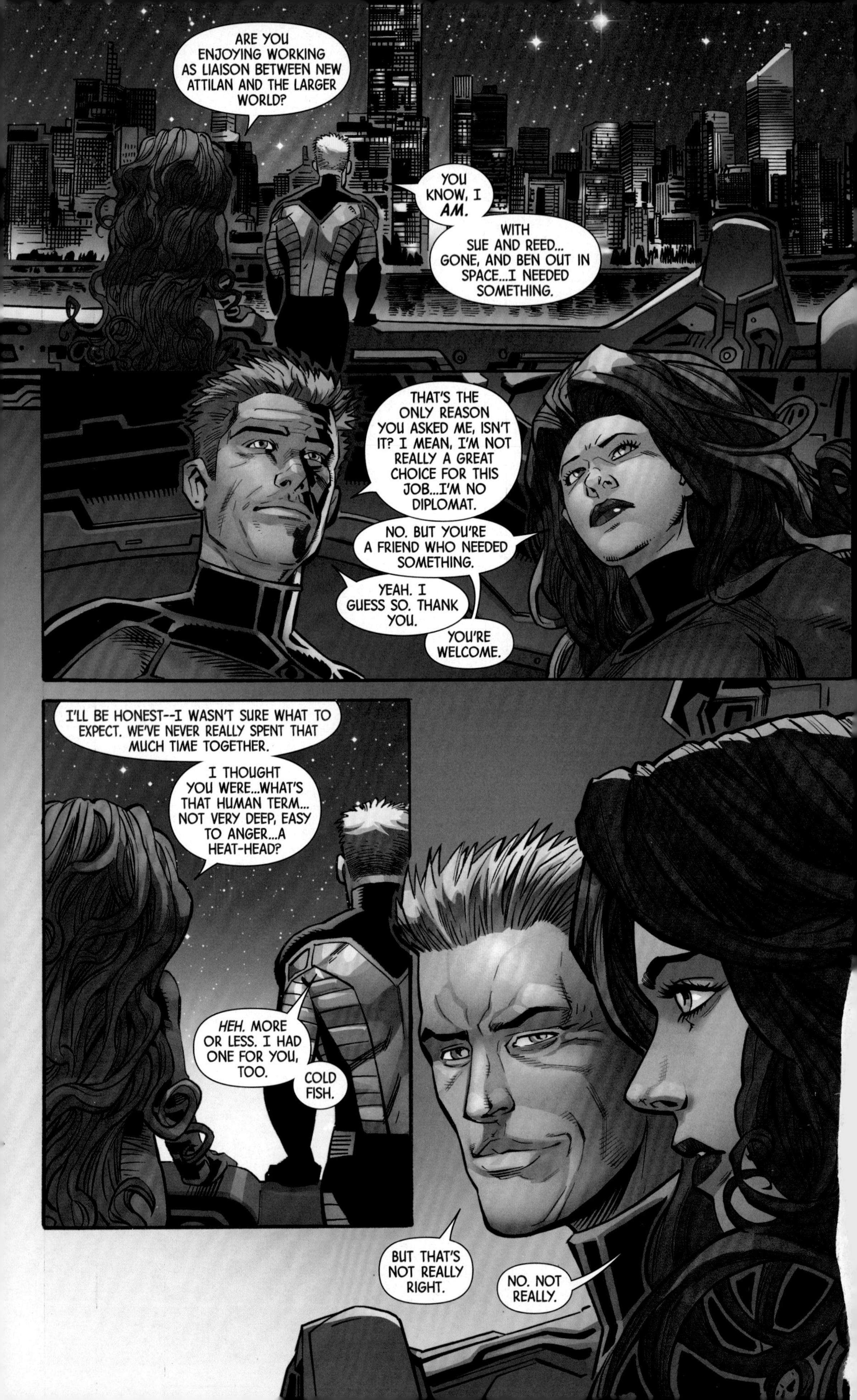
ARE YOU ENJOYING WORKING AS LIAISON BETWEEN NEW ATTILAN AND THE LARGER WORLD?
YOU KNOW, I *AM.*
WITH SUE AND REED... GONE, AND BEN OUT IN SPACE...I NEEDED SOMETHING.
THAT'S THE ONLY REASON YOU ASKED ME, ISN'T IT? I MEAN, I'M NOT REALLY A GREAT CHOICE FOR THIS JOB...I'M NO DIPLOMAT.
NO. BUT YOU'RE A FRIEND WHO NEEDED SOMETHING.
YEAH. I GUESS SO. THANK YOU.
YOU'RE WELCOME.
I'LL BE HONEST--I WASN'T SURE WHAT TO EXPECT. WE'VE NEVER REALLY SPENT THAT MUCH TIME TOGETHER.
I THOUGHT YOU WERE...WHAT'S THAT HUMAN TERM... NOT VERY DEEP, EASY TO ANGER...A HEAT-HEAD?
HEH. MORE OR LESS. I HAD ONE FOR YOU, TOO.
COLD FISH.
BUT THAT'S NOT REALLY RIGHT.
NO. NOT REALLY.

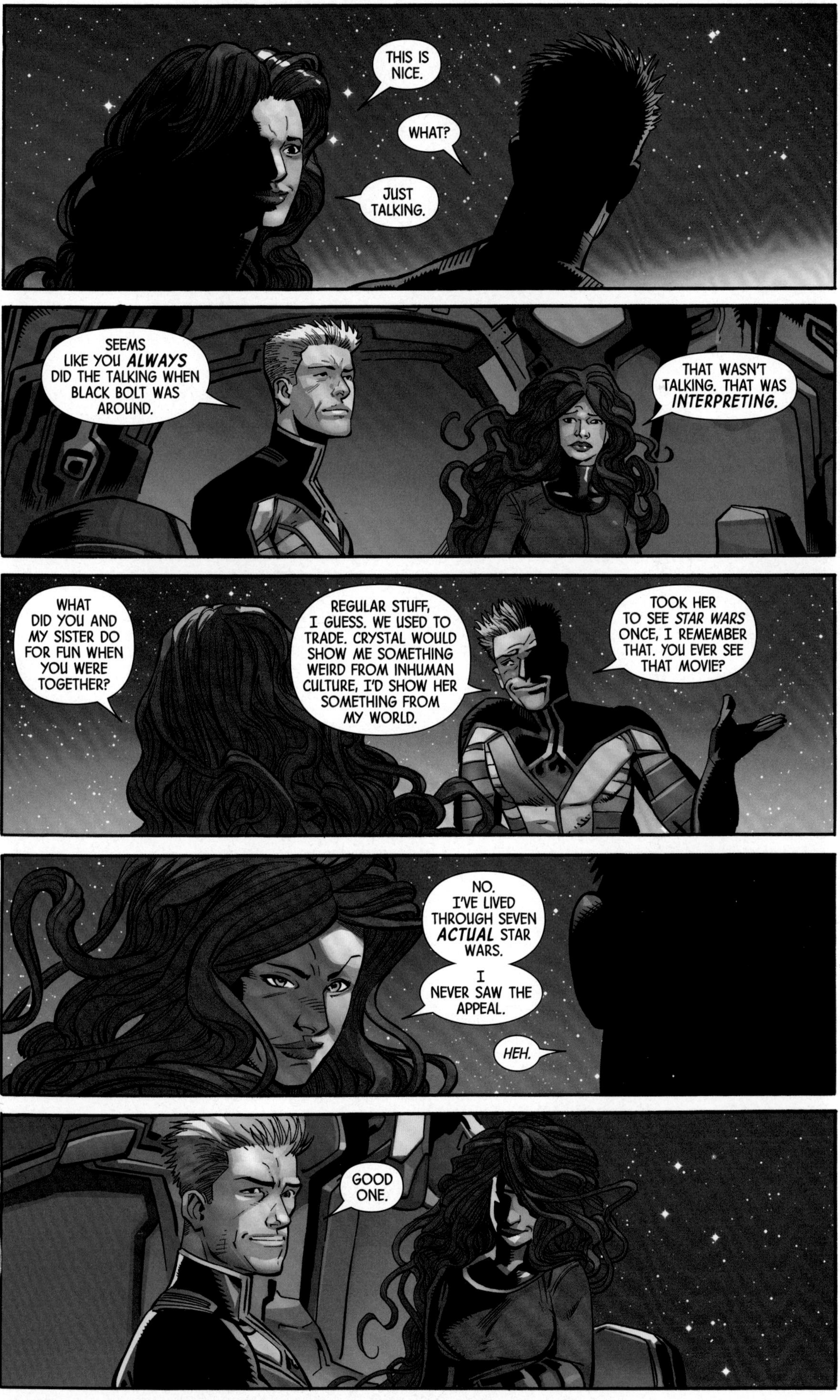
THIS IS NICE.
WHAT?
JUST TALKING.
SEEMS LIKE YOU *ALWAYS* DID THE TALKING WHEN BLACK BOLT WAS AROUND.
THAT WASN'T TALKING. THAT WAS *INTERPRETING.*
WHAT DID YOU AND MY SISTER DO FOR FUN WHEN YOU WERE TOGETHER?
REGULAR STUFF, I GUESS. WE USED TO TRADE. CRYSTAL WOULD SHOW ME SOMETHING WEIRD FROM INHUMAN CULTURE, I'D SHOW HER SOMETHING FROM MY WORLD.
TOOK HER TO SEE *STAR WARS* ONCE, I REMEMBER THAT. YOU EVER SEE THAT MOVIE?
NO. I'VE LIVED THROUGH SEVEN *ACTUAL* STAR WARS.
I NEVER SAW THE APPEAL.
HEH.
GOOD ONE.

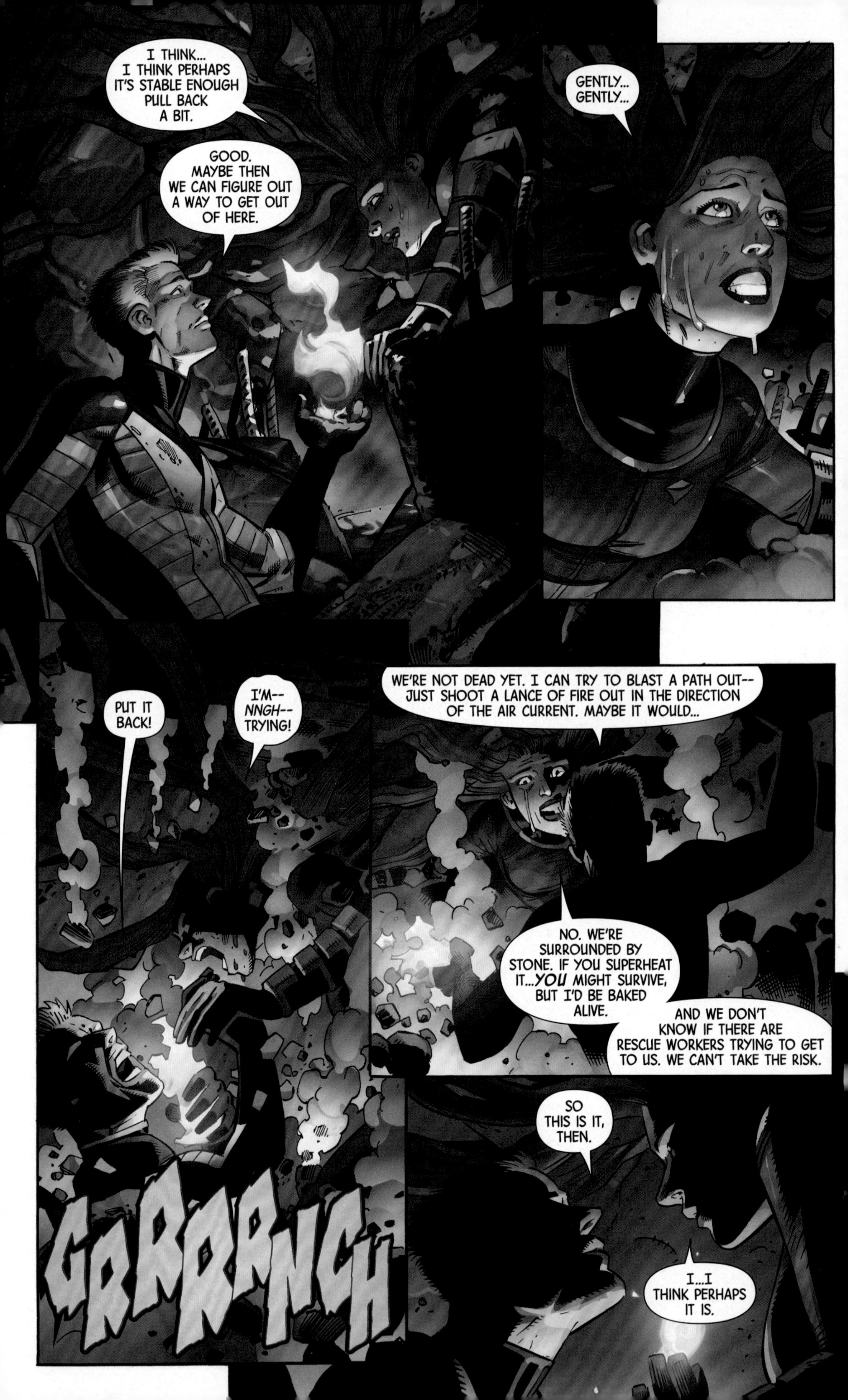
I THINK... I THINK PERHAPS IT'S STABLE ENOUGH PULL BACK A BIT.
GOOD. MAYBE THEN WE CAN FIGURE OUT A WAY TO GET OUT OF HERE.
GENTLY... GENTLY...
PUT IT BACK!
I'M-- NNGH-- TRYING!
GRRANCH
WE'RE NOT DEAD YET. I CAN TRY TO BLAST A PATH OUT-- JUST SHOOT A LANCE OF FIRE OUT IN THE DIRECTION OF THE AIR CURRENT. MAYBE IT WOULD...
NO. WE'RE SURROUNDED BY STONE. IF YOU SUPERHEAT IT...YOU MIGHT SURVIVE, BUT I'D BE BAKED ALIVE.
AND WE DON'T KNOW IF THERE ARE RESCUE WORKERS TRYING TO GET TO US. WE CAN'T TAKE THE RISK.
SO THIS IS IT, THEN.
I...I THINK PERHAPS IT IS.

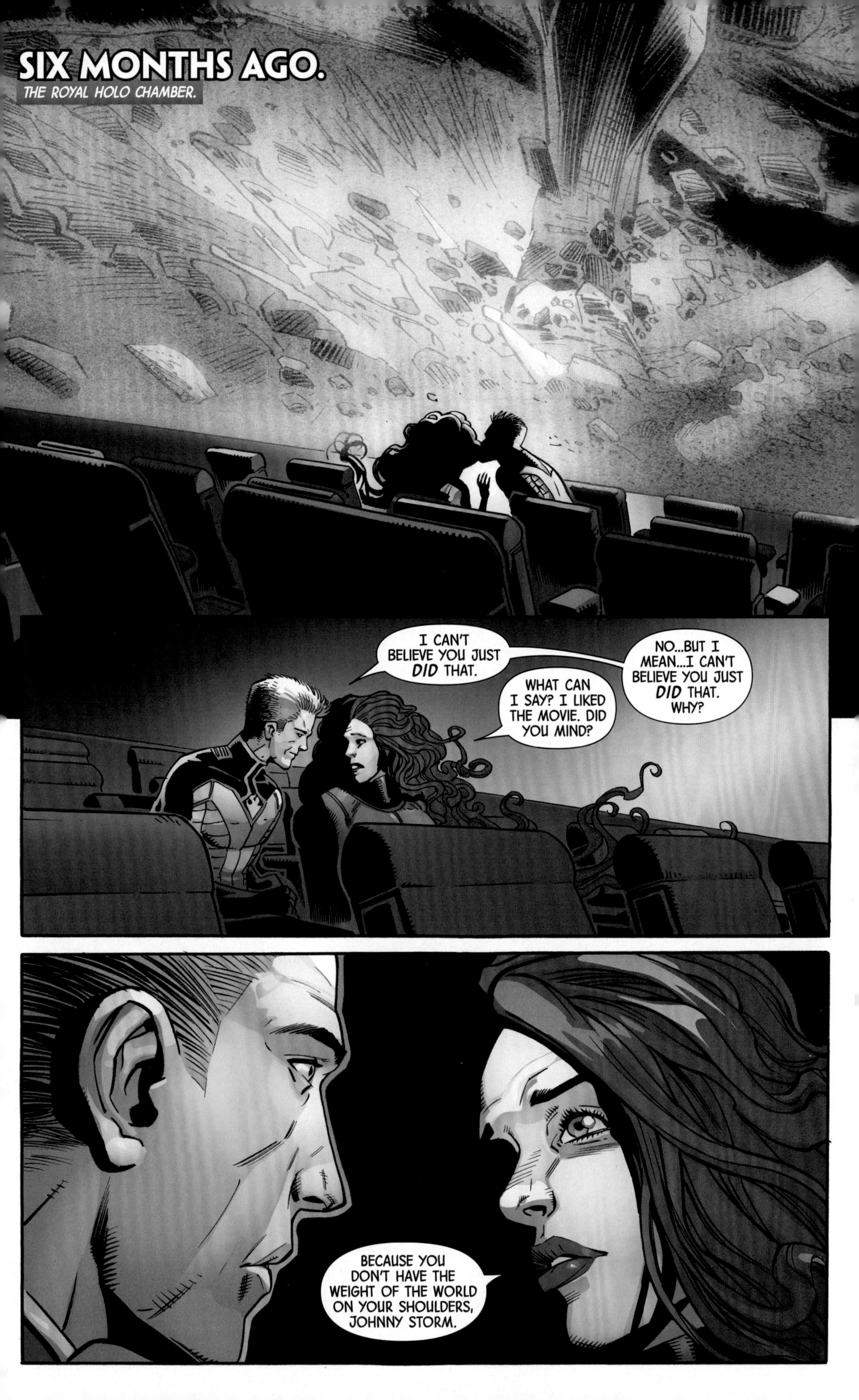
SIX MONTHS AGO.
THE ROYAL HOLO CHAMBER.
I CAN'T BELIEVE YOU JUST DID THAT.
WHAT CAN I SAY? I LIKED THE MOVIE. DID YOU MIND?
NO...BUT I MEAN...I CAN'T BELIEVE YOU JUST DID THAT. WHY?
BECAUSE YOU DON'T HAVE THE WEIGHT OF THE WORLD ON YOUR SHOULDERS, JOHNNY STORM.

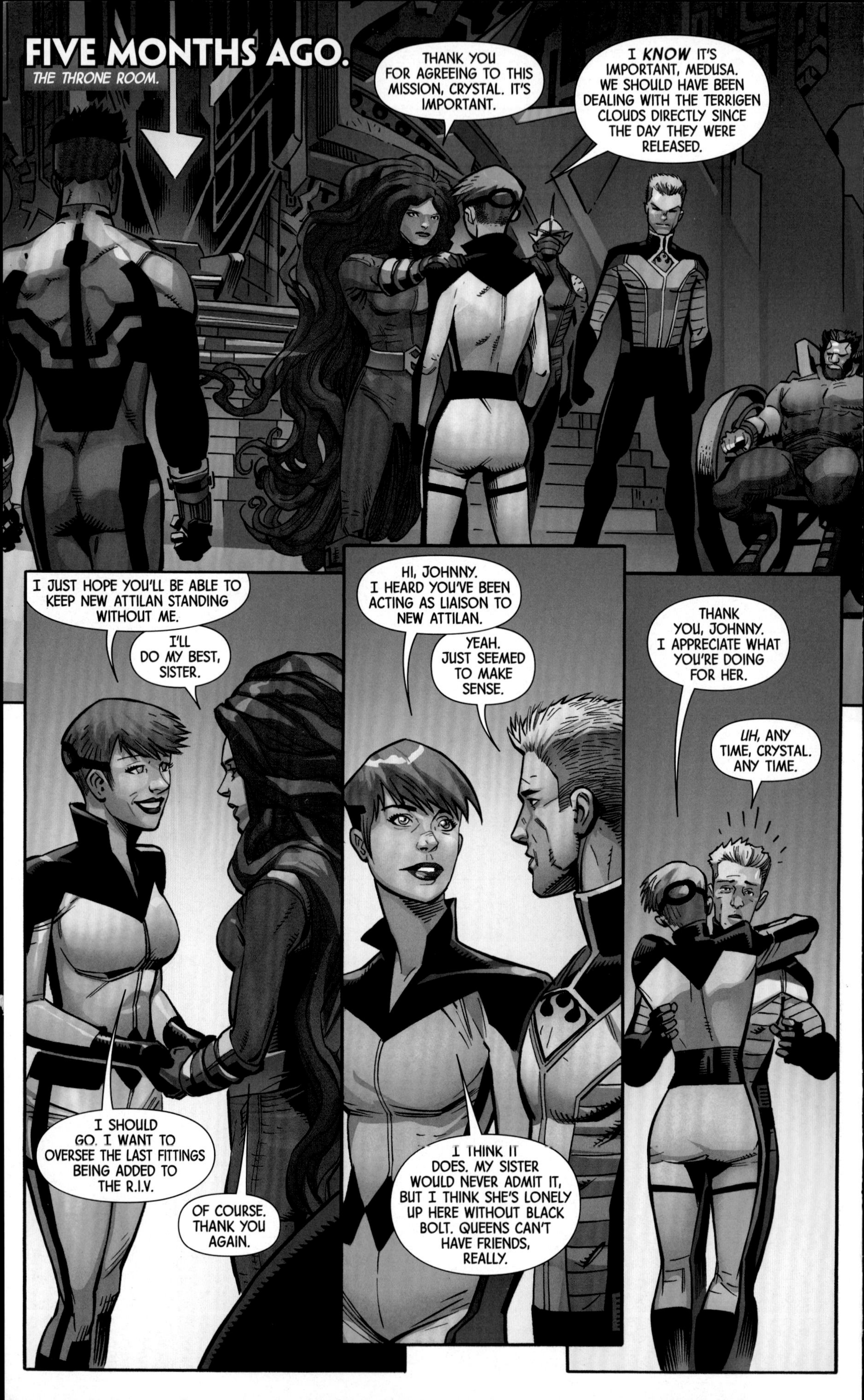
FIVE MONTHS AGO.
THE THRONE ROOM.
THANK YOU FOR AGREEING TO THIS MISSION, CRYSTAL. IT'S IMPORTANT.
I KNOW IT'S IMPORTANT, MEDUSA. WE SHOULD HAVE BEEN DEALING WITH THE TERRIGEN CLOUDS DIRECTLY SINCE THE DAY THEY WERE RELEASED.
I JUST HOPE YOU'LL BE ABLE TO KEEP NEW ATTILAN STANDING WITHOUT ME.
I'LL DO MY BEST, SISTER.
I SHOULD GO. I WANT TO OVERSEE THE LAST FITTINGS BEING ADDED TO THE R.I.V.
OF COURSE. THANK YOU AGAIN.
HI, JOHNNY. I HEARD YOU'VE BEEN ACTING AS LIAISON TO NEW ATTILAN.
YEAH. JUST SEEMED TO MAKE SENSE.
I THINK IT DOES. MY SISTER WOULD NEVER ADMIT IT, BUT I THINK SHE'S LONELY UP HERE WITHOUT BLACK BOLT. QUEENS CAN'T HAVE FRIENDS, REALLY.
THANK YOU, JOHNNY. I APPRECIATE WHAT YOU'RE DOING FOR HER.
UH, ANY TIME, CRYSTAL. ANY TIME.

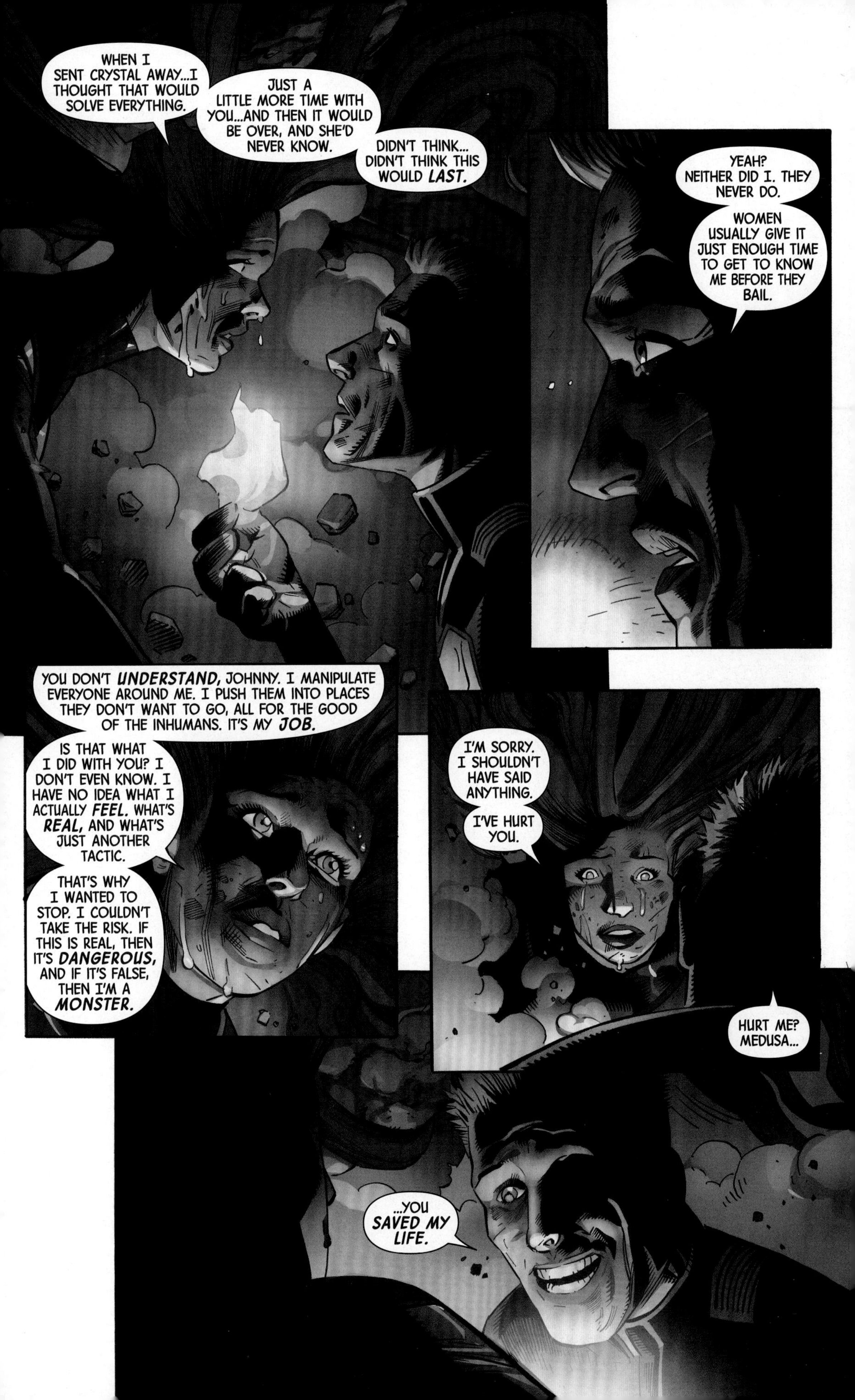
WHEN I SENT CRYSTAL AWAY...I THOUGHT THAT WOULD SOLVE EVERYTHING.
JUST A LITTLE MORE TIME WITH YOU...AND THEN IT WOULD BE OVER, AND SHE'D NEVER KNOW.
DIDN'T THINK... DIDN'T THINK THIS WOULD LAST.
YEAH? NEITHER DID I. THEY NEVER DO.
WOMEN USUALLY GIVE IT JUST ENOUGH TIME TO GET TO KNOW ME BEFORE THEY BAIL.
YOU DON'T UNDERSTAND, JOHNNY. I MANIPULATE EVERYONE AROUND ME. I PUSH THEM INTO PLACES THEY DON'T WANT TO GO, ALL FOR THE GOOD OF THE INHUMANS. IT'S MY JOB.
IS THAT WHAT I DID WITH YOU? I DON'T EVEN KNOW. I HAVE NO IDEA WHAT I ACTUALLY FEEL. WHAT'S REAL, AND WHAT'S JUST ANOTHER TACTIC.
THAT'S WHY I WANTED TO STOP. I COULDN'T TAKE THE RISK. IF THIS IS REAL, THEN IT'S DANGEROUS, AND IF IT'S FALSE, THEN I'M A MONSTER.
I'M SORRY. I SHOULDN'T HAVE SAID ANYTHING.
I'VE HURT YOU.
HURT ME? MEDUSA...
...YOU SAVED MY LIFE.

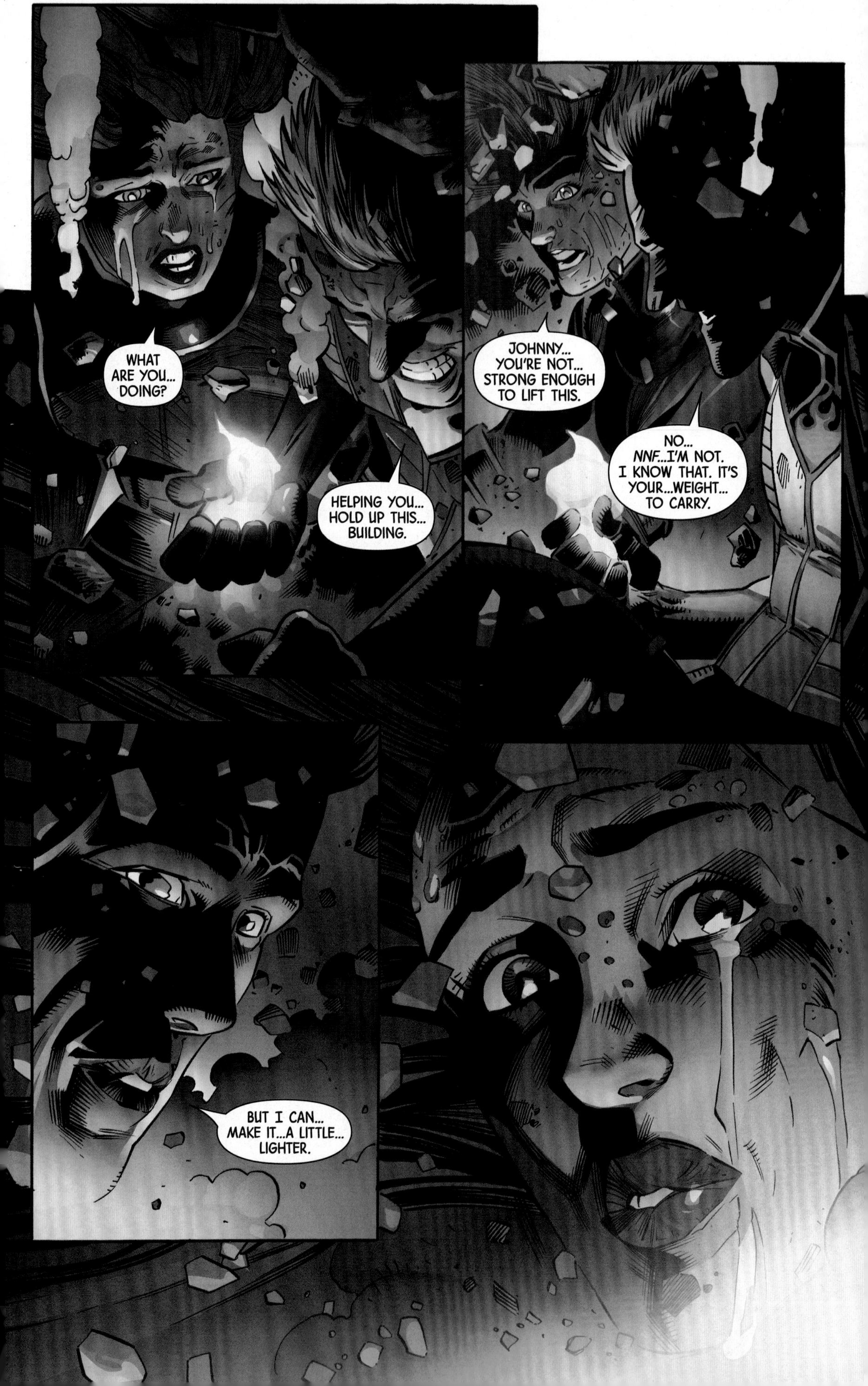
WHAT ARE YOU... DOING?
HELPING YOU... HOLD UP THIS... BUILDING.
JOHNNY... YOU'RE NOT... STRONG ENOUGH TO LIFT THIS.
NO... NNF...I'M NOT. I KNOW THAT. IT'S YOUR...WEIGHT... TO CARRY.
BUT I CAN... MAKE IT...A LITTLE... LIGHTER.

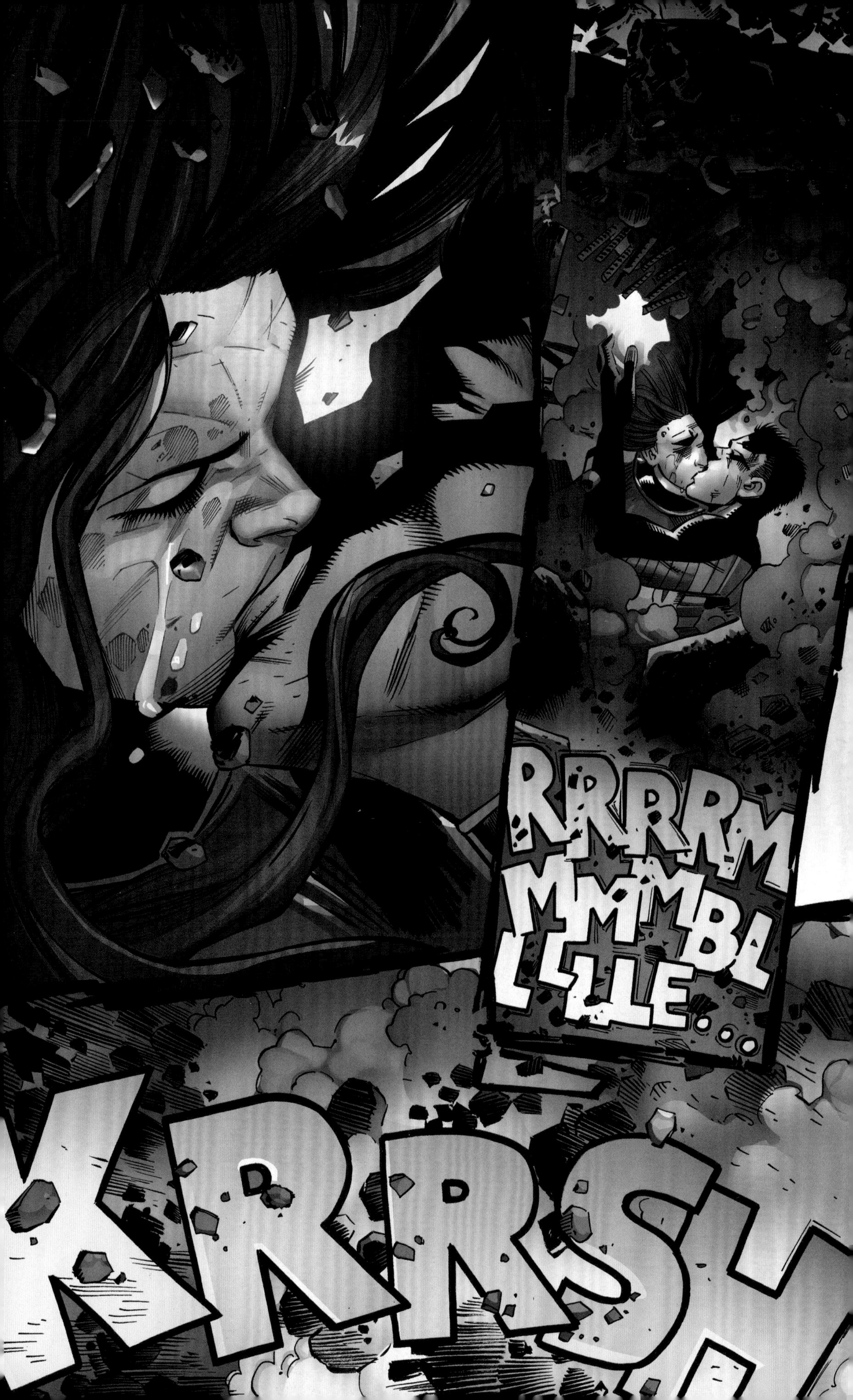
RRRR
MMMBL
LLLE...
KRRS

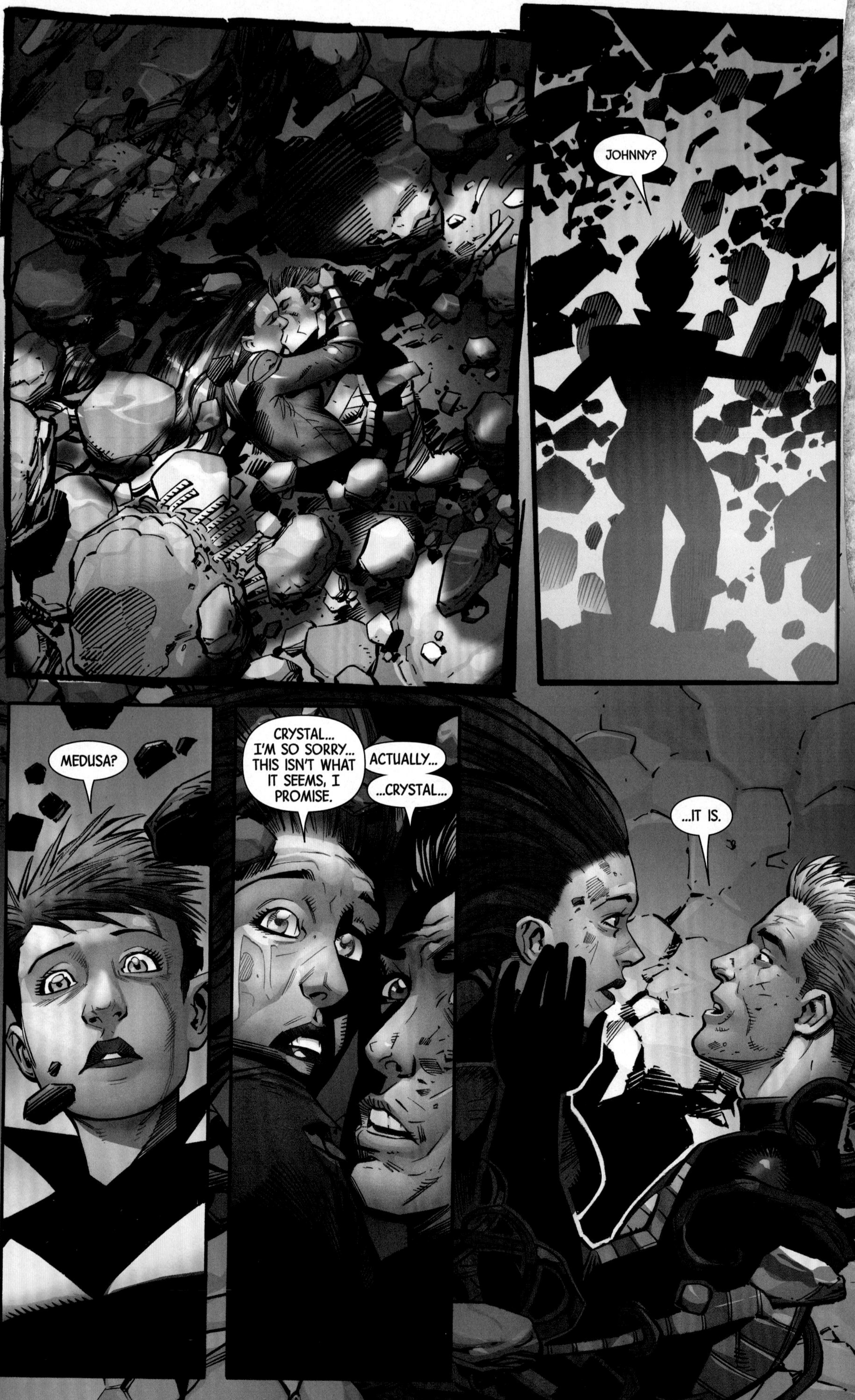
JOHNNY?
MEDUSA?
CRYSTAL... I'M SO SORRY... THIS ISN'T WHAT IT SEEMS, I PROMISE.
ACTUALLY...
...CRYSTAL...
...IT IS.

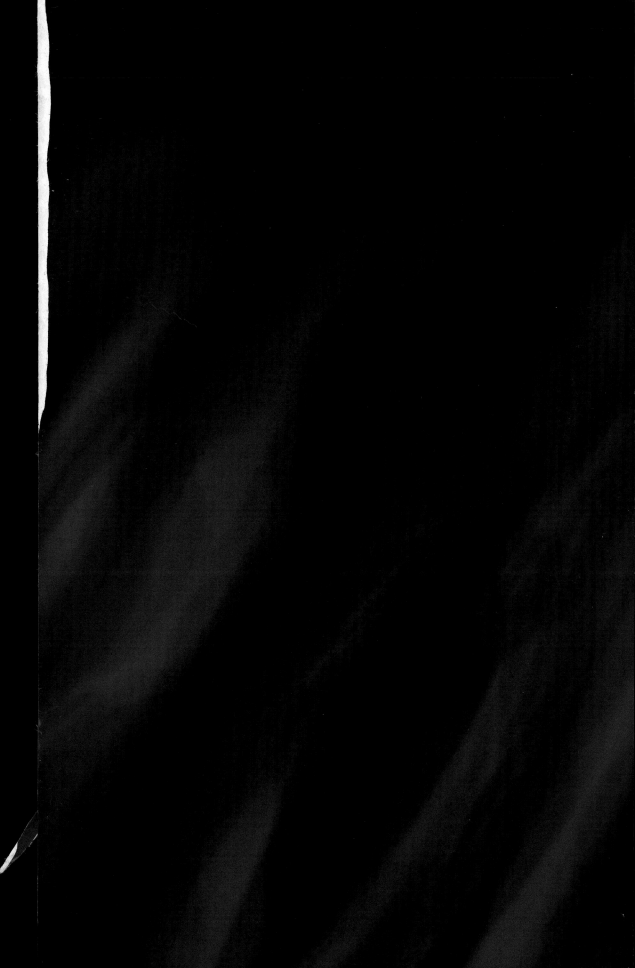

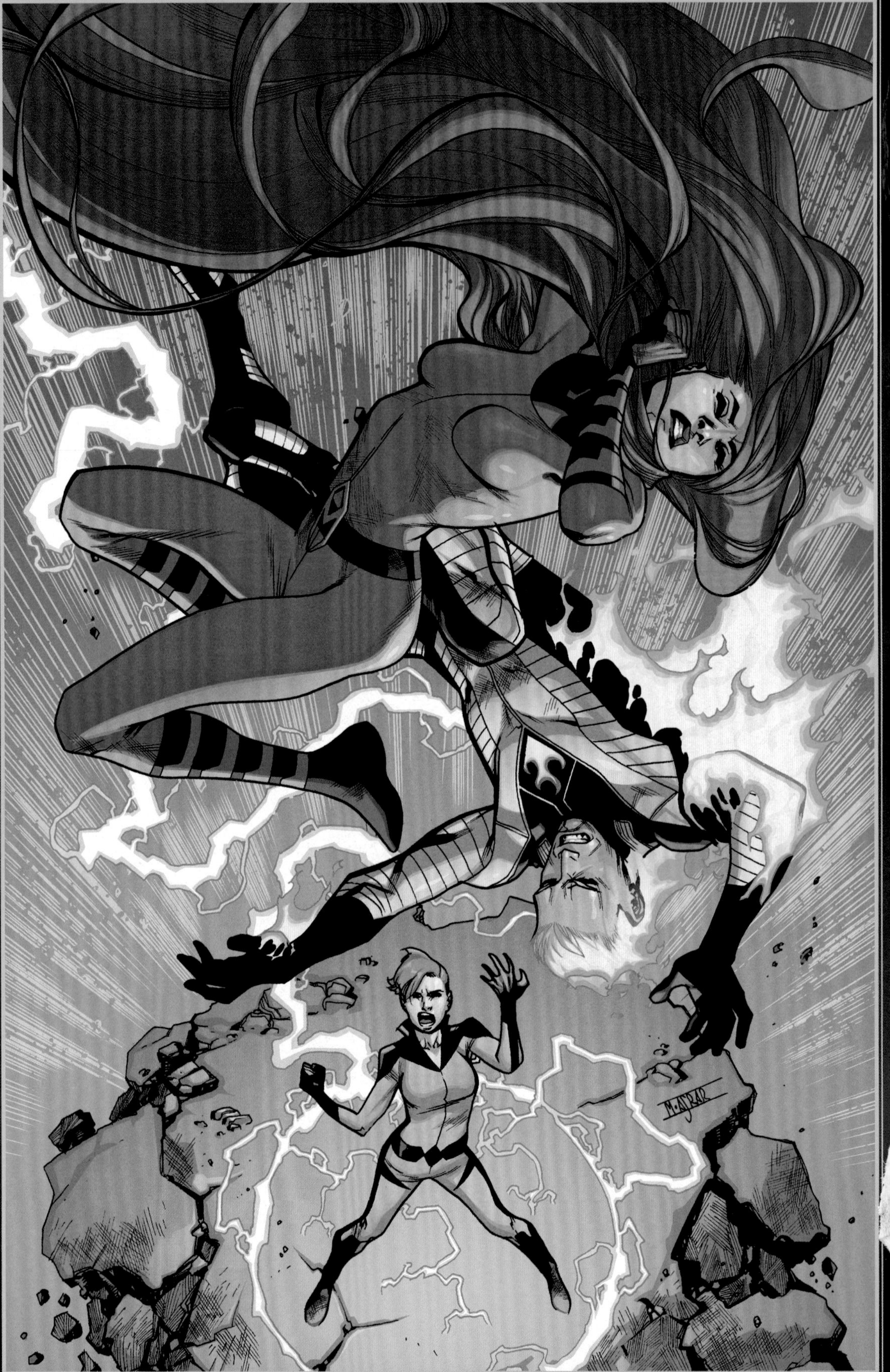
M.ASRAR

9

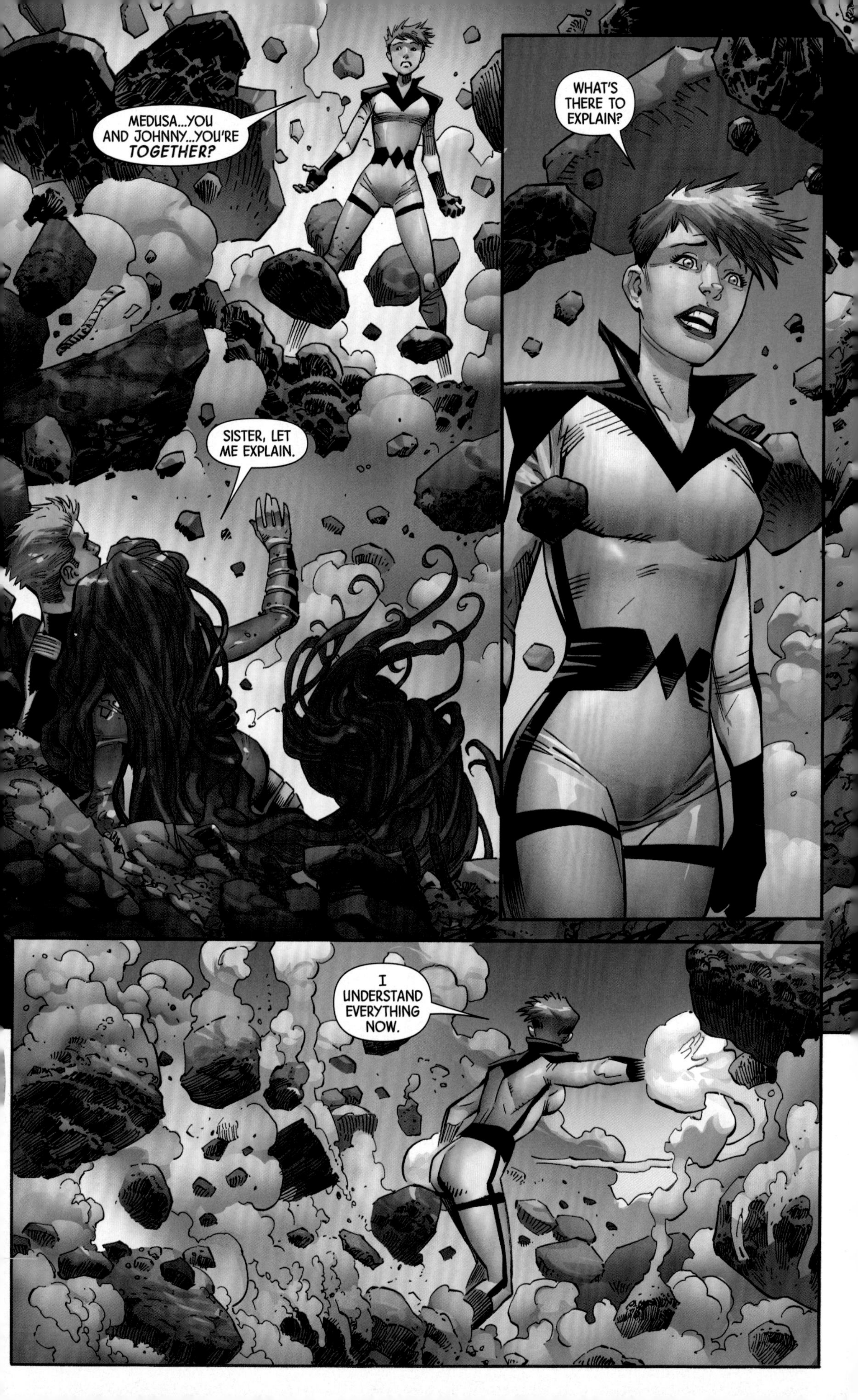
MEDUSA...YOU AND JOHNNY...YOU'RE *TOGETHER?*
WHAT'S THERE TO EXPLAIN?
SISTER, LET ME EXPLAIN.
I UNDERSTAND EVERYTHING NOW.

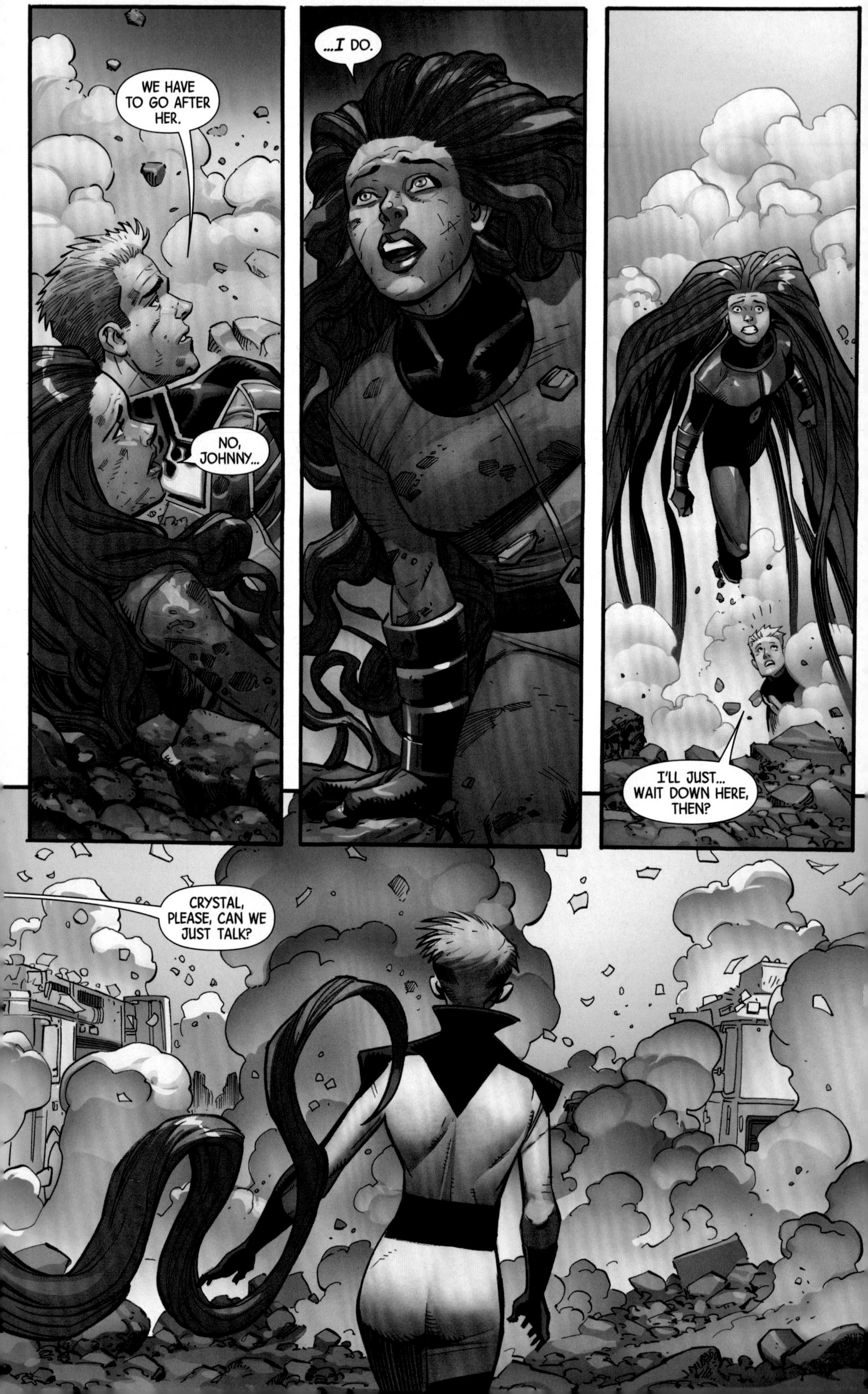
WE HAVE TO GO AFTER HER.
NO, JOHNNY...
...I DO.
I'LL JUST... WAIT DOWN HERE, THEN?
CRYSTAL, PLEASE, CAN WE JUST TALK?

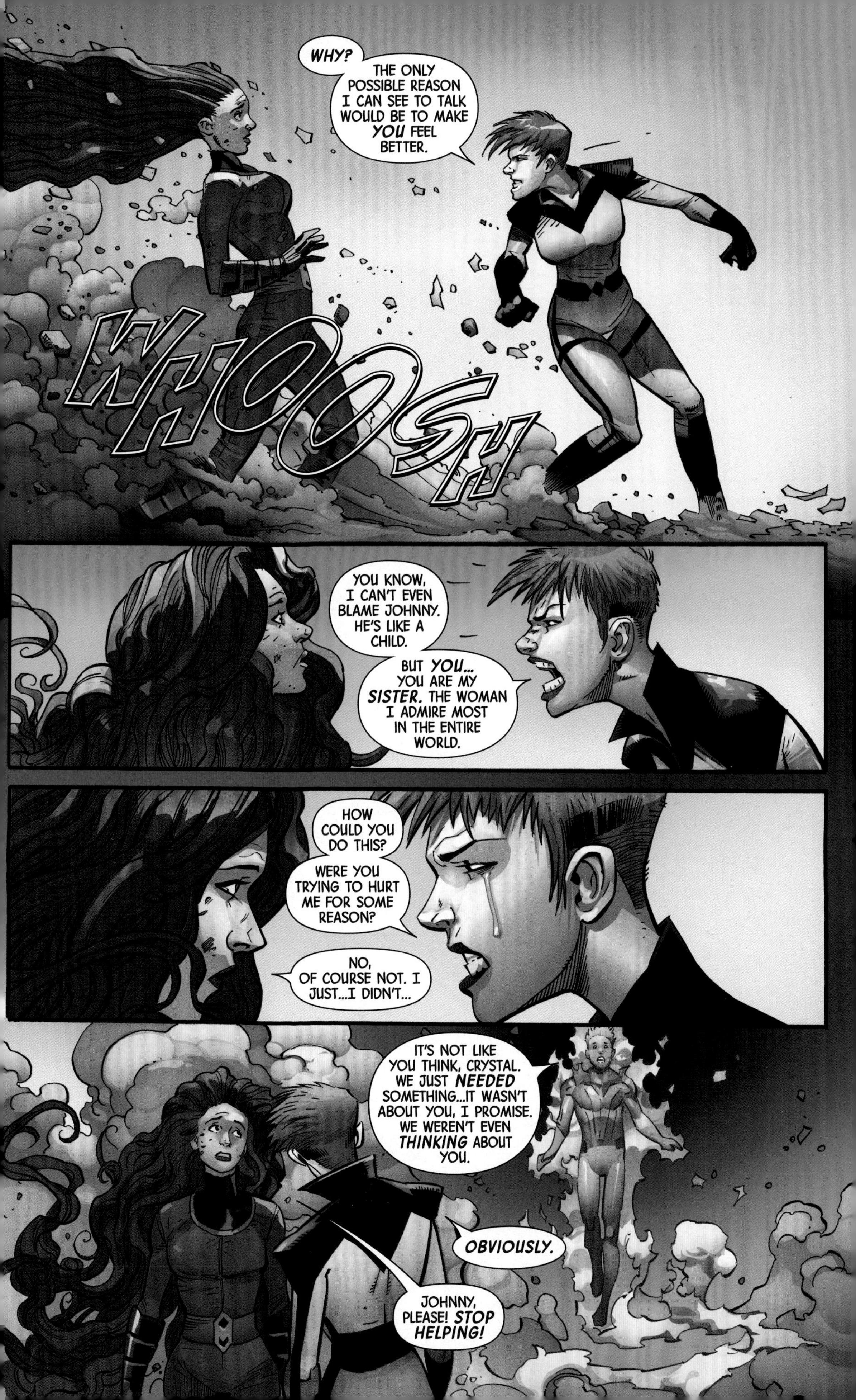
WHY?
THE ONLY POSSIBLE REASON I CAN SEE TO TALK WOULD BE TO MAKE YOU FEEL BETTER.
WHOOSH
YOU KNOW, I CAN'T EVEN BLAME JOHNNY. HE'S LIKE A CHILD.
BUT YOU... YOU ARE MY SISTER. THE WOMAN I ADMIRE MOST IN THE ENTIRE WORLD.
HOW COULD YOU DO THIS?
WERE YOU TRYING TO HURT ME FOR SOME REASON?
NO, OF COURSE NOT. I JUST...I DIDN'T...
IT'S NOT LIKE YOU THINK, CRYSTAL. WE JUST NEEDED SOMETHING...IT WASN'T ABOUT YOU, I PROMISE. WE WEREN'T EVEN THINKING ABOUT YOU.
OBVIOUSLY.
JOHNNY, PLEASE! STOP HELPING!

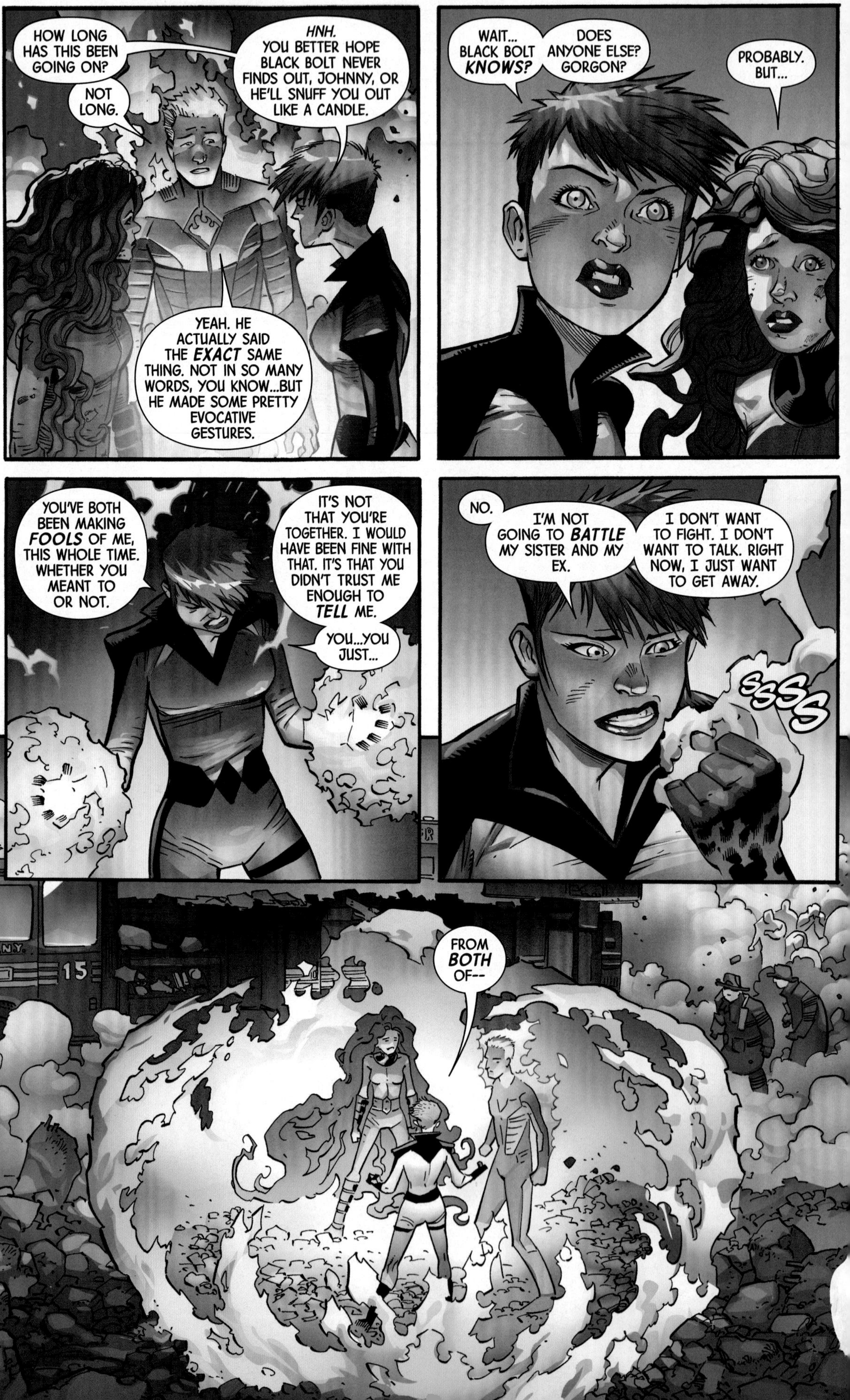

HOW LONG HAS THIS BEEN GOING ON?
NOT LONG.
HNH. YOU BETTER HOPE BLACK BOLT NEVER FINDS OUT, JOHNNY, OR HE'LL SNUFF YOU OUT LIKE A CANDLE.
YEAH. HE ACTUALLY SAID THE EXACT SAME THING. NOT IN SO MANY WORDS, YOU KNOW...BUT HE MADE SOME PRETTY EVOCATIVE GESTURES.
WAIT... BLACK BOLT KNOWS?
DOES ANYONE ELSE? GORGON?
PROBABLY. BUT...
YOU'VE BOTH BEEN MAKING FOOLS OF ME, THIS WHOLE TIME. WHETHER YOU MEANT TO OR NOT.
IT'S NOT THAT YOU'RE TOGETHER. I WOULD HAVE BEEN FINE WITH THAT. IT'S THAT YOU DIDN'T TRUST ME ENOUGH TO TELL ME.
YOU...YOU JUST...
NO.
I'M NOT GOING TO BATTLE MY SISTER AND MY EX.
I DON'T WANT TO FIGHT. I DON'T WANT TO TALK. RIGHT NOW, I JUST WANT TO GET AWAY.
SSSS
F.D.N.Y.
15
FROM BOTH OF--

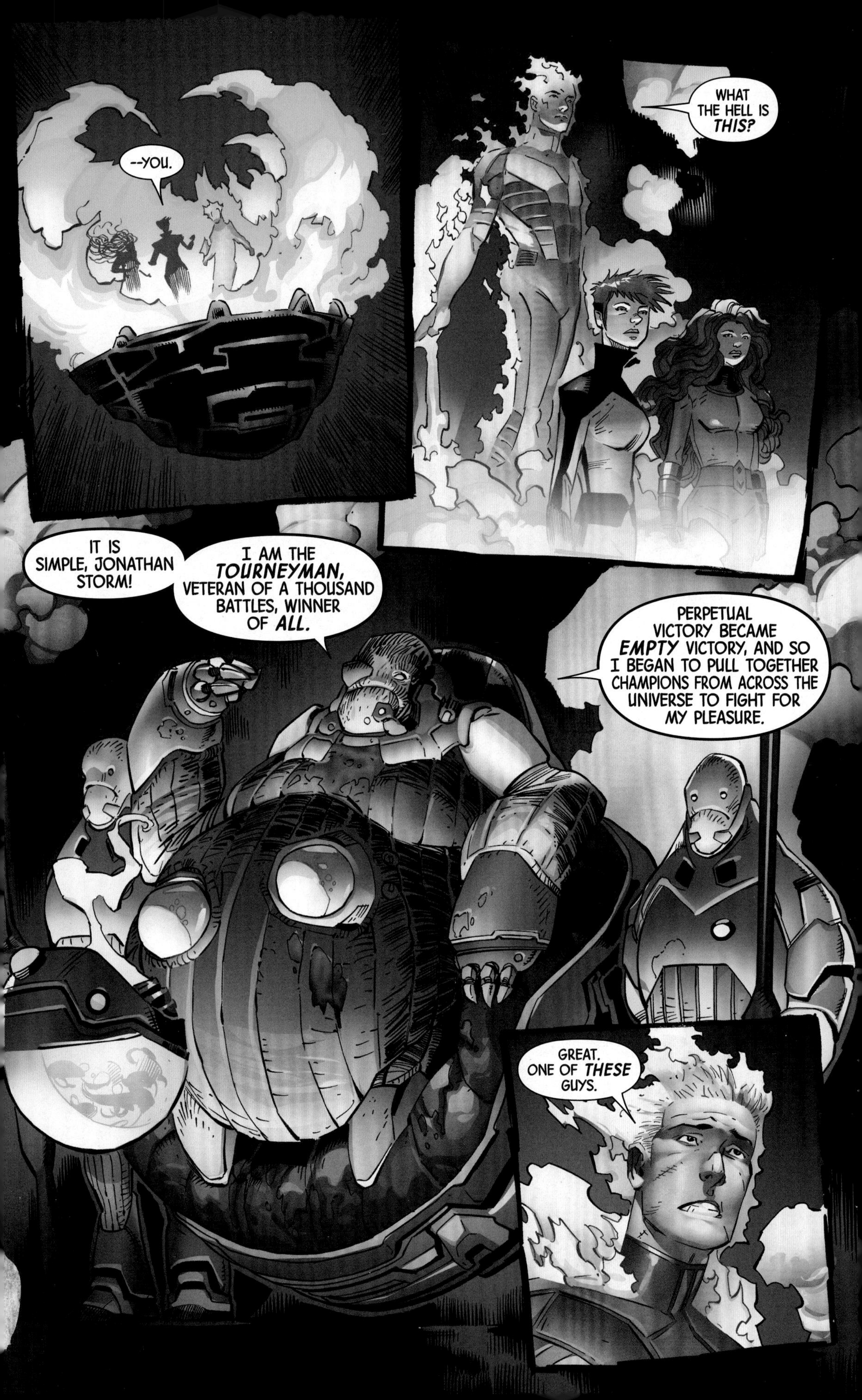

--YOU.
WHAT THE HELL IS THIS?
IT IS SIMPLE, JONATHAN STORM!
I AM THE TOURNEYMAN, VETERAN OF A THOUSAND BATTLES, WINNER OF ALL.
PERPETUAL VICTORY BECAME EMPTY VICTORY, AND SO I BEGAN TO PULL TOGETHER CHAMPIONS FROM ACROSS THE UNIVERSE TO FIGHT FOR MY PLEASURE.
GREAT. ONE OF THESE GUYS.

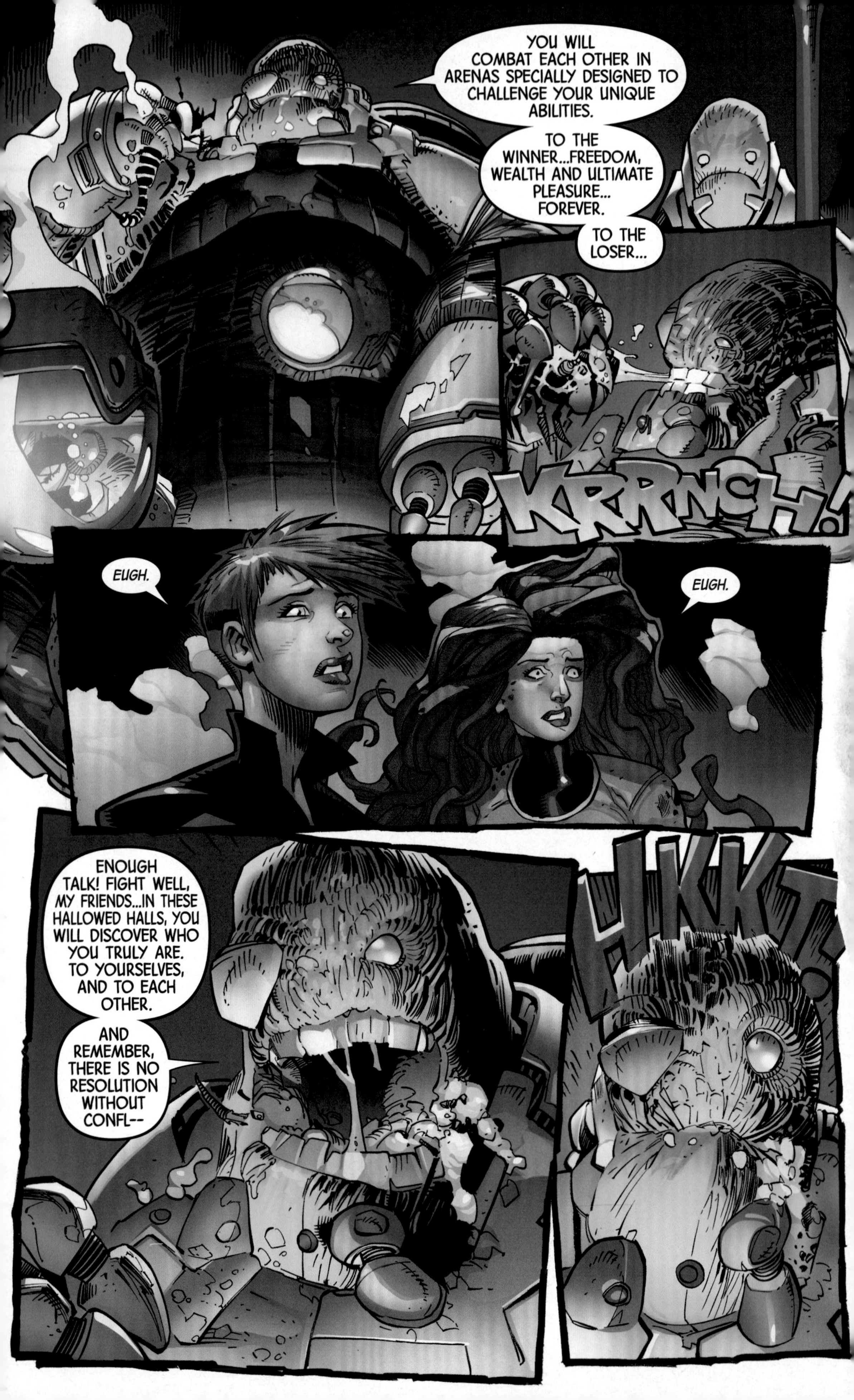
YOU WILL COMBAT EACH OTHER IN ARENAS SPECIALLY DESIGNED TO CHALLENGE YOUR UNIQUE ABILITIES.
TO THE WINNER...FREEDOM, WEALTH AND ULTIMATE PLEASURE... FOREVER.
TO THE LOSER...
KRRNCH!
EUGH.
EUGH.
ENOUGH TALK! FIGHT WELL, MY FRIENDS...IN THESE HALLOWED HALLS, YOU WILL DISCOVER WHO YOU TRULY ARE. TO YOURSELVES, AND TO EACH OTHER.
AND REMEMBER, THERE IS NO RESOLUTION WITHOUT CONFL--

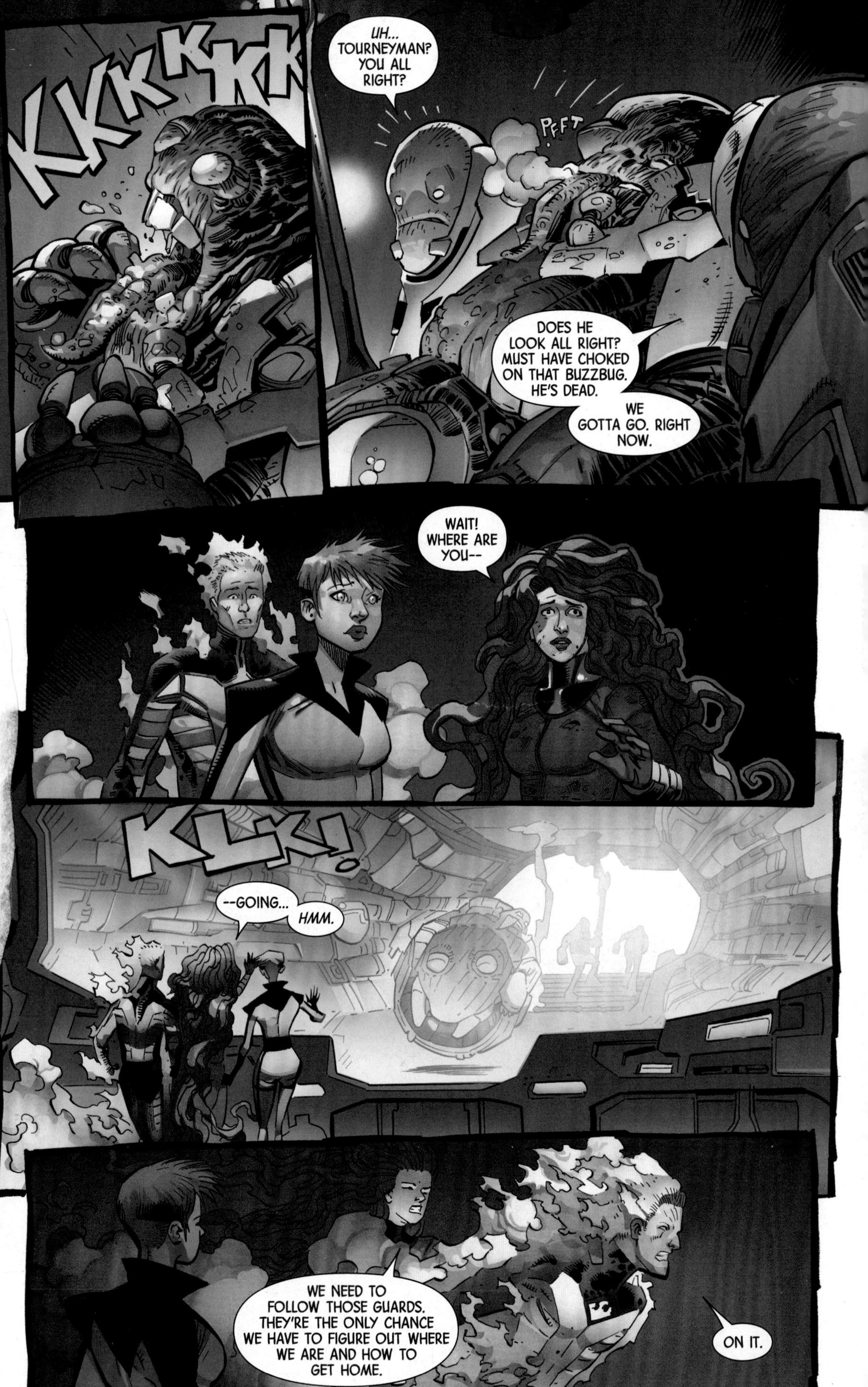

KKKKKK
UH... TOURNEYMAN? YOU ALL RIGHT?
PFFT
DOES HE LOOK ALL RIGHT? MUST HAVE CHOKED ON THAT BUZZBUG. HE'S DEAD.
WE GOTTA GO. RIGHT NOW.
WAIT! WHERE ARE YOU--
KLK!
--GOING...
HMM.
WE NEED TO FOLLOW THOSE GUARDS. THEY'RE THE ONLY CHANCE WE HAVE TO FIGURE OUT WHERE WE ARE AND HOW TO GET HOME.
ON IT.

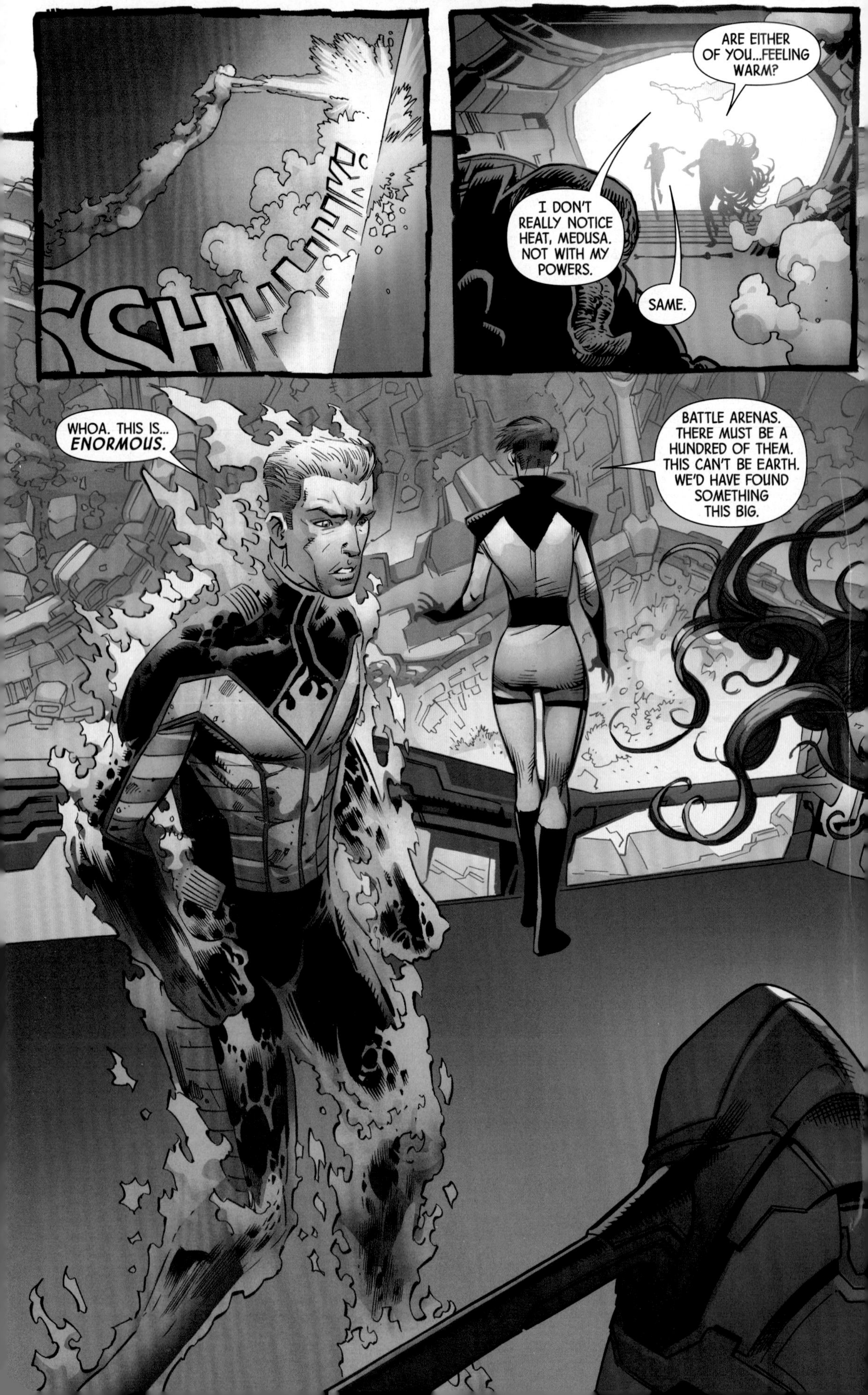
ARE EITHER OF YOU...FEELING WARM?
I DON'T REALLY NOTICE HEAT, MEDUSA. NOT WITH MY POWERS.
SAME.
WHOA. THIS IS... *ENORMOUS.*
BATTLE ARENAS. THERE MUST BE A HUNDRED OF THEM. THIS CAN'T BE EARTH. WE'D HAVE FOUND SOMETHING THIS BIG.

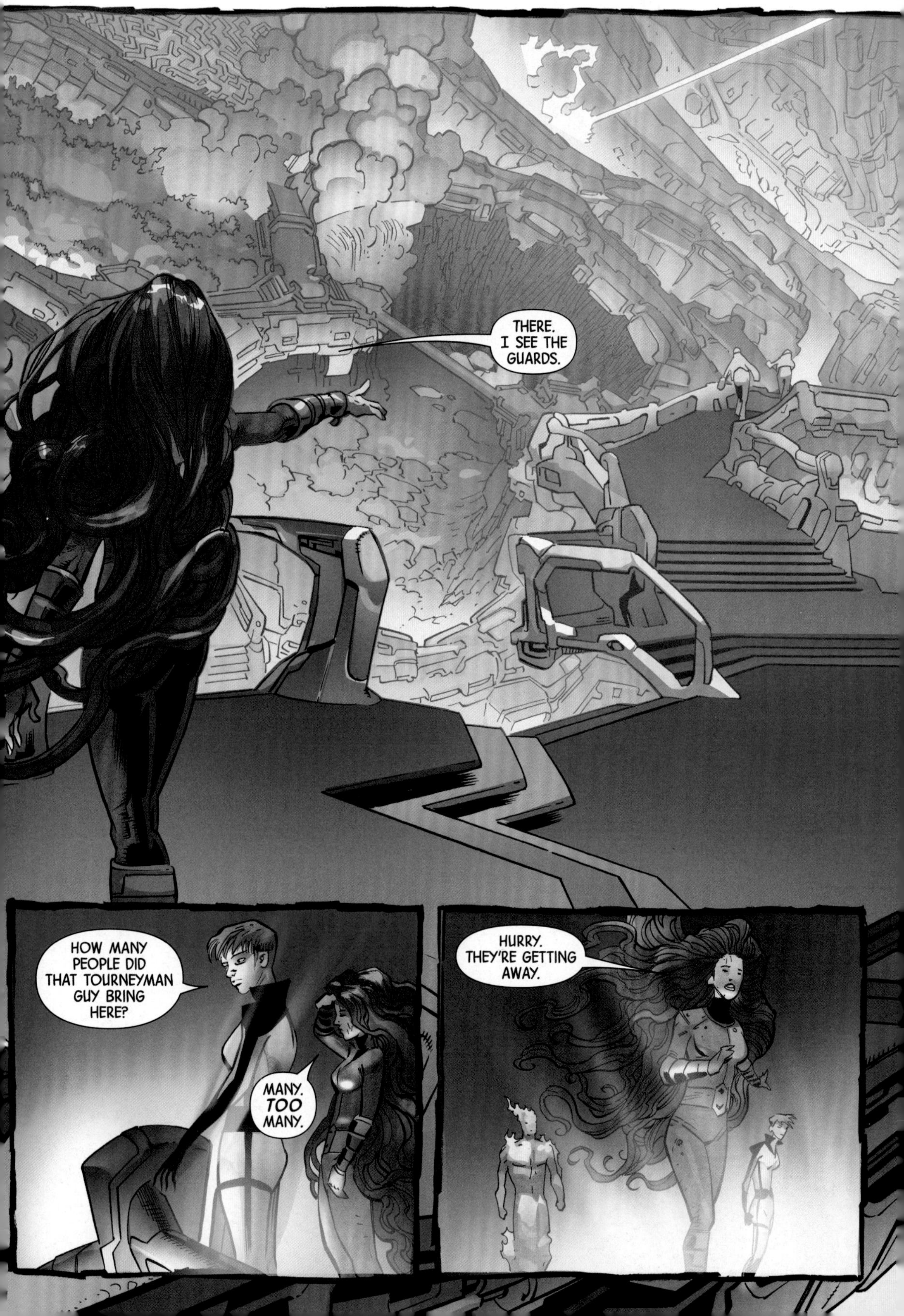
THERE. I SEE THE GUARDS.
HOW MANY PEOPLE DID THAT TOURNEYMAN GUY BRING HERE?
MANY. *TOO* MANY.
HURRY. THEY'RE GETTING AWAY.

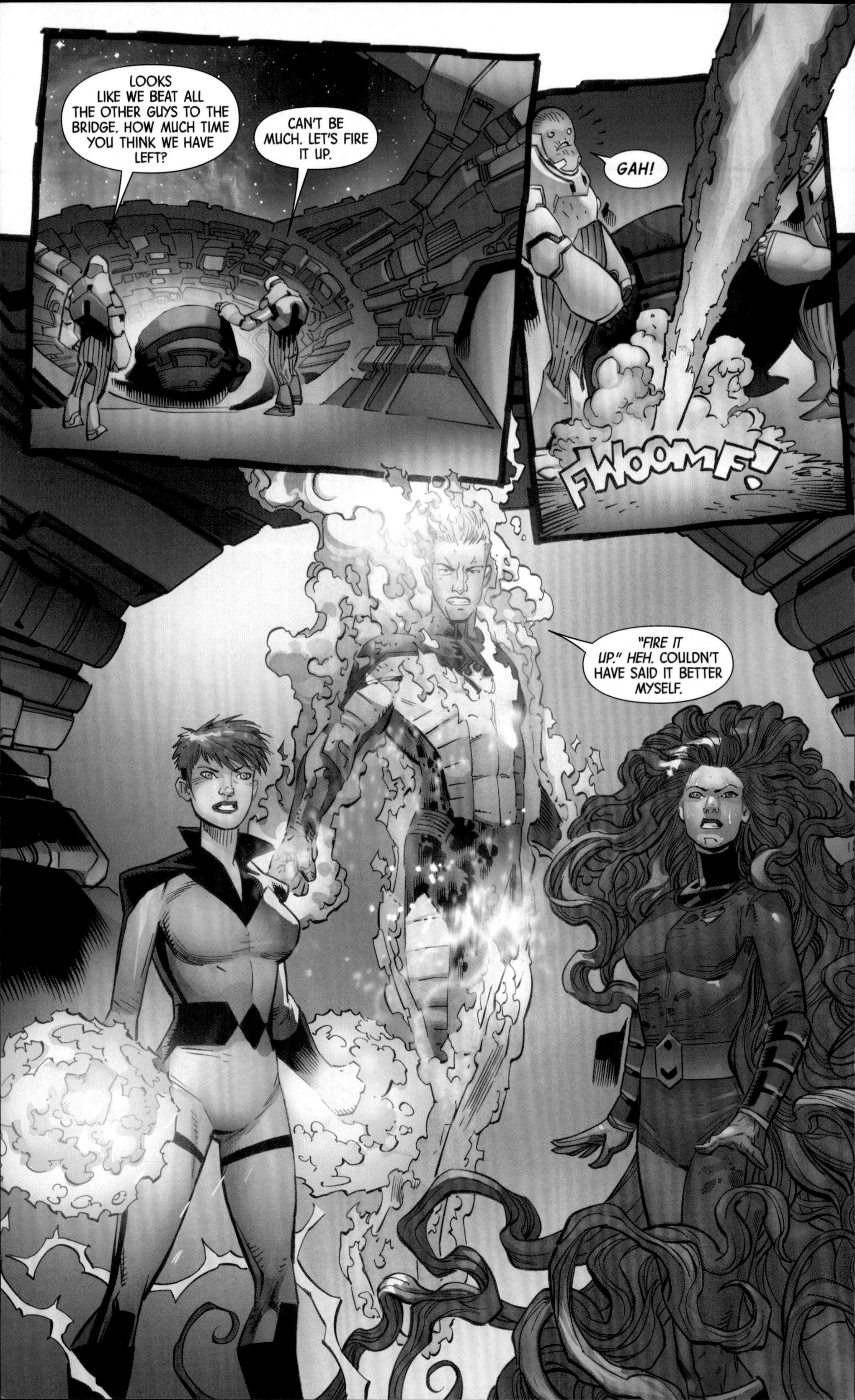
LOOKS LIKE WE BEAT ALL THE OTHER GUYS TO THE BRIDGE. HOW MUCH TIME YOU THINK WE HAVE LEFT?
CAN'T BE MUCH. LET'S FIRE IT UP.
GAH!
FWOOMF!
"FIRE IT UP." HEH. COULDN'T HAVE SAID IT BETTER MYSELF.

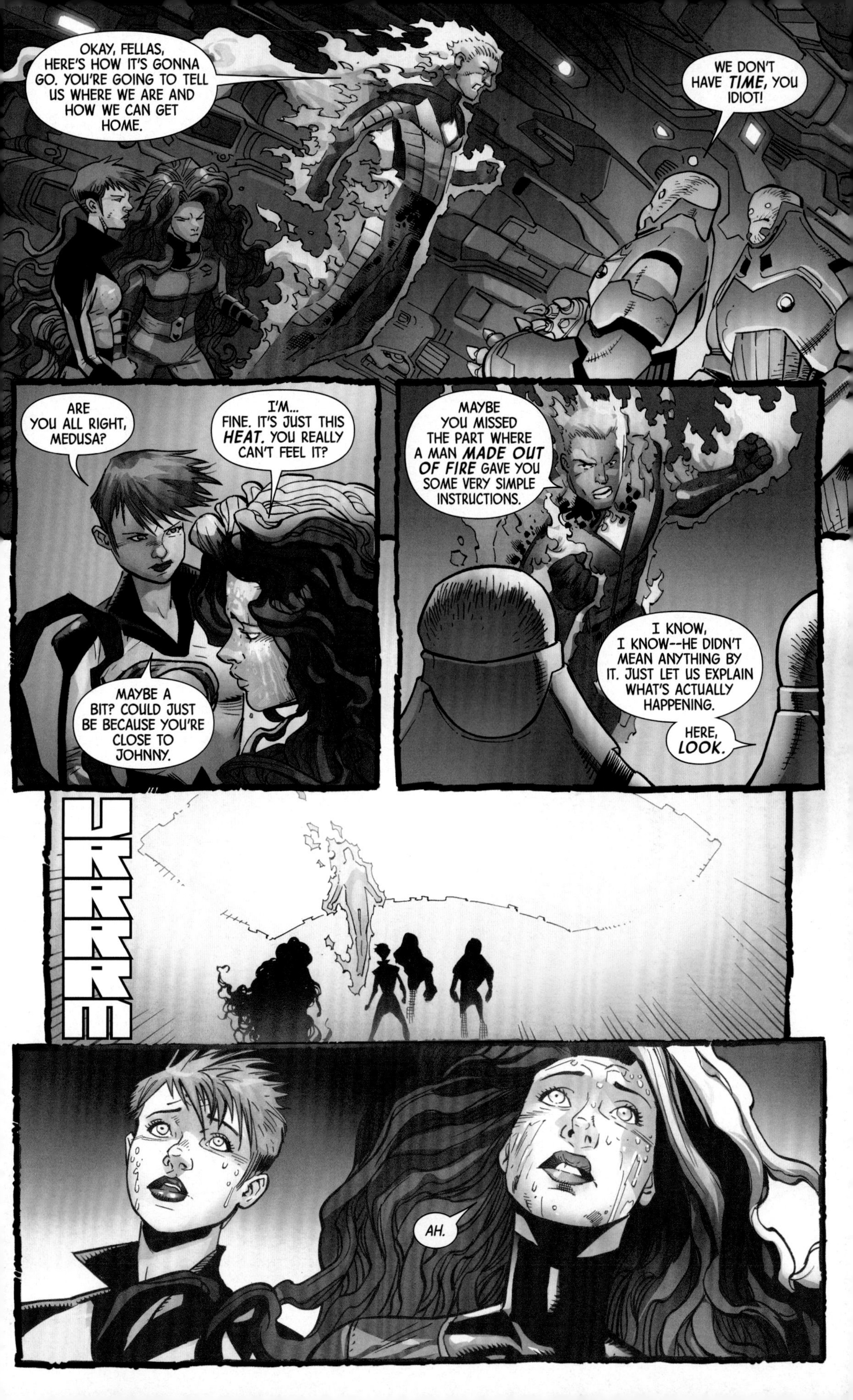
OKAY, FELLAS, HERE'S HOW IT'S GONNA GO. YOU'RE GOING TO TELL US WHERE WE ARE AND HOW WE CAN GET HOME.
WE DON'T HAVE TIME, YOU IDIOT!
ARE YOU ALL RIGHT, MEDUSA?
I'M... FINE. IT'S JUST THIS HEAT. YOU REALLY CAN'T FEEL IT?
MAYBE A BIT? COULD JUST BE BECAUSE YOU'RE CLOSE TO JOHNNY.
MAYBE YOU MISSED THE PART WHERE A MAN MADE OUT OF FIRE GAVE YOU SOME VERY SIMPLE INSTRUCTIONS.
I KNOW, I KNOW--HE DIDN'T MEAN ANYTHING BY IT. JUST LET US EXPLAIN WHAT'S ACTUALLY HAPPENING.
HERE, LOOK.
URRRRM
AH.

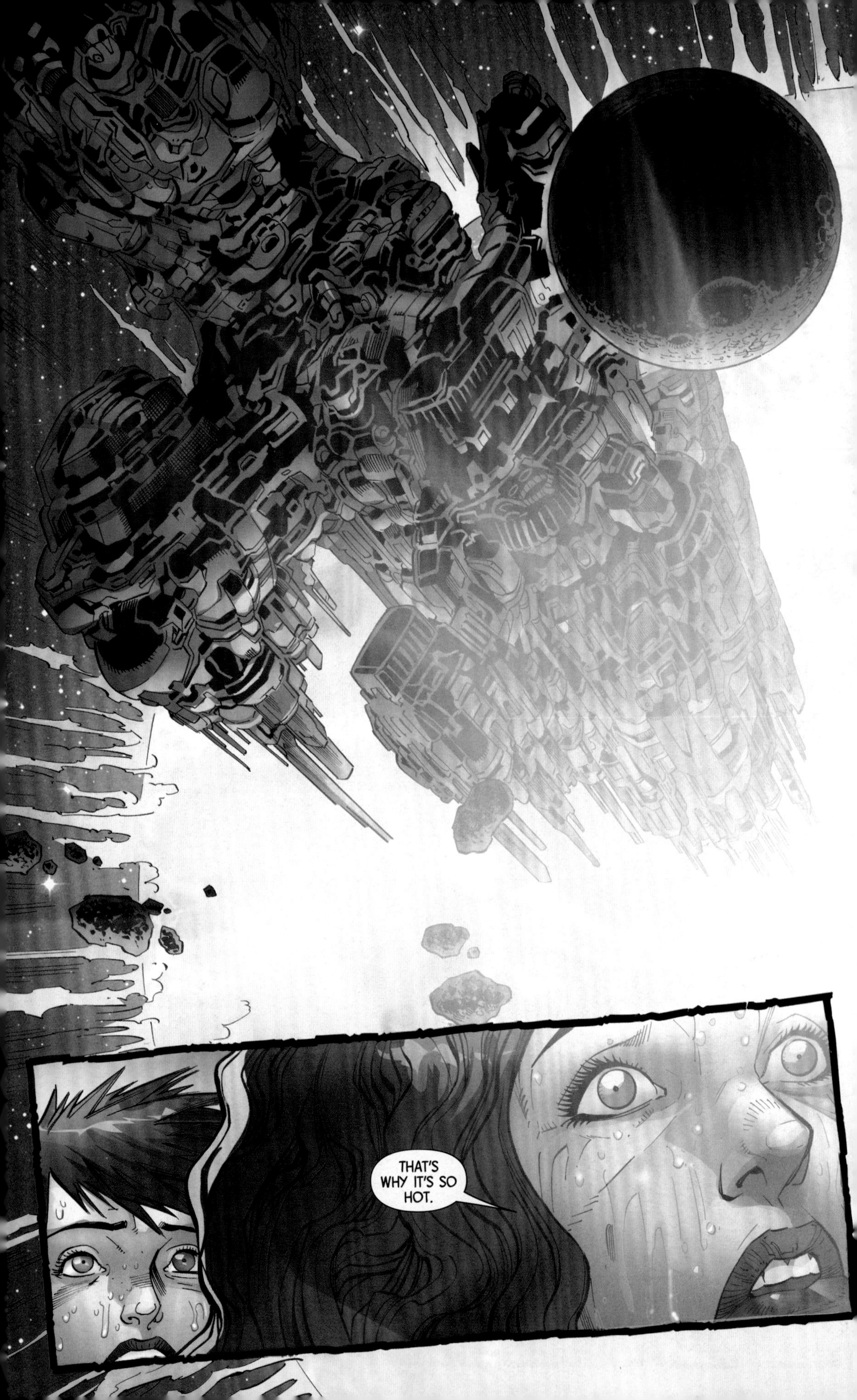
THAT'S WHY IT'S SO HOT.

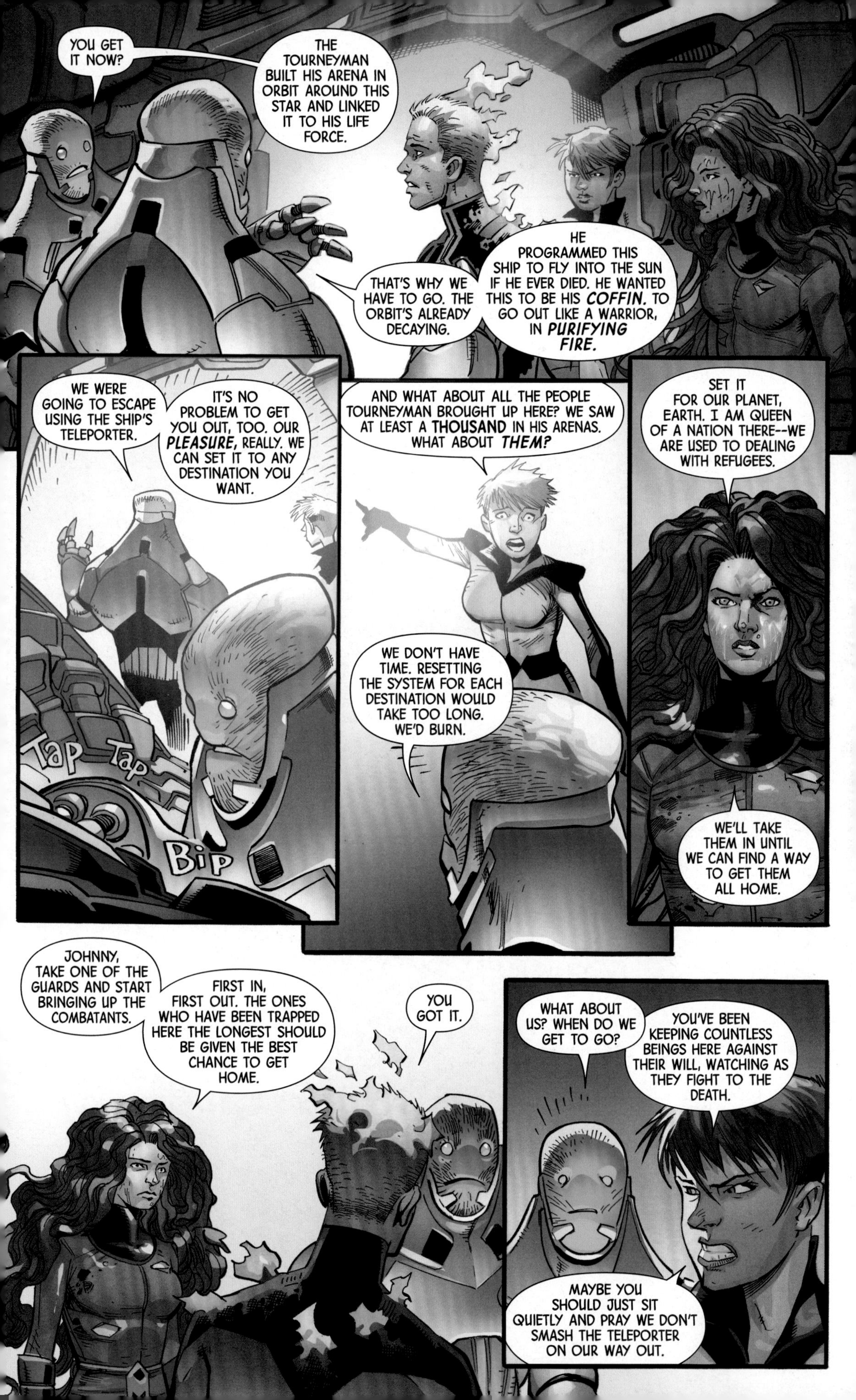

YOU GET IT NOW?
THE TOURNEYMAN BUILT HIS ARENA IN ORBIT AROUND THIS STAR AND LINKED IT TO HIS LIFE FORCE.
HE PROGRAMMED THIS SHIP TO FLY INTO THE SUN IF HE EVER DIED. HE WANTED THIS TO BE HIS COFFIN. TO GO OUT LIKE A WARRIOR, IN PURIFYING FIRE.
THAT'S WHY WE HAVE TO GO. THE ORBIT'S ALREADY DECAYING.
WE WERE GOING TO ESCAPE USING THE SHIP'S TELEPORTER.
IT'S NO PROBLEM TO GET YOU OUT, TOO. OUR PLEASURE, REALLY. WE CAN SET IT TO ANY DESTINATION YOU WANT.
TAP TAP
BIP
AND WHAT ABOUT ALL THE PEOPLE TOURNEYMAN BROUGHT UP HERE? WE SAW AT LEAST A THOUSAND IN HIS ARENAS. WHAT ABOUT THEM?
WE DON'T HAVE TIME. RESETTING THE SYSTEM FOR EACH DESTINATION WOULD TAKE TOO LONG. WE'D BURN.
SET IT FOR OUR PLANET, EARTH. I AM QUEEN OF A NATION THERE--WE ARE USED TO DEALING WITH REFUGEES.
WE'LL TAKE THEM IN UNTIL WE CAN FIND A WAY TO GET THEM ALL HOME.
JOHNNY, TAKE ONE OF THE GUARDS AND START BRINGING UP THE COMBATANTS.
FIRST IN, FIRST OUT. THE ONES WHO HAVE BEEN TRAPPED HERE THE LONGEST SHOULD BE GIVEN THE BEST CHANCE TO GET HOME.
YOU GOT IT.
WHAT ABOUT US? WHEN DO WE GET TO GO?
YOU'VE BEEN KEEPING COUNTLESS BEINGS HERE AGAINST THEIR WILL, WATCHING AS THEY FIGHT TO THE DEATH.
MAYBE YOU SHOULD JUST SIT QUIETLY AND PRAY WE DON'T SMASH THE TELEPORTER ON OUR WAY OUT.

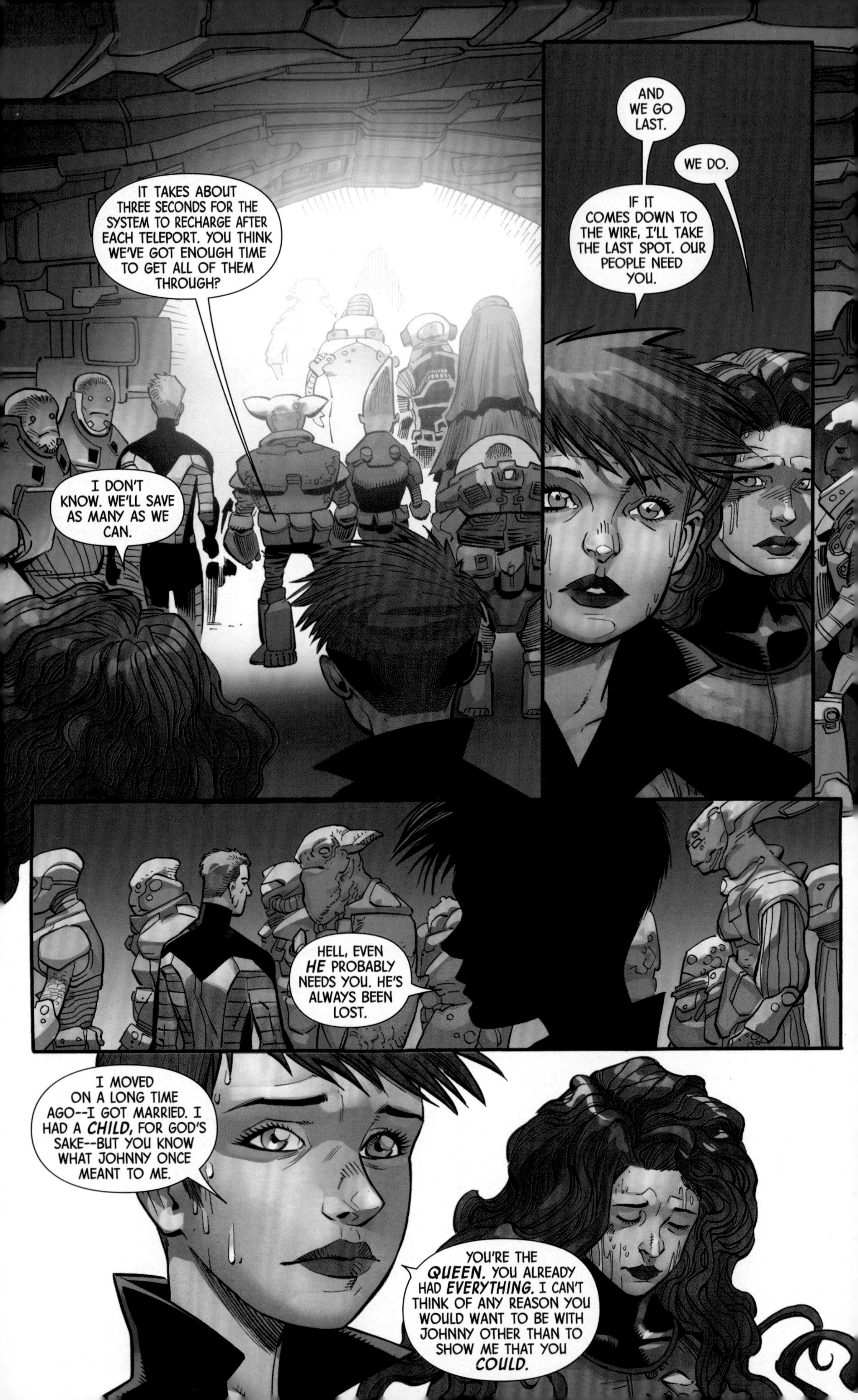
IT TAKES ABOUT THREE SECONDS FOR THE SYSTEM TO RECHARGE AFTER EACH TELEPORT. YOU THINK WE'VE GOT ENOUGH TIME TO GET ALL OF THEM THROUGH?
I DON'T KNOW. WE'LL SAVE AS MANY AS WE CAN.
AND WE GO LAST.
WE DO.
IF IT COMES DOWN TO THE WIRE, I'LL TAKE THE LAST SPOT. OUR PEOPLE NEED YOU.
HELL, EVEN *HE* PROBABLY NEEDS YOU. HE'S ALWAYS BEEN LOST.
I MOVED ON A LONG TIME AGO--I GOT MARRIED. I HAD A *CHILD,* FOR GOD'S SAKE--BUT YOU KNOW WHAT JOHNNY ONCE MEANT TO ME.
YOU'RE THE *QUEEN.* YOU ALREADY HAD *EVERYTHING.* I CAN'T THINK OF ANY REASON YOU WOULD WANT TO BE WITH JOHNNY OTHER THAN TO SHOW ME THAT YOU *COULD.*

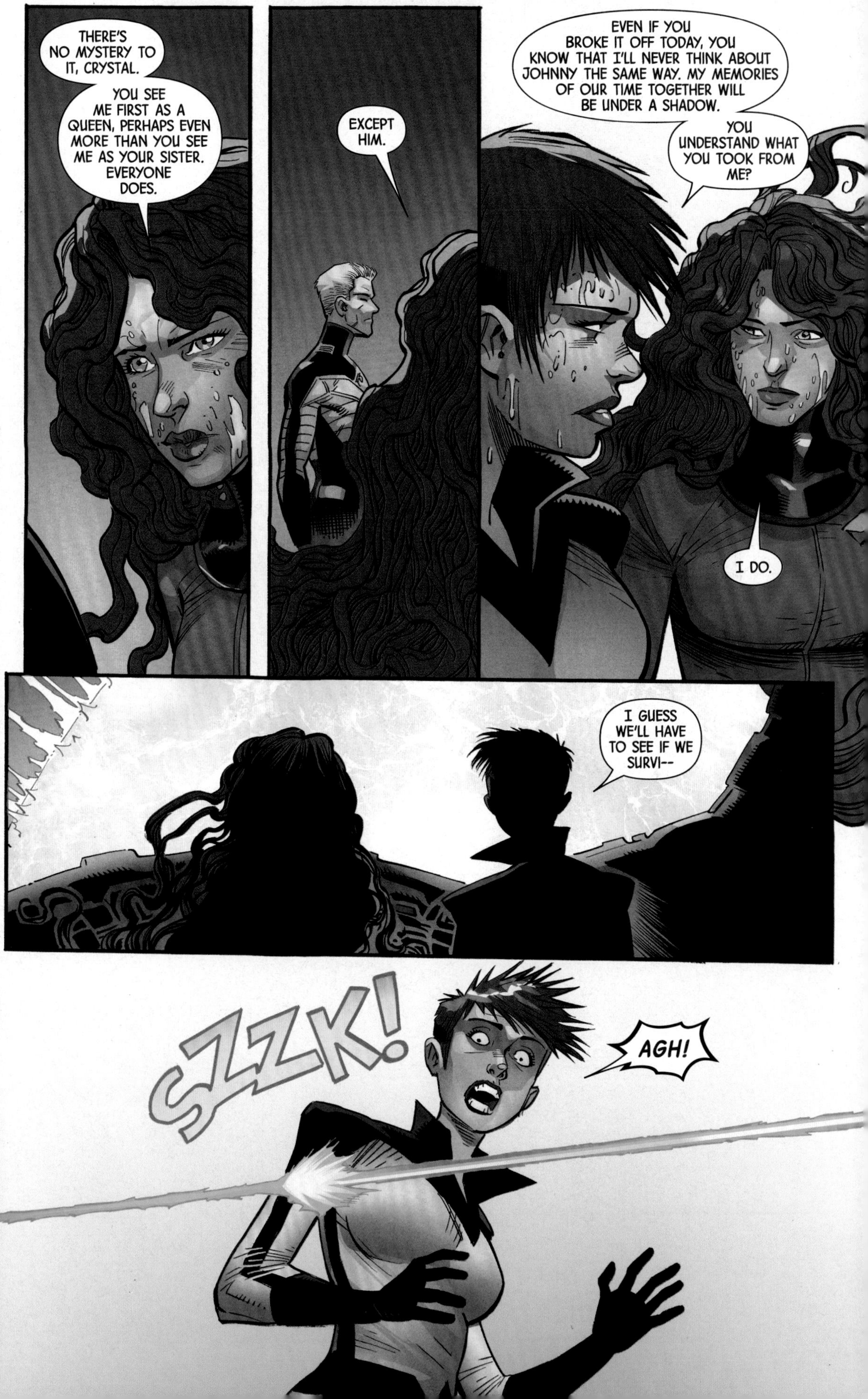
THERE'S NO MYSTERY TO IT, CRYSTAL.
YOU SEE ME FIRST AS A QUEEN, PERHAPS EVEN MORE THAN YOU SEE ME AS YOUR SISTER. EVERYONE DOES.
EXCEPT HIM.
EVEN IF YOU BROKE IT OFF TODAY, YOU KNOW THAT I'LL NEVER THINK ABOUT JOHNNY THE SAME WAY. MY MEMORIES OF OUR TIME TOGETHER WILL BE UNDER A SHADOW.
YOU UNDERSTAND WHAT YOU TOOK FROM ME?
I DO.
I GUESS WE'LL HAVE TO SEE IF WE SURVI--
SZZK!
AGH!

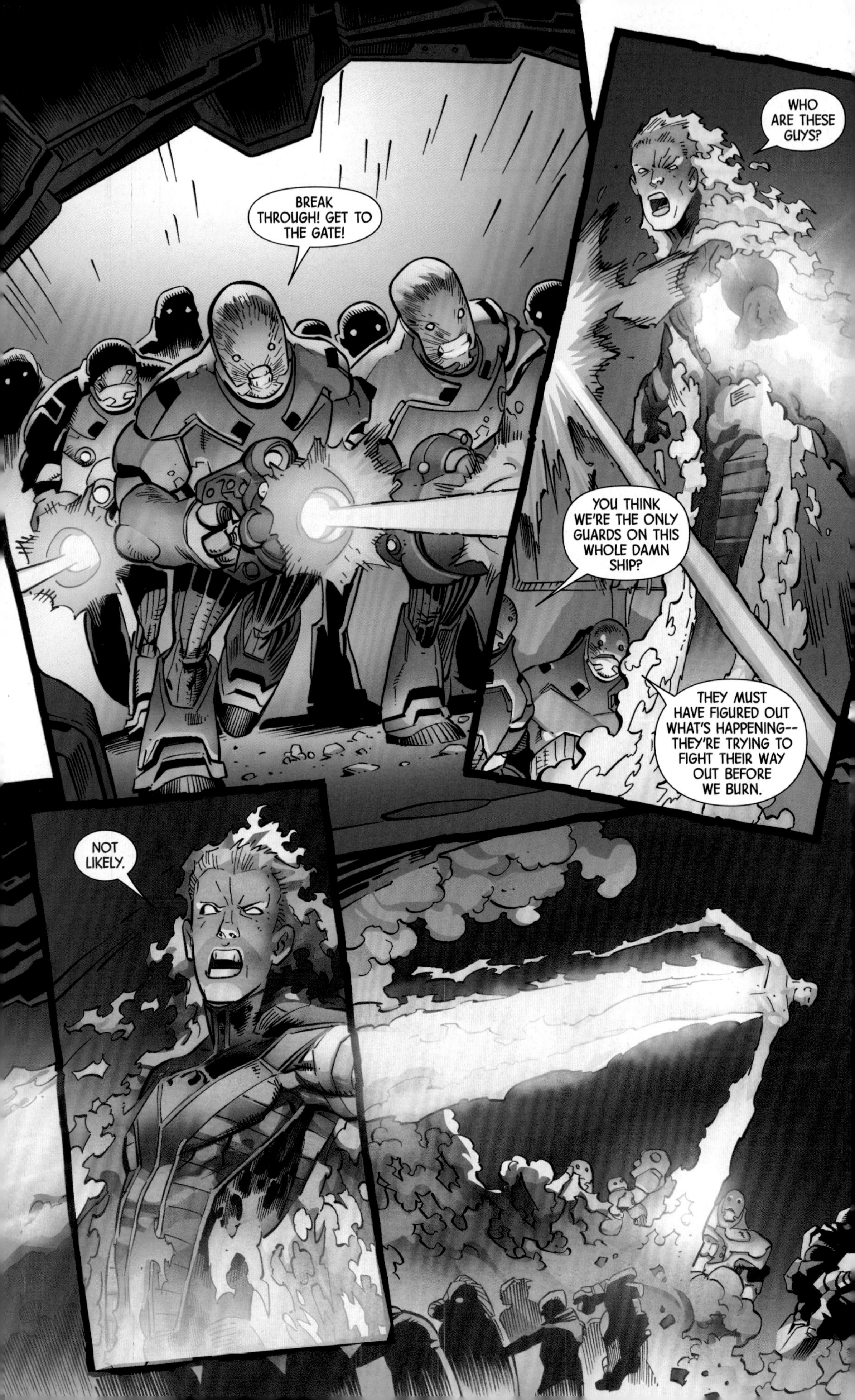
BREAK THROUGH! GET TO THE GATE!
WHO ARE THESE GUYS?
YOU THINK WE'RE THE ONLY GUARDS ON THIS WHOLE DAMN SHIP?
THEY MUST HAVE FIGURED OUT WHAT'S HAPPENING-- THEY'RE TRYING TO FIGHT THEIR WAY OUT BEFORE WE BURN.
NOT LIKELY.

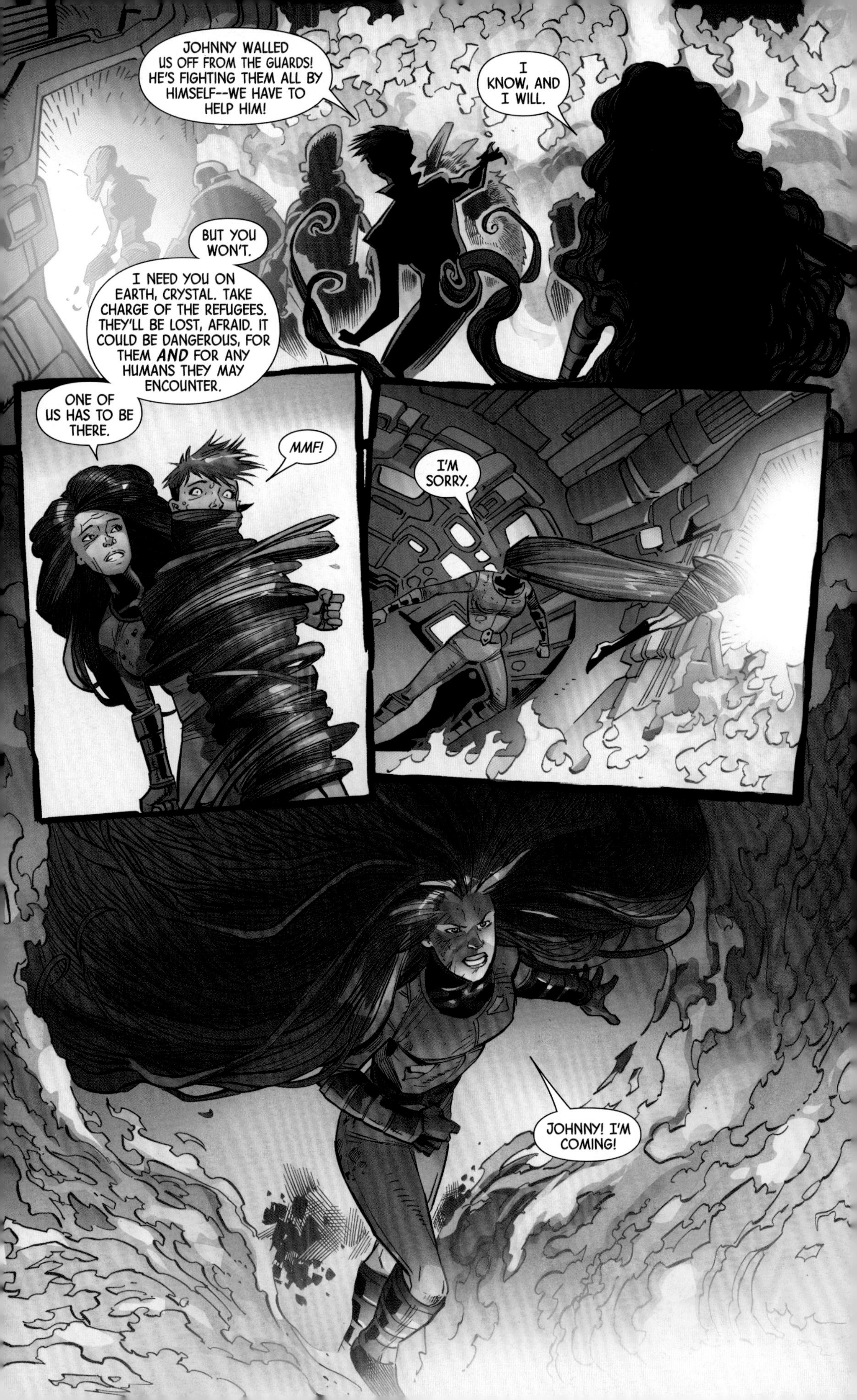
JOHNNY WALLED US OFF FROM THE GUARDS! HE'S FIGHTING THEM ALL BY HIMSELF--WE HAVE TO HELP HIM!
I KNOW, AND I WILL.
BUT YOU WON'T.
I NEED YOU ON EARTH, CRYSTAL. TAKE CHARGE OF THE REFUGEES. THEY'LL BE LOST, AFRAID. IT COULD BE DANGEROUS, FOR THEM ***AND*** FOR ANY HUMANS THEY MAY ENCOUNTER.
ONE OF US HAS TO BE THERE.
MMF!
I'M SORRY.
JOHNNY! I'M COMING!

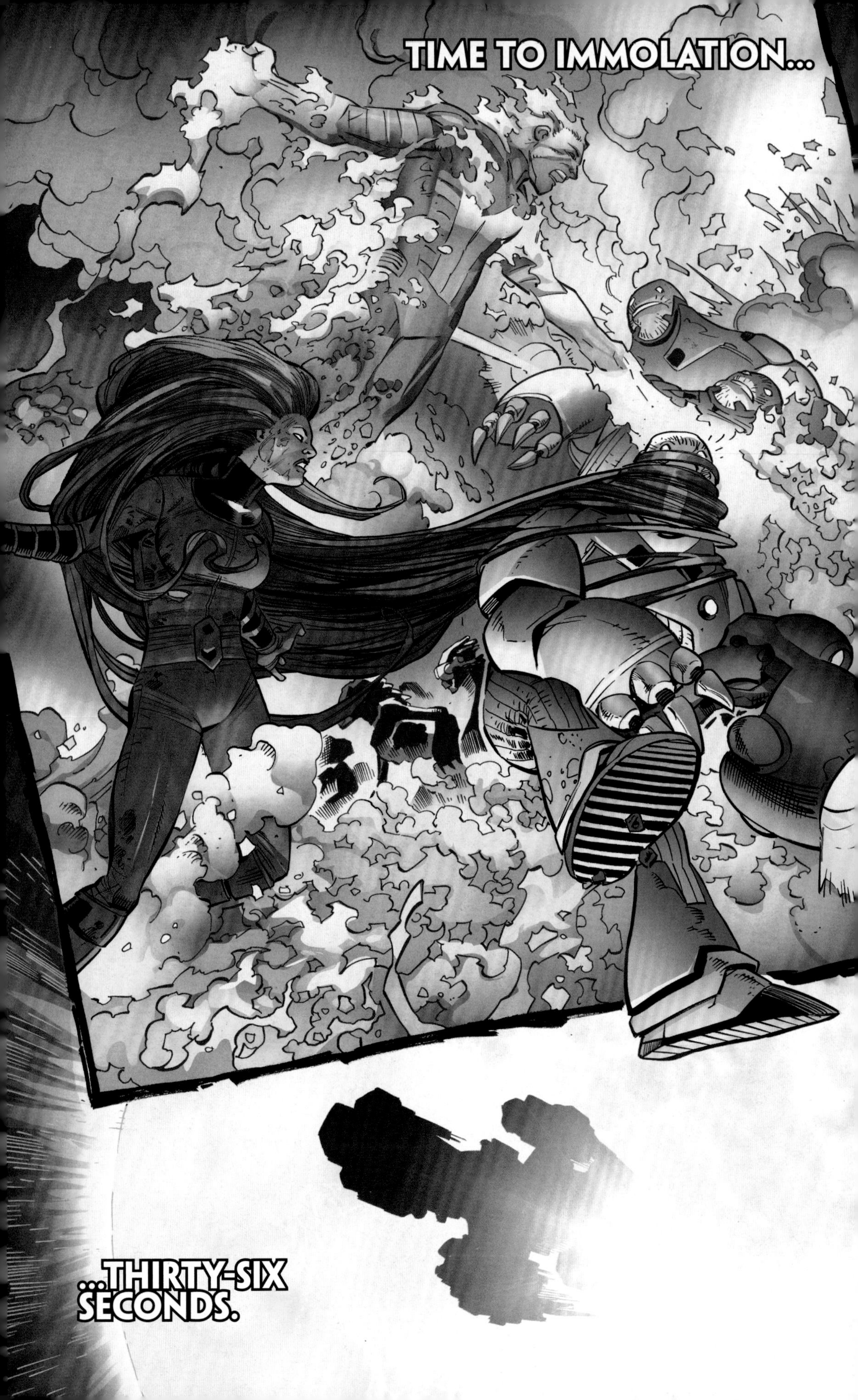
TIME TO IMMOLATION...
...THIRTY-SIX SECONDS.

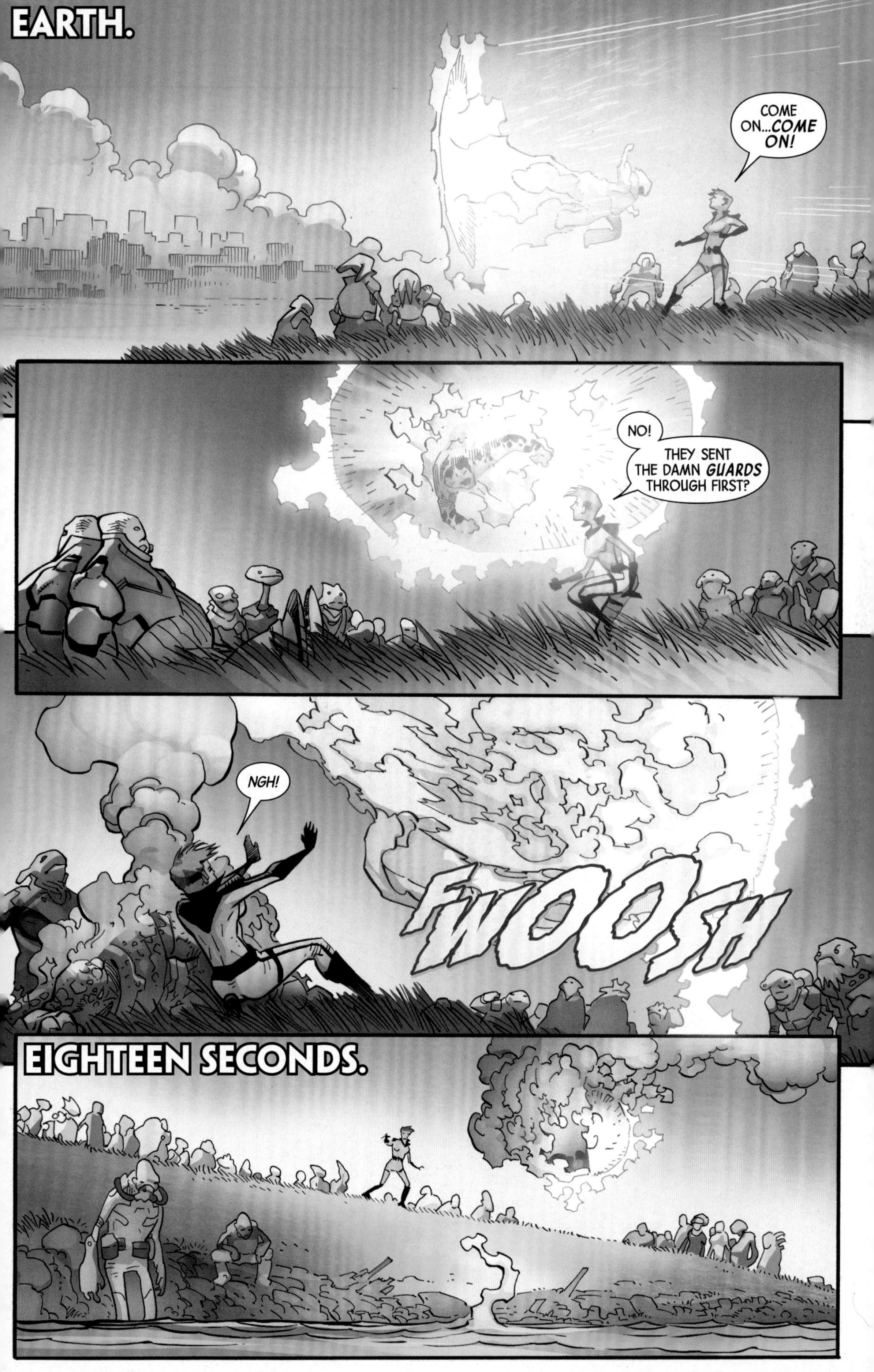
EARTH.
COME ON...COME ON!
NO!
THEY SENT THE DAMN GUARDS THROUGH FIRST?
NGH!
FWOOSH
EIGHTEEN SECONDS.

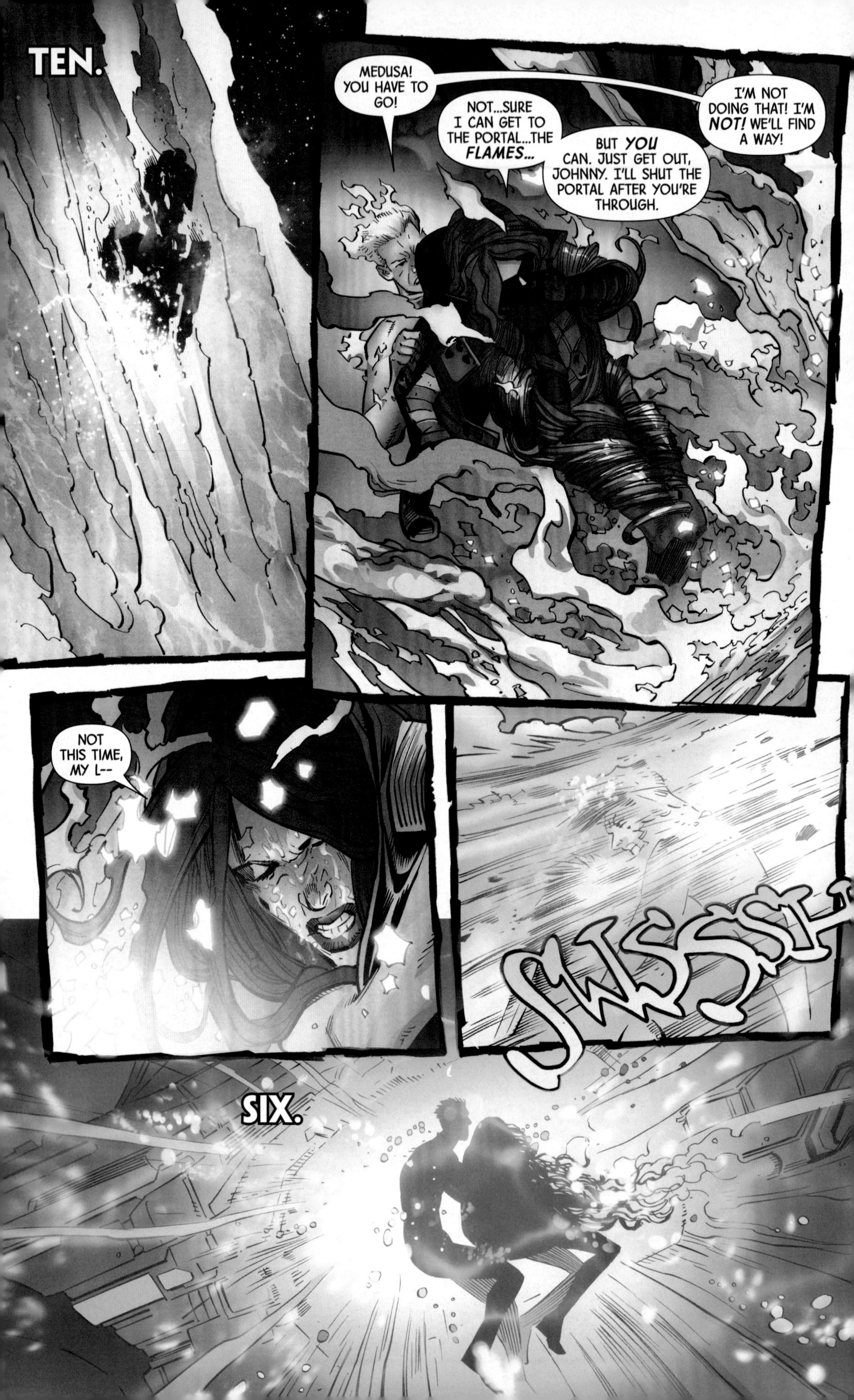
TEN.
MEDUSA! YOU HAVE TO GO!
NOT...SURE I CAN GET TO THE PORTAL...THE FLAMES...
BUT YOU CAN. JUST GET OUT, JOHNNY. I'LL SHUT THE PORTAL AFTER YOU'RE THROUGH.
I'M NOT DOING THAT! I'M NOT! WE'LL FIND A WAY!
NOT THIS TIME, MY L--
SWSSH
SIX.

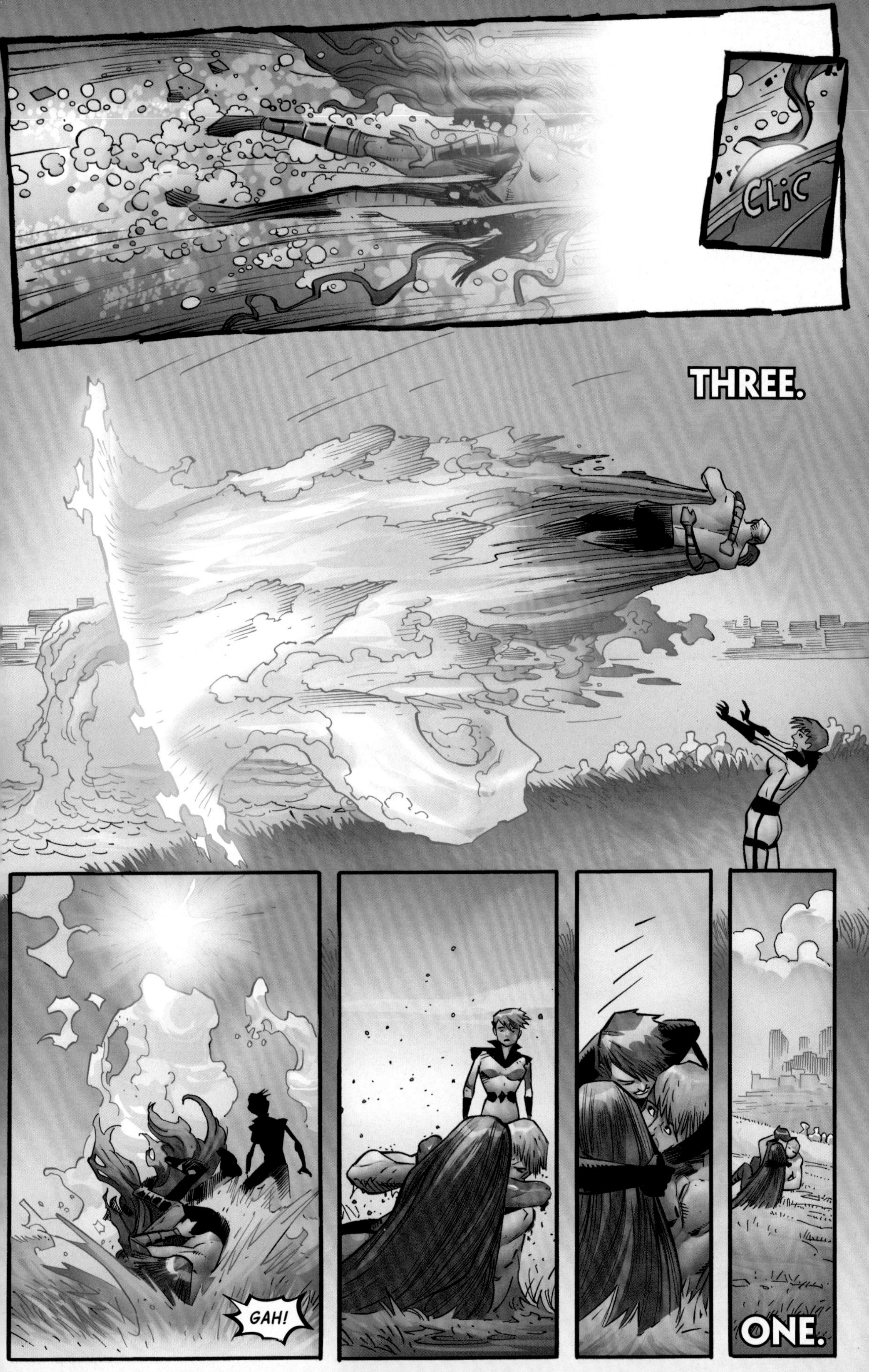
CLIC
THREE.
GAH!
ONE.

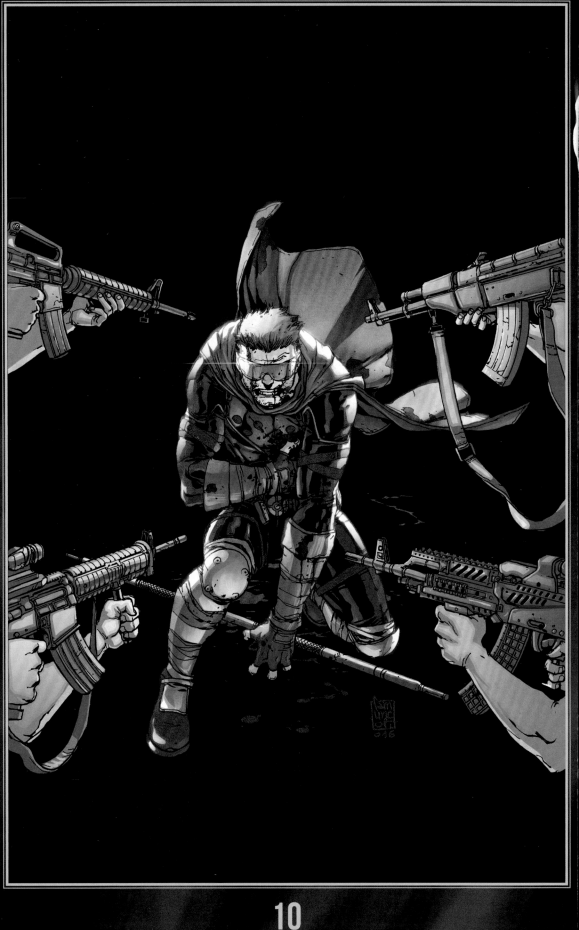

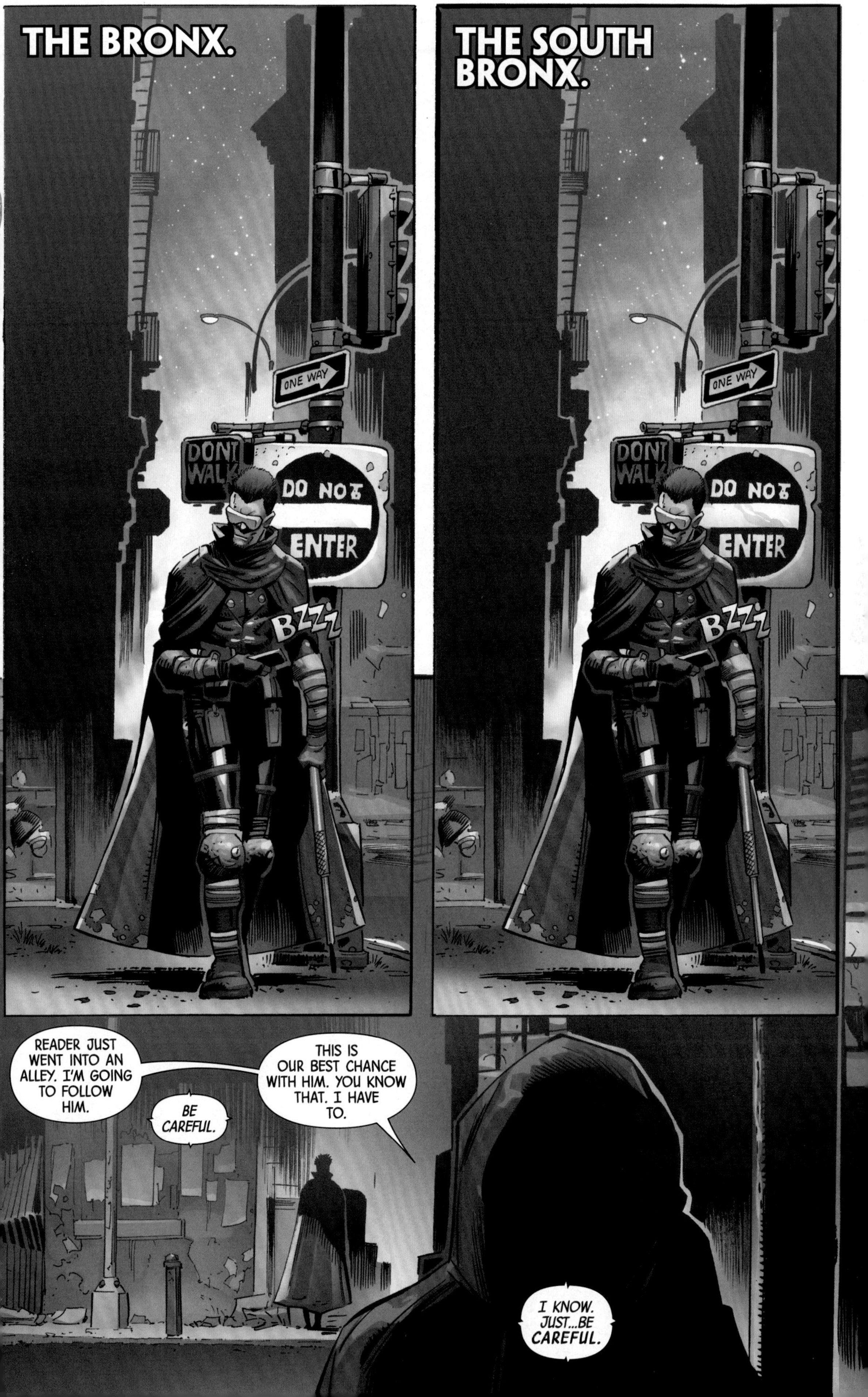
THE BRONX.
ONE WAY
DON'T WALK
DO NOT ENTER
BZZZ
THE SOUTH BRONX.
ONE WAY
DON'T WALK
DO NOT ENTER
BZZZ
READER JUST WENT INTO AN ALLEY. I'M GOING TO FOLLOW HIM.
BE CAREFUL.
THIS IS OUR BEST CHANCE WITH HIM. YOU KNOW THAT. I HAVE TO.
I KNOW. JUST...BE CAREFUL.

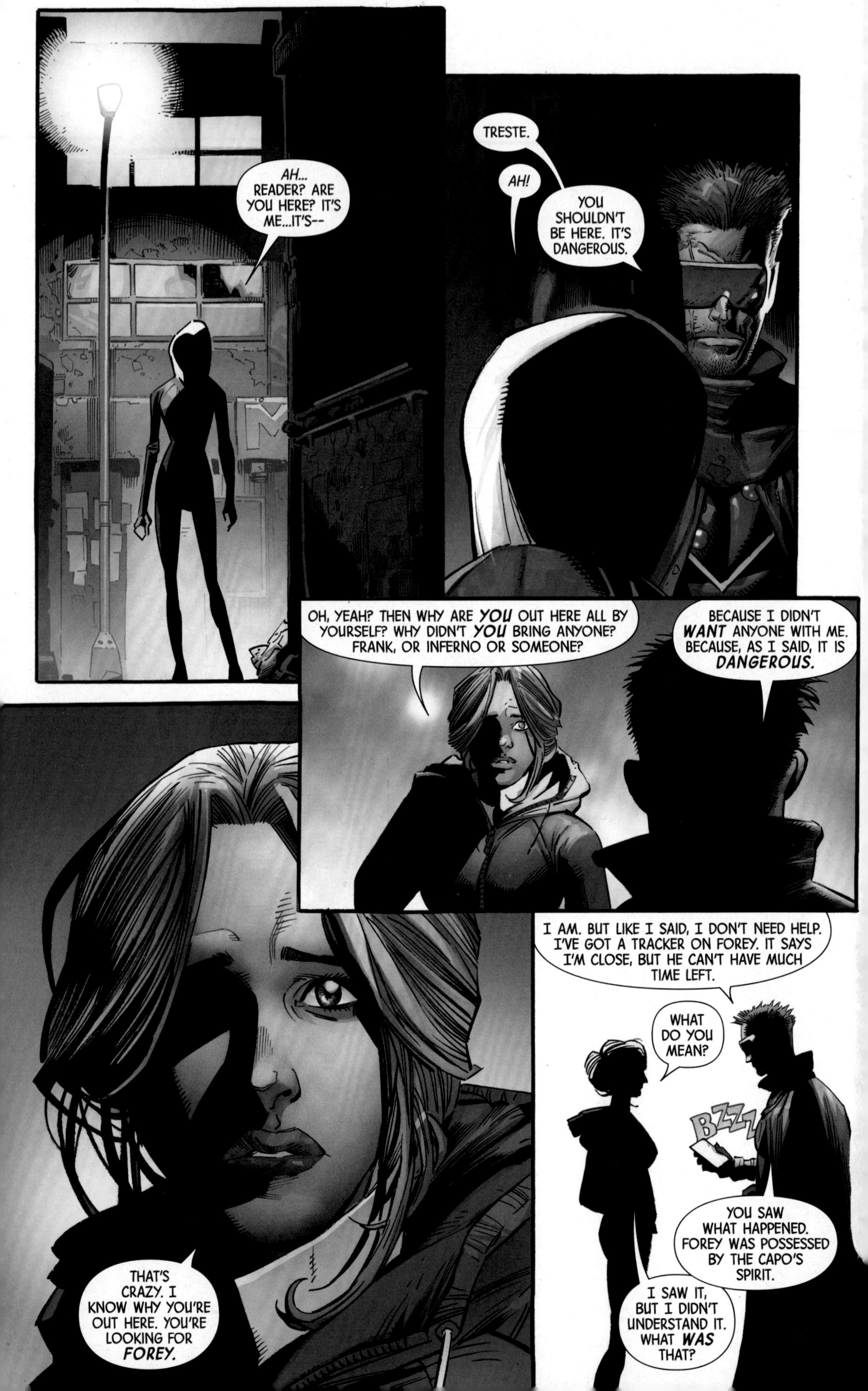
AH... READER? ARE YOU HERE? IT'S ME...IT'S--
TRESTE.
AH!
YOU SHOULDN'T BE HERE. IT'S DANGEROUS.
OH, YEAH? THEN WHY ARE YOU OUT HERE ALL BY YOURSELF? WHY DIDN'T YOU BRING ANYONE? FRANK, OR INFERNO OR SOMEONE?
BECAUSE I DIDN'T WANT ANYONE WITH ME. BECAUSE, AS I SAID, IT IS DANGEROUS.
THAT'S CRAZY. I KNOW WHY YOU'RE OUT HERE. YOU'RE LOOKING FOR FOREY.
I AM. BUT LIKE I SAID, I DON'T NEED HELP. I'VE GOT A TRACKER ON FOREY. IT SAYS I'M CLOSE, BUT HE CAN'T HAVE MUCH TIME LEFT.
WHAT DO YOU MEAN?
BZZZ
YOU SAW WHAT HAPPENED. FOREY WAS POSSESSED BY THE CAPO'S SPIRIT.
I SAW IT, BUT I DIDN'T UNDERSTAND IT. WHAT WAS THAT?

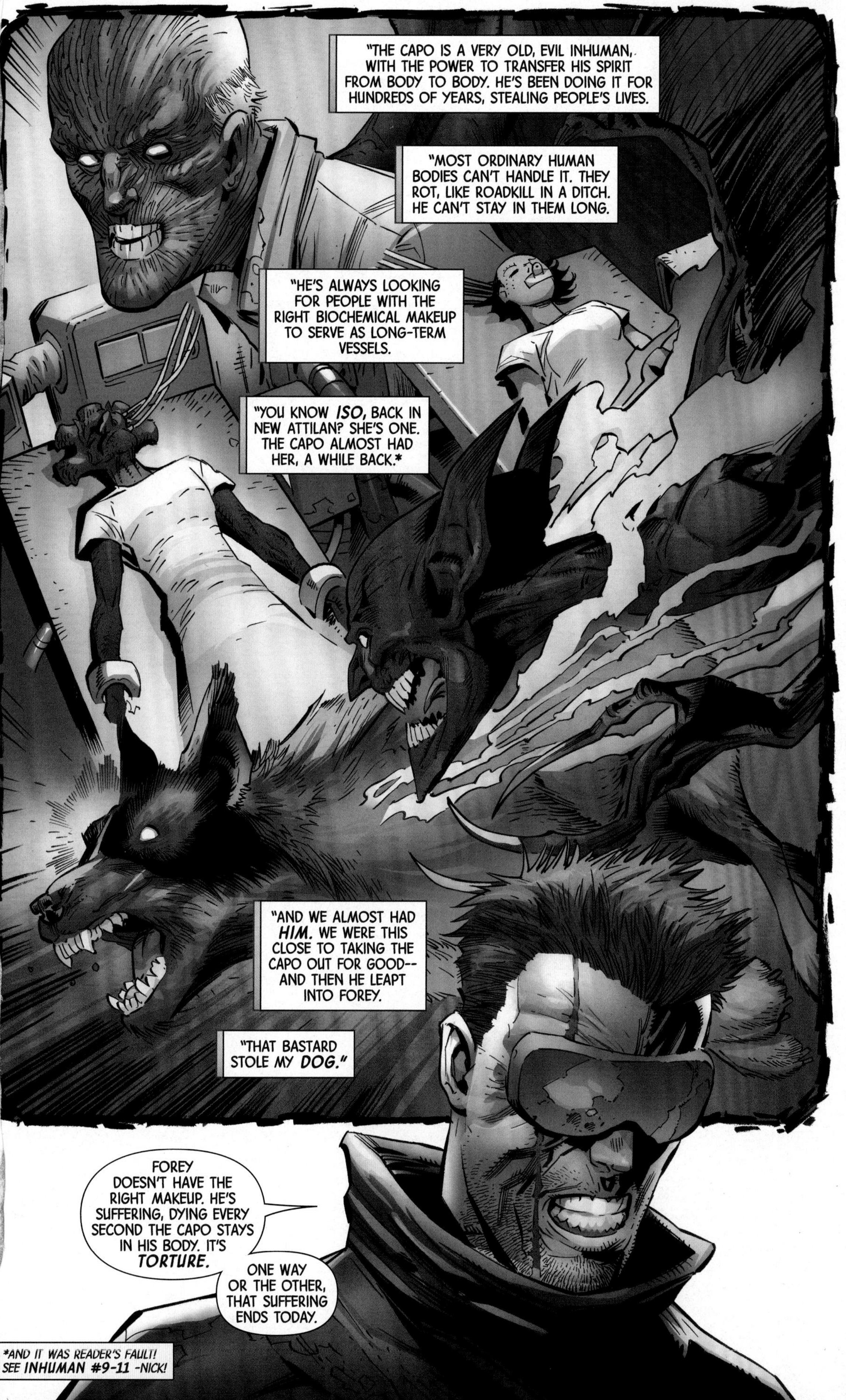
"THE CAPO IS A VERY OLD, EVIL INHUMAN, WITH THE POWER TO TRANSFER HIS SPIRIT FROM BODY TO BODY. HE'S BEEN DOING IT FOR HUNDREDS OF YEARS, STEALING PEOPLE'S LIVES.
"MOST ORDINARY HUMAN BODIES CAN'T HANDLE IT. THEY ROT, LIKE ROADKILL IN A DITCH. HE CAN'T STAY IN THEM LONG.
"HE'S ALWAYS LOOKING FOR PEOPLE WITH THE RIGHT BIOCHEMICAL MAKEUP TO SERVE AS LONG-TERM VESSELS.
"YOU KNOW *ISO,* BACK IN NEW ATTILAN? SHE'S ONE. THE CAPO ALMOST HAD HER, A WHILE BACK.*
"AND WE ALMOST HAD *HIM.* WE WERE THIS CLOSE TO TAKING THE CAPO OUT FOR GOOD-- AND THEN HE LEAPT INTO FOREY.
"THAT BASTARD STOLE MY *DOG.*"
FOREY DOESN'T HAVE THE RIGHT MAKEUP. HE'S SUFFERING, DYING EVERY SECOND THE CAPO STAYS IN HIS BODY. IT'S *TORTURE.*
ONE WAY OR THE OTHER, THAT SUFFERING ENDS TODAY.
*AND IT WAS READER'S FAULT! SEE **INHUMAN #9-11** -NICK!

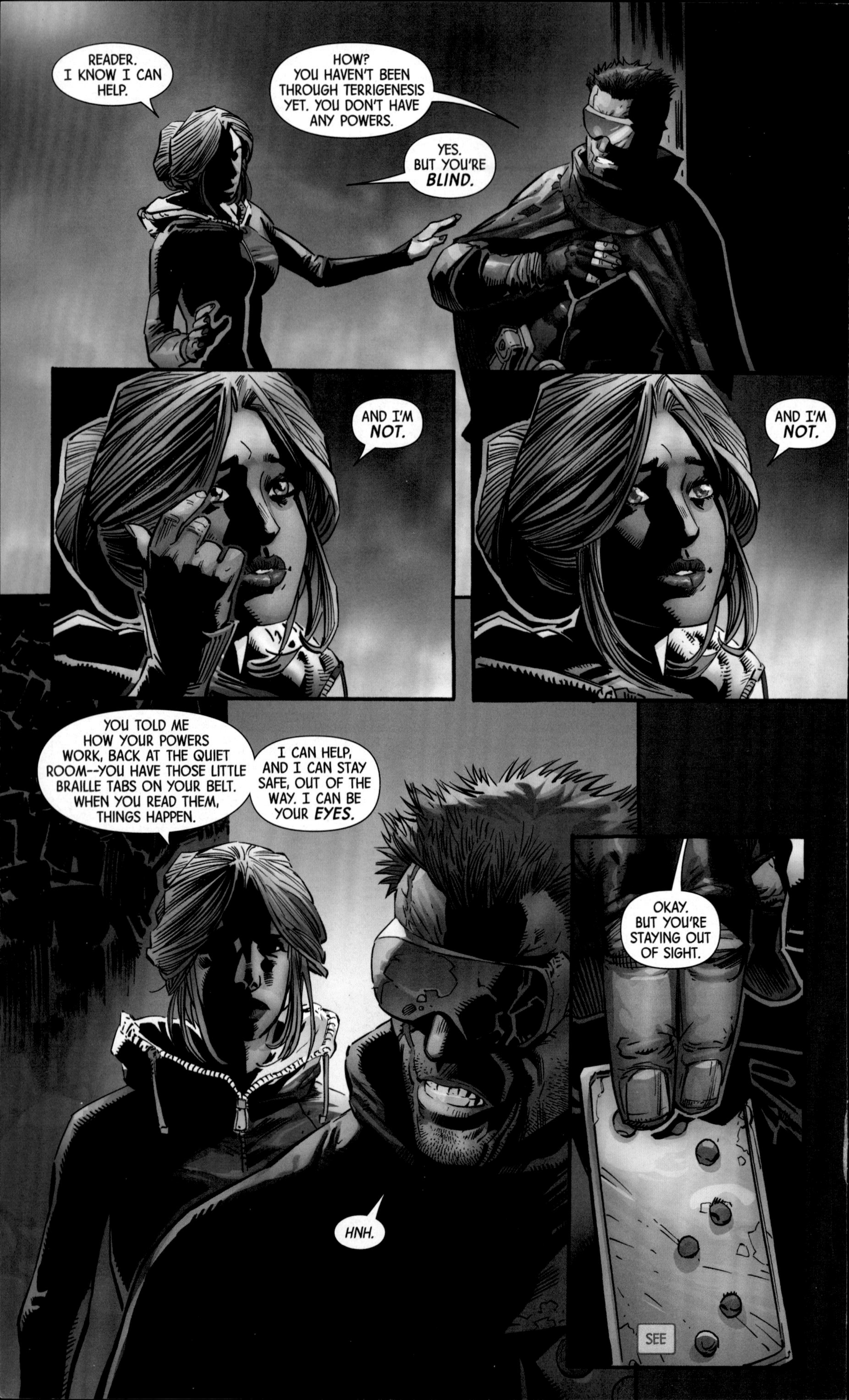
READER. I KNOW I CAN HELP.
HOW? YOU HAVEN'T BEEN THROUGH TERRIGENESIS YET. YOU DON'T HAVE ANY POWERS.
YES. BUT YOU'RE *BLIND.*
AND I'M *NOT.*
AND I'M *NOT.*
YOU TOLD ME HOW YOUR POWERS WORK, BACK AT THE QUIET ROOM--YOU HAVE THOSE LITTLE BRAILLE TABS ON YOUR BELT. WHEN YOU READ THEM, THINGS HAPPEN.
I CAN HELP, AND I CAN STAY SAFE, OUT OF THE WAY. I CAN BE YOUR *EYES.*
OKAY. BUT YOU'RE STAYING OUT OF SIGHT.
HNH.
SEE

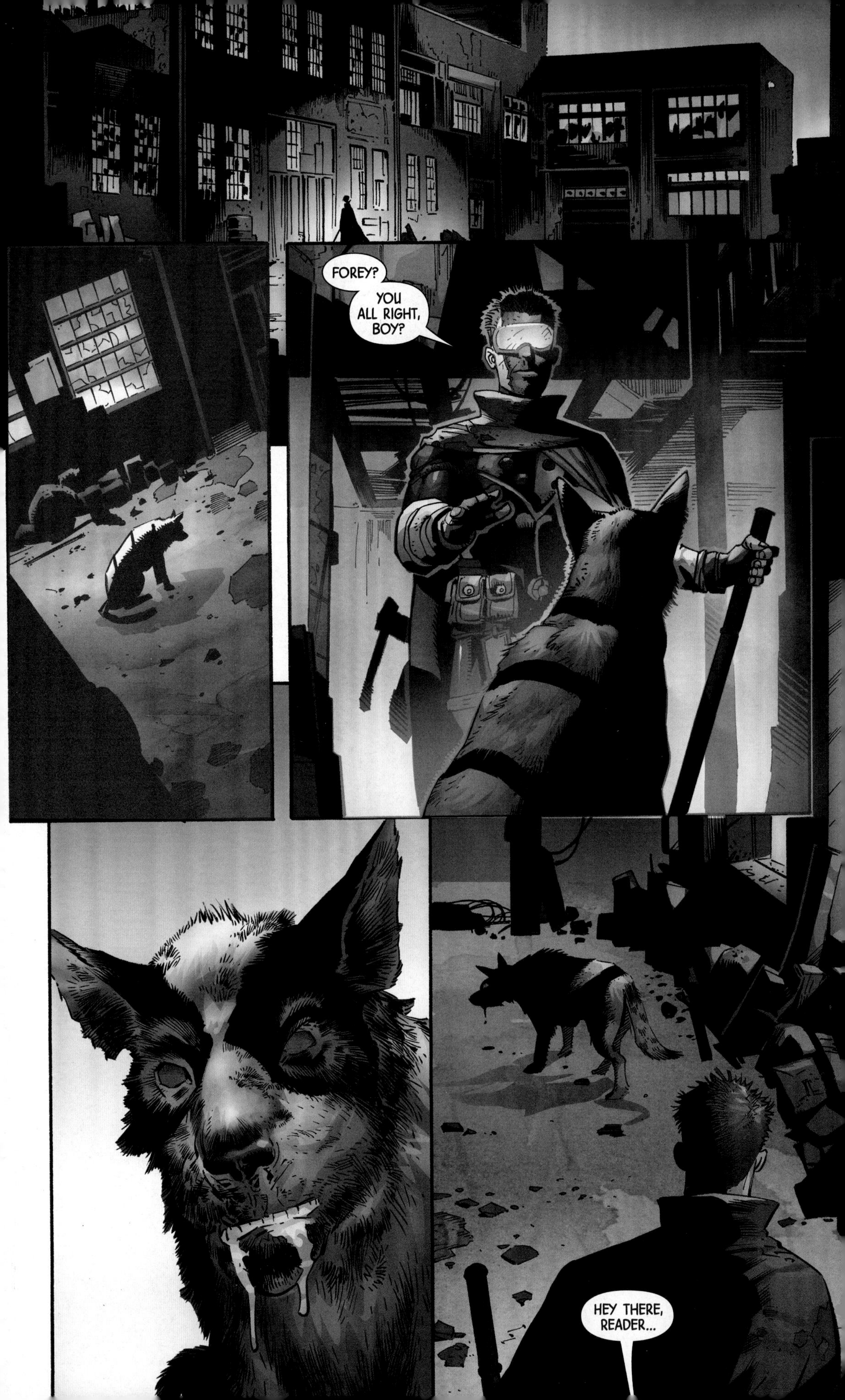
FOREY?
YOU ALL RIGHT, BOY?
HEY THERE, READER...

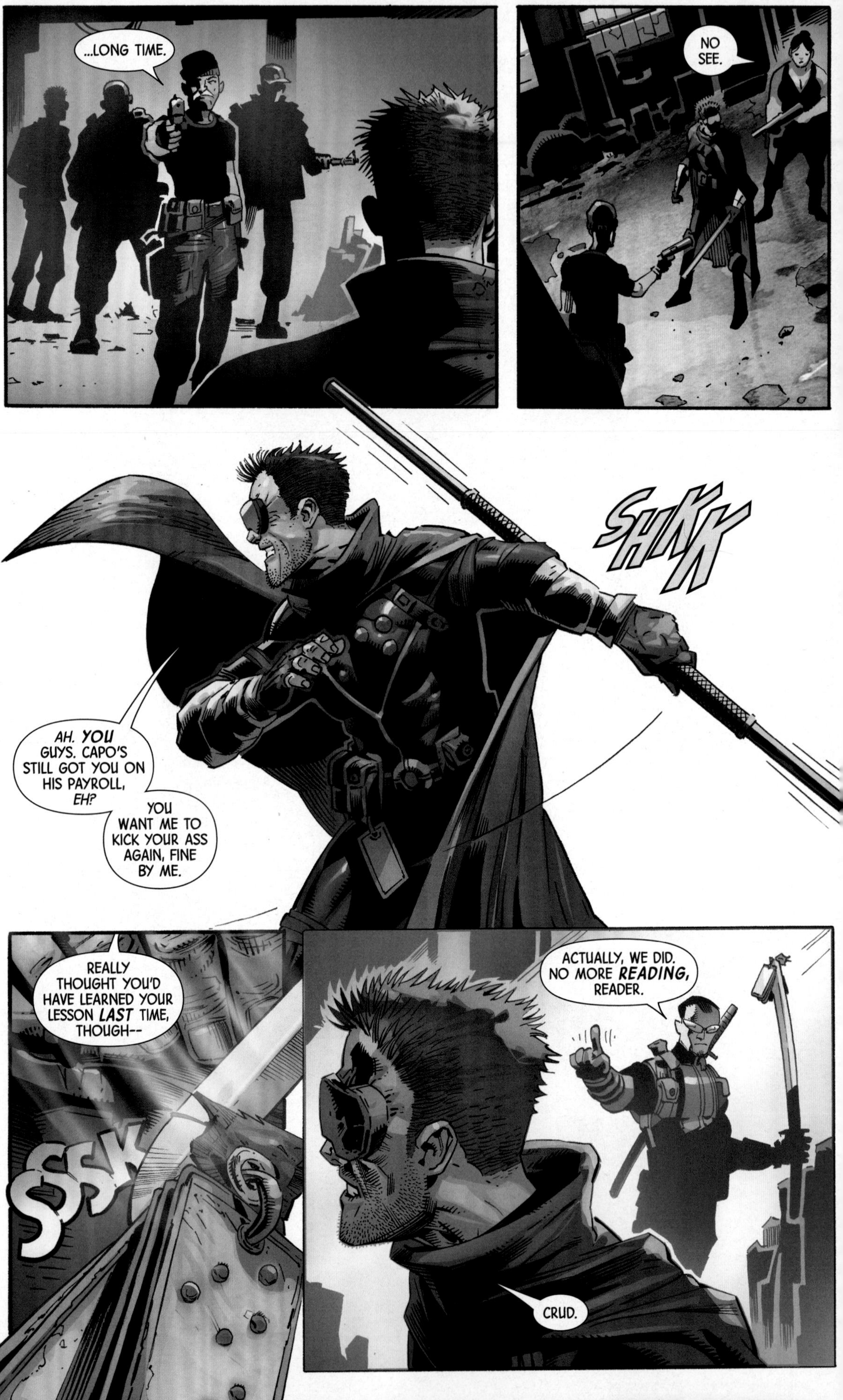
...LONG TIME.
NO SEE.
SHIKK
AH. *YOU* GUYS. CAPO'S STILL GOT YOU ON HIS PAYROLL, *EH?*
YOU WANT ME TO KICK YOUR ASS AGAIN, FINE BY ME.
REALLY THOUGHT YOU'D HAVE LEARNED YOUR LESSON *LAST* TIME, THOUGH--
SSK
ACTUALLY, WE DID. NO MORE *READING*, READER.
CRUD.

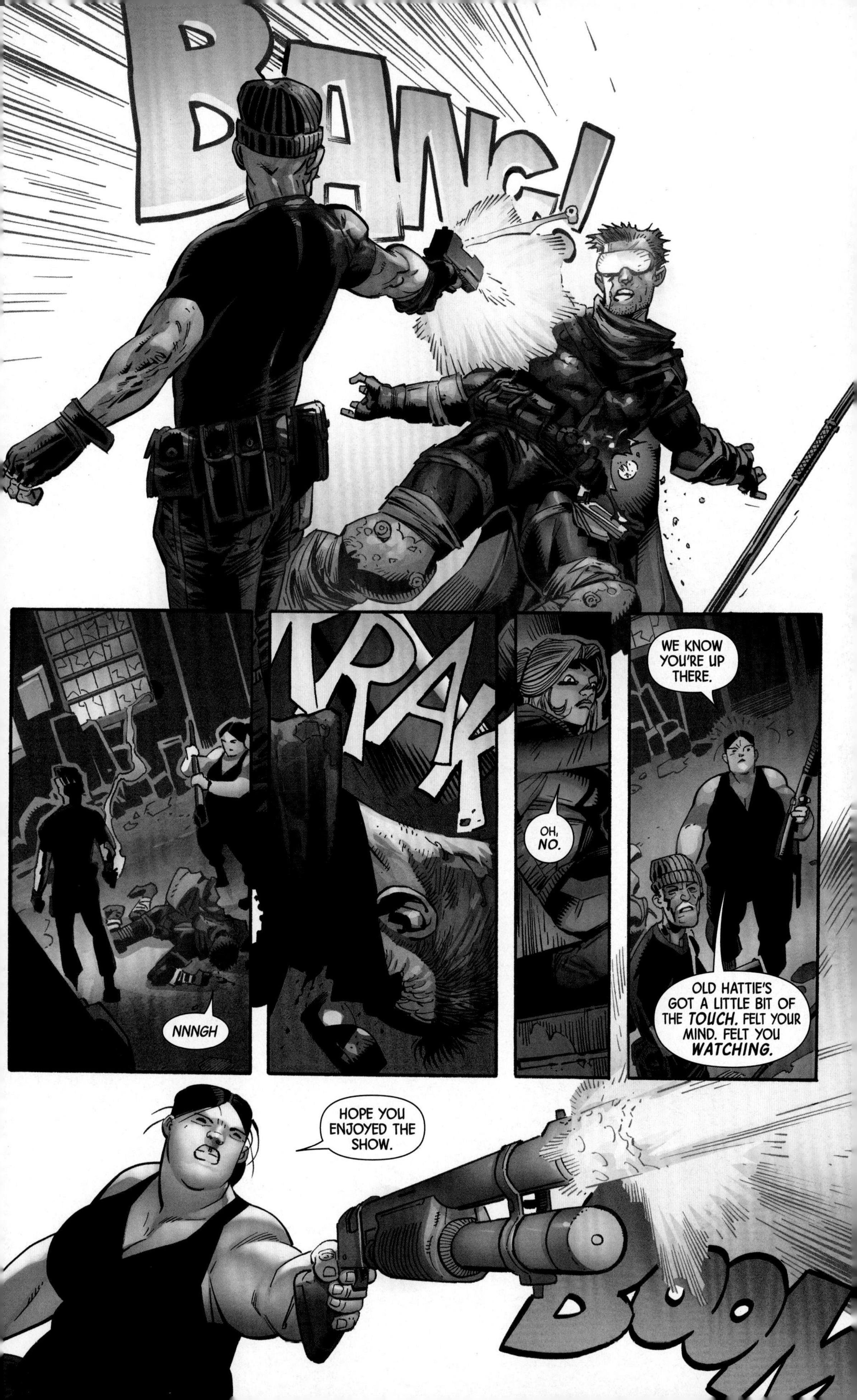
BANG!
NNNGH
TRAK
OH, NO.
WE KNOW YOU'RE UP THERE.
OLD HATTIE'S GOT A LITTLE BIT OF THE TOUCH. FELT YOUR MIND. FELT YOU WATCHING.
HOPE YOU ENJOYED THE SHOW.
BOOM

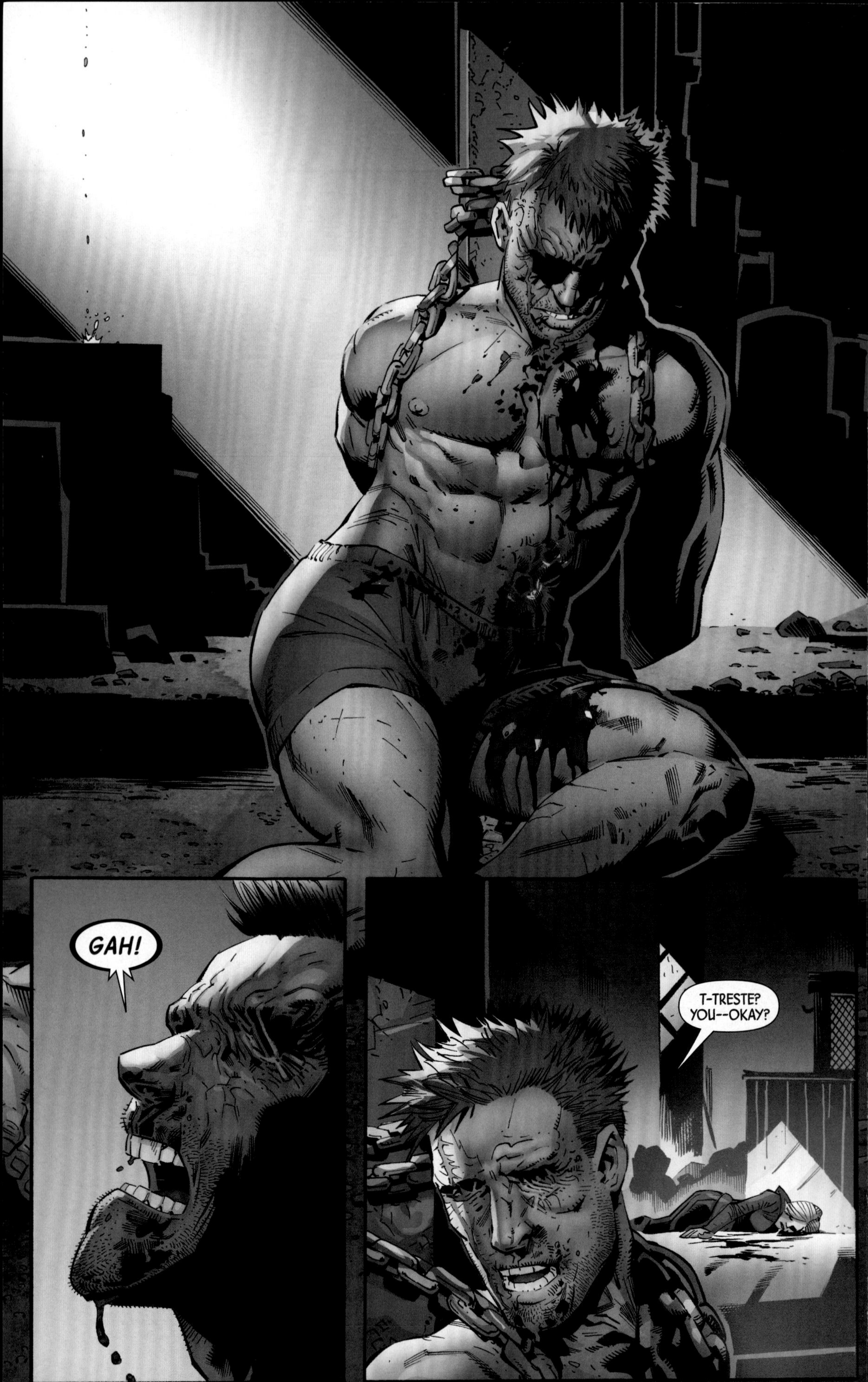
GAH!
T-TRESTE? YOU--OKAY?

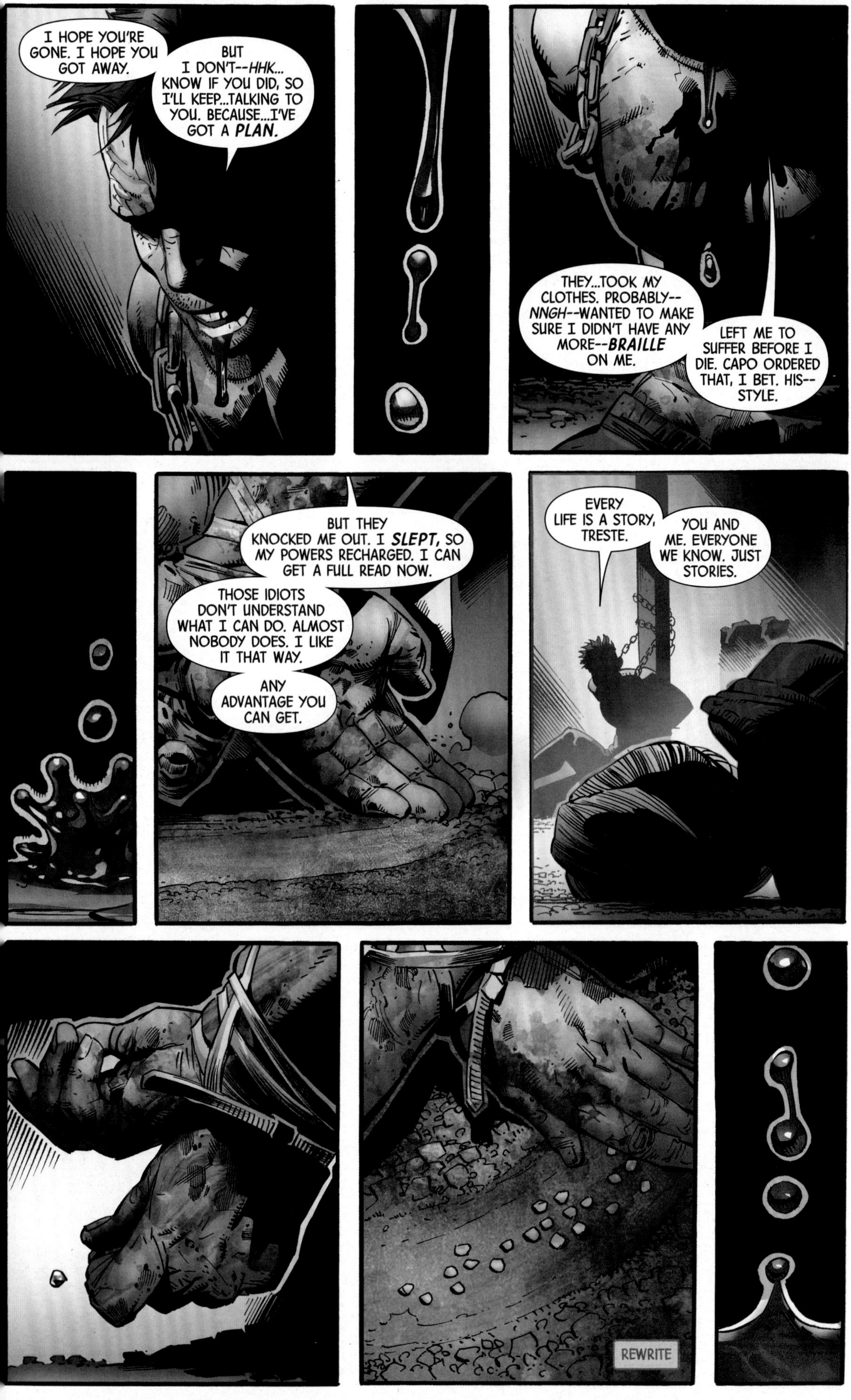
I HOPE YOU'RE GONE. I HOPE YOU GOT AWAY.
BUT I DON'T--*HHK*... KNOW IF YOU DID, SO I'LL KEEP...TALKING TO YOU. BECAUSE...I'VE GOT A ***PLAN.***
THEY...TOOK MY CLOTHES. PROBABLY-- *NNGH*--WANTED TO MAKE SURE I DIDN'T HAVE ANY MORE--***BRAILLE*** ON ME.
LEFT ME TO SUFFER BEFORE I DIE. CAPO ORDERED THAT, I BET. HIS-- STYLE.
BUT THEY KNOCKED ME OUT. I ***SLEPT,*** SO MY POWERS RECHARGED. I CAN GET A FULL READ NOW.
THOSE IDIOTS DON'T UNDERSTAND WHAT I CAN DO. ALMOST NOBODY DOES. I LIKE IT THAT WAY.
ANY ADVANTAGE YOU CAN GET.
EVERY LIFE IS A STORY, TRESTE.
YOU AND ME. EVERYONE WE KNOW. JUST STORIES.
REWRITE

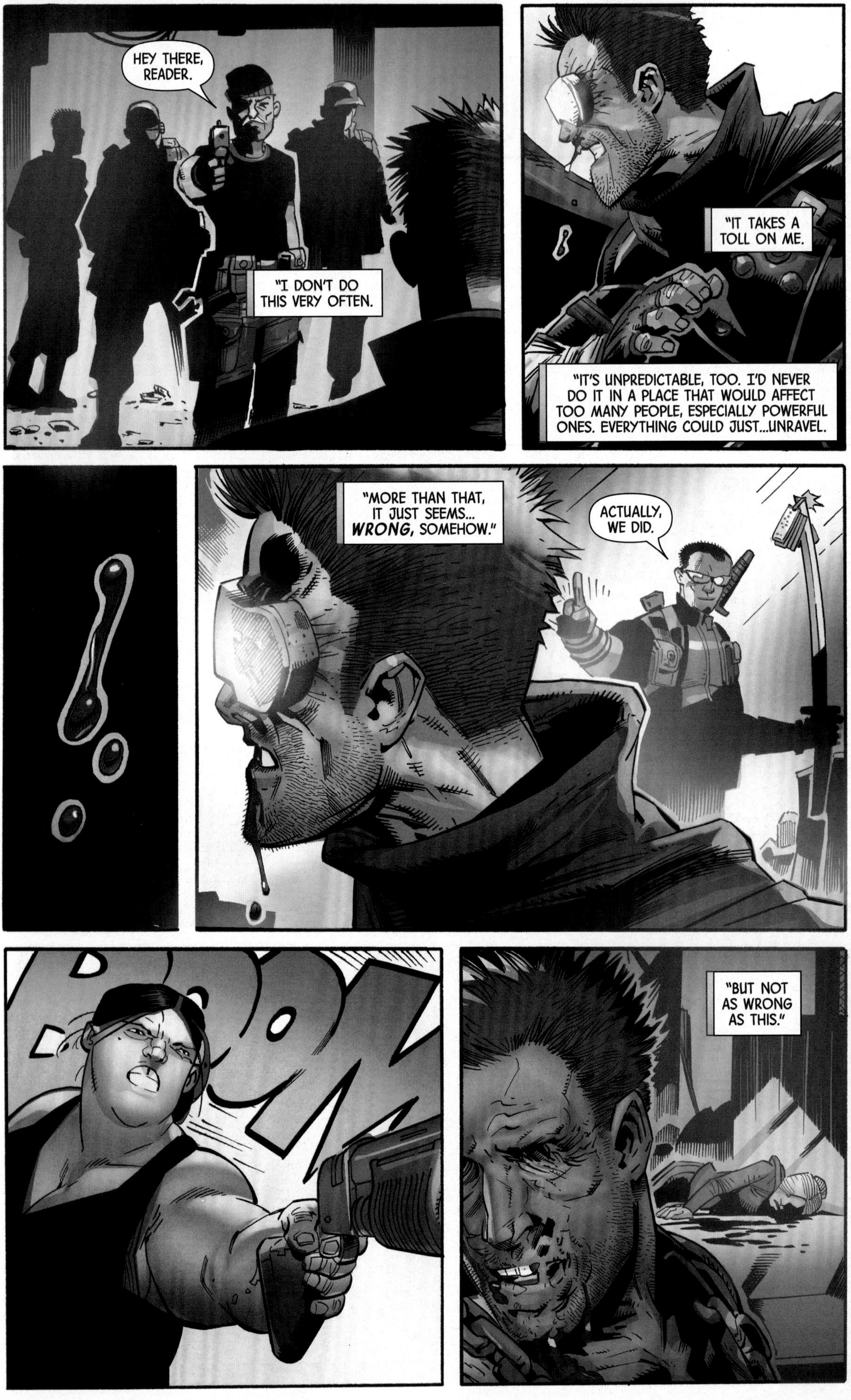
HEY THERE, READER.
"I DON'T DO THIS VERY OFTEN.
"IT TAKES A TOLL ON ME.
"IT'S UNPREDICTABLE, TOO. I'D NEVER DO IT IN A PLACE THAT WOULD AFFECT TOO MANY PEOPLE, ESPECIALLY POWERFUL ONES. EVERYTHING COULD JUST...UNRAVEL.
"MORE THAN THAT, IT JUST SEEMS... WRONG, SOMEHOW."
ACTUALLY, WE DID.
"BUT NOT AS WRONG AS THIS."

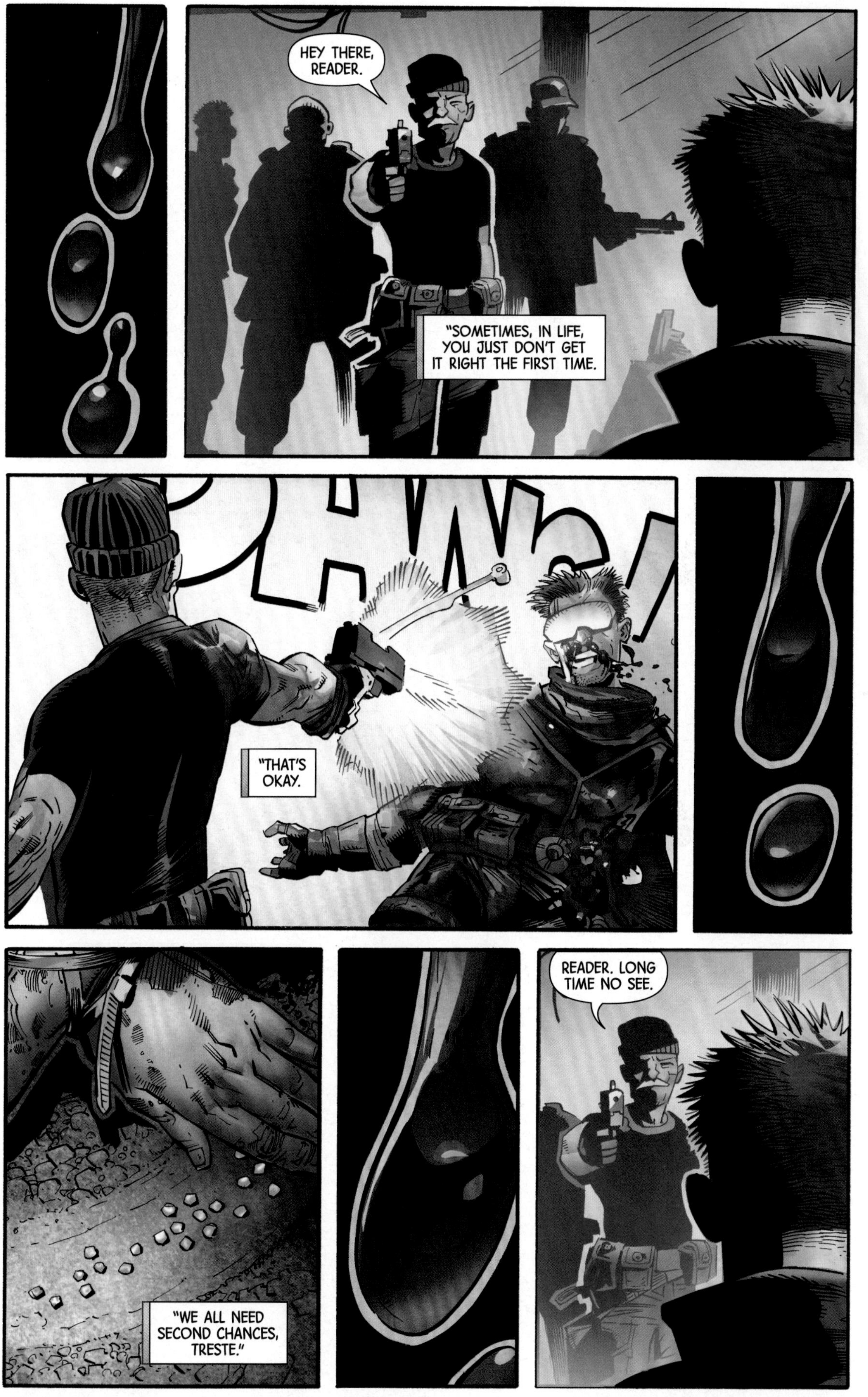
HEY THERE, READER.
"SOMETIMES, IN LIFE, YOU JUST DON'T GET IT RIGHT THE FIRST TIME.
"THAT'S OKAY.
"WE ALL NEED SECOND CHANCES, TRESTE."
READER. LONG TIME NO SEE.

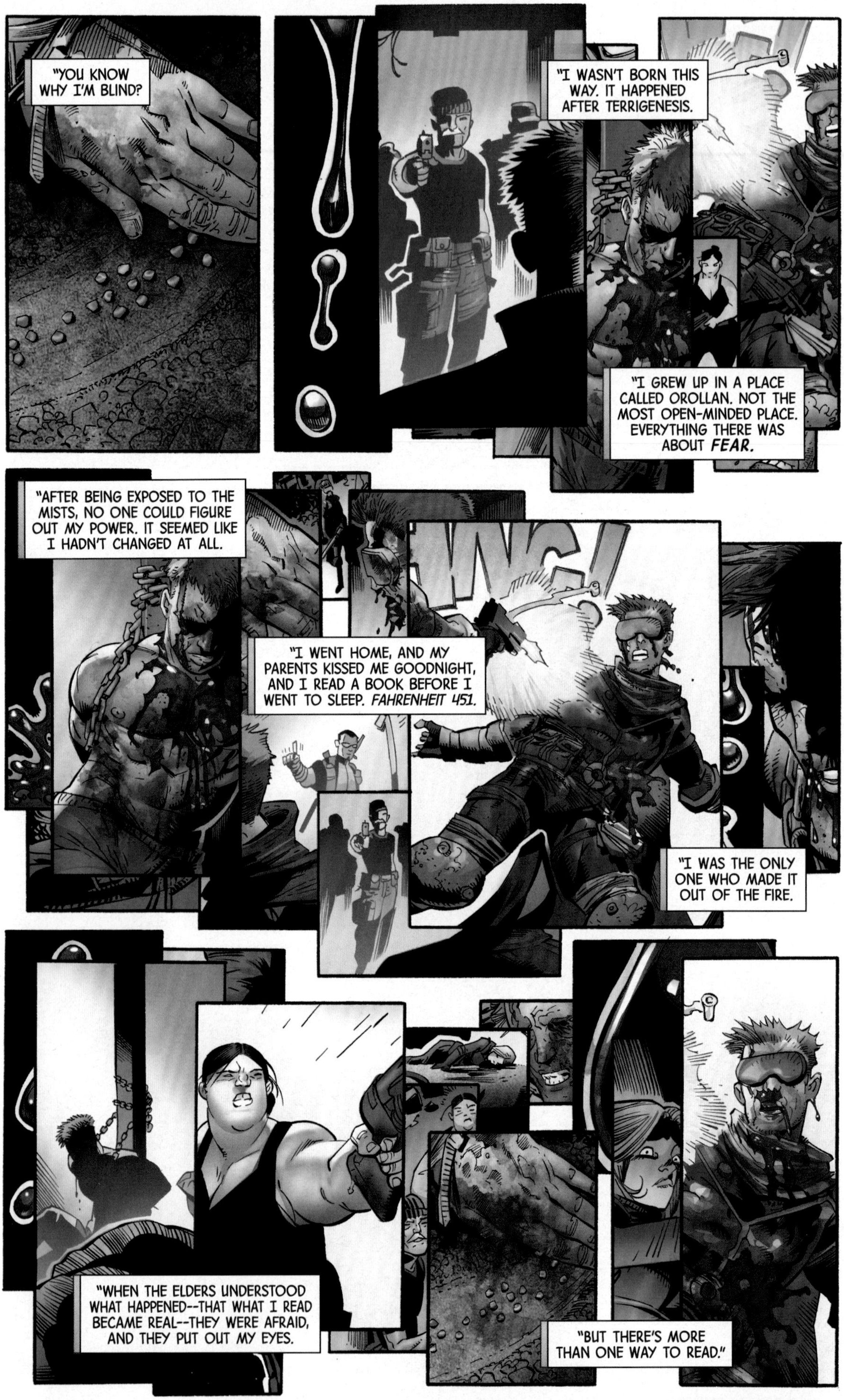
"YOU KNOW WHY I'M BLIND?
"I WASN'T BORN THIS WAY. IT HAPPENED AFTER TERRIGENESIS.
"I GREW UP IN A PLACE CALLED OROLLAN. NOT THE MOST OPEN-MINDED PLACE. EVERYTHING THERE WAS ABOUT *FEAR.*
"AFTER BEING EXPOSED TO THE MISTS, NO ONE COULD FIGURE OUT MY POWER. IT SEEMED LIKE I HADN'T CHANGED AT ALL.
"I WENT HOME, AND MY PARENTS KISSED ME GOODNIGHT, AND I READ A BOOK BEFORE I WENT TO SLEEP. *FAHRENHEIT 451.*
"I WAS THE ONLY ONE WHO MADE IT OUT OF THE FIRE.
"WHEN THE ELDERS UNDERSTOOD WHAT HAPPENED--THAT WHAT I READ BECAME REAL--THEY WERE AFRAID, AND THEY PUT OUT MY EYES.
"BUT THERE'S MORE THAN ONE WAY TO READ."

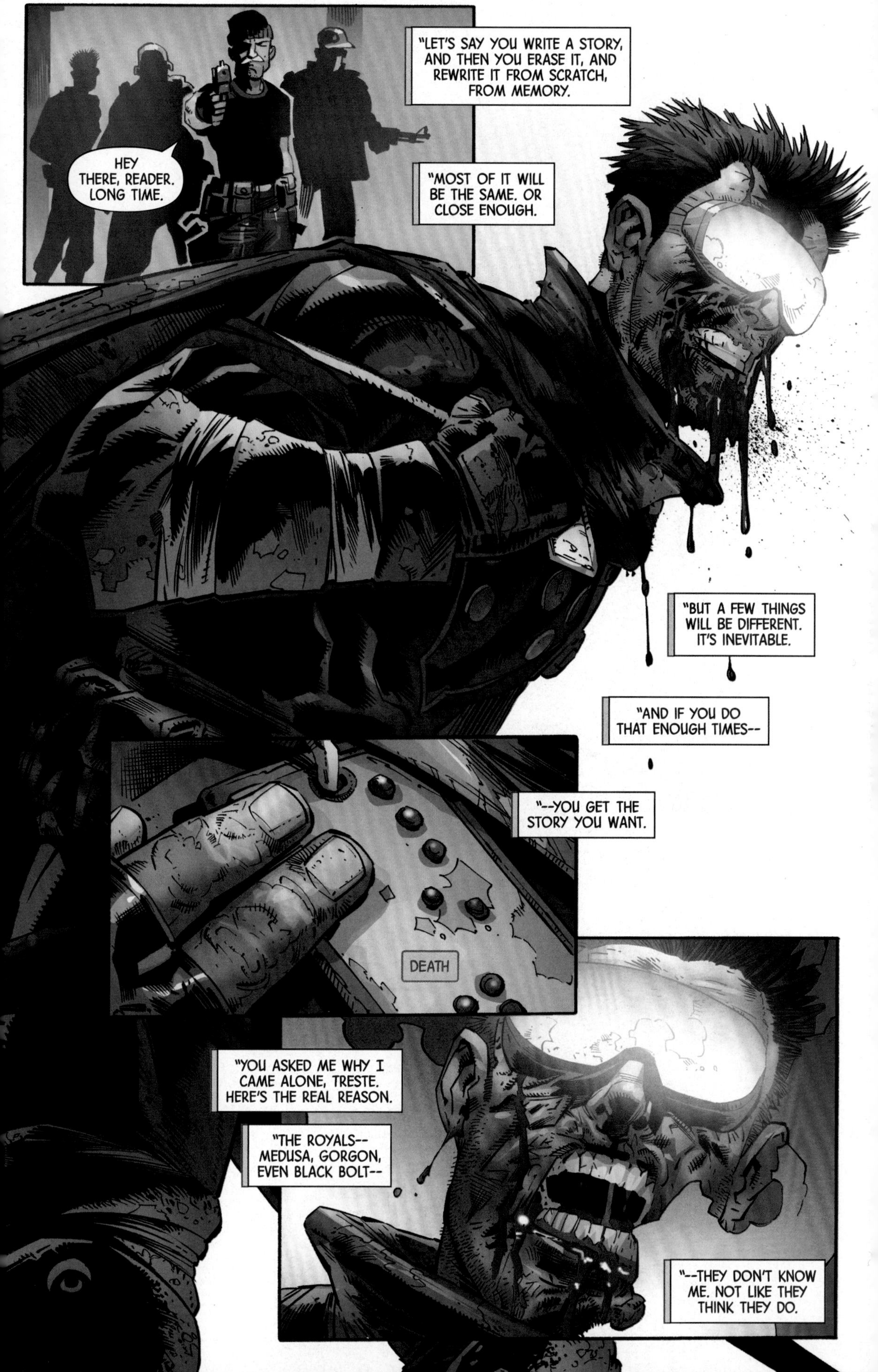

"LET'S SAY YOU WRITE A STORY, AND THEN YOU ERASE IT, AND REWRITE IT FROM SCRATCH, FROM MEMORY.
HEY THERE, READER. LONG TIME.
"MOST OF IT WILL BE THE SAME. OR CLOSE ENOUGH.
"BUT A FEW THINGS WILL BE DIFFERENT. IT'S INEVITABLE.
"AND IF YOU DO THAT ENOUGH TIMES--
"--YOU GET THE STORY YOU WANT.
DEATH
"YOU ASKED ME WHY I CAME ALONE, TRESTE. HERE'S THE REAL REASON.
"THE ROYALS-- MEDUSA, GORGON, EVEN BLACK BOLT--
"--THEY DON'T KNOW ME. NOT LIKE THEY THINK THEY DO.

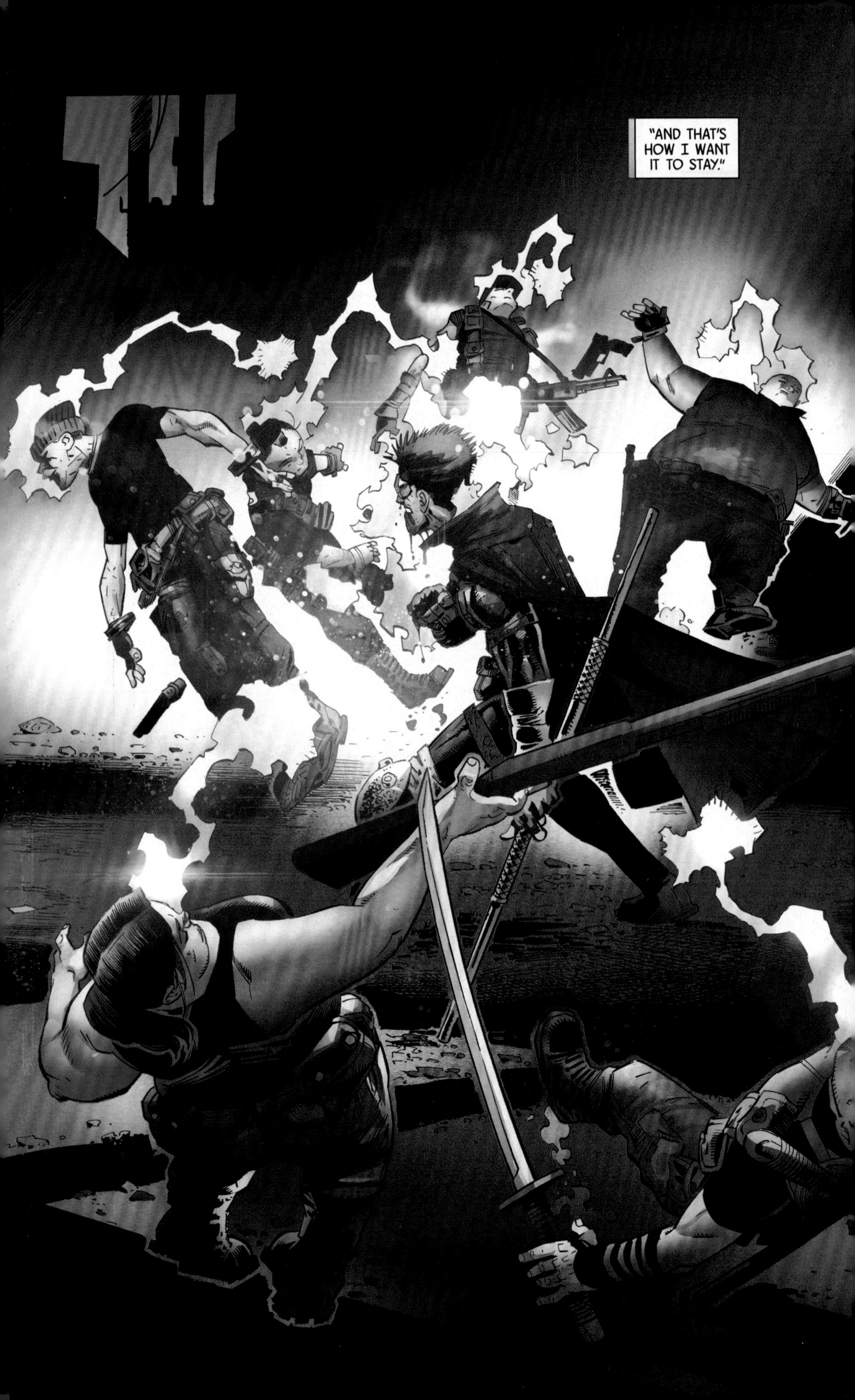
"AND THAT'S HOW I WANT IT TO STAY."

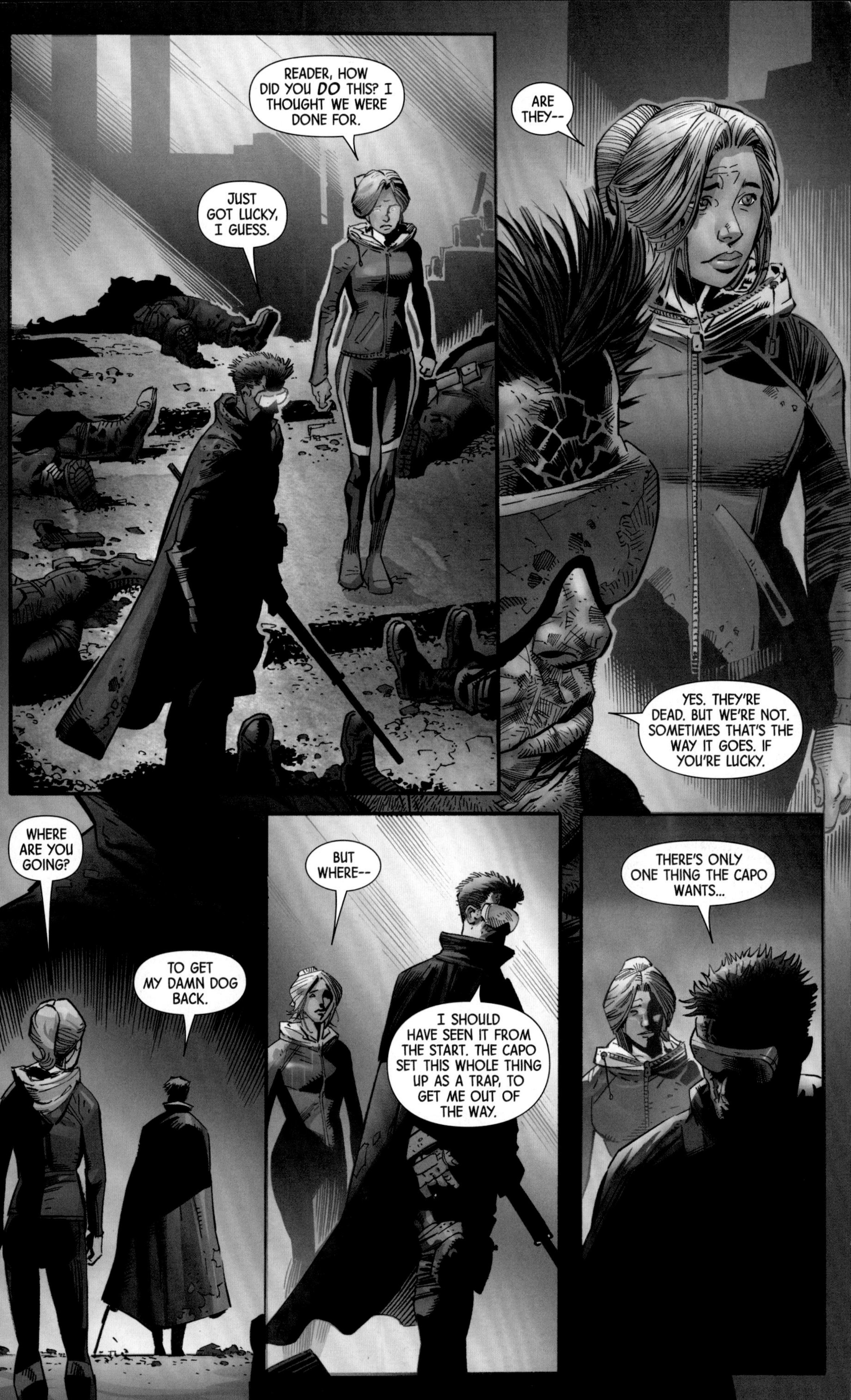

READER, HOW DID YOU DO THIS? I THOUGHT WE WERE DONE FOR.
JUST GOT LUCKY, I GUESS.
ARE THEY--
YES. THEY'RE DEAD. BUT WE'RE NOT. SOMETIMES THAT'S THE WAY IT GOES. IF YOU'RE LUCKY.
WHERE ARE YOU GOING?
TO GET MY DAMN DOG BACK.
BUT WHERE--
I SHOULD HAVE SEEN IT FROM THE START. THE CAPO SET THIS WHOLE THING UP AS A TRAP, TO GET ME OUT OF THE WAY.
THERE'S ONLY ONE THING THE CAPO WANTS...

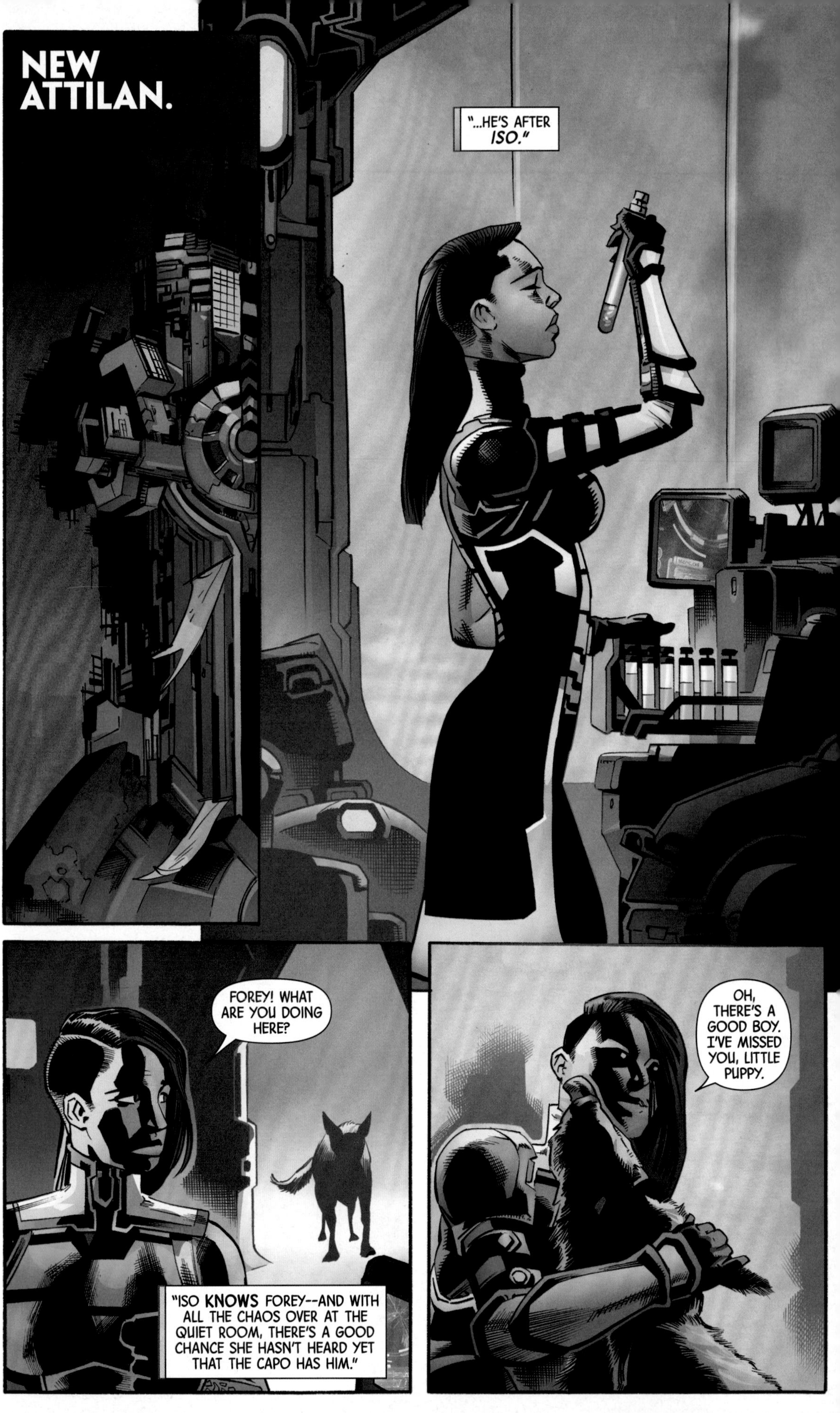
NEW ATTILAN.
"...HE'S AFTER ISO."
FOREY! WHAT ARE YOU DOING HERE?
"ISO KNOWS FOREY--AND WITH ALL THE CHAOS OVER AT THE QUIET ROOM, THERE'S A GOOD CHANCE SHE HASN'T HEARD YET THAT THE CAPO HAS HIM."
OH, THERE'S A GOOD BOY. I'VE MISSED YOU, LITTLE PUPPY.

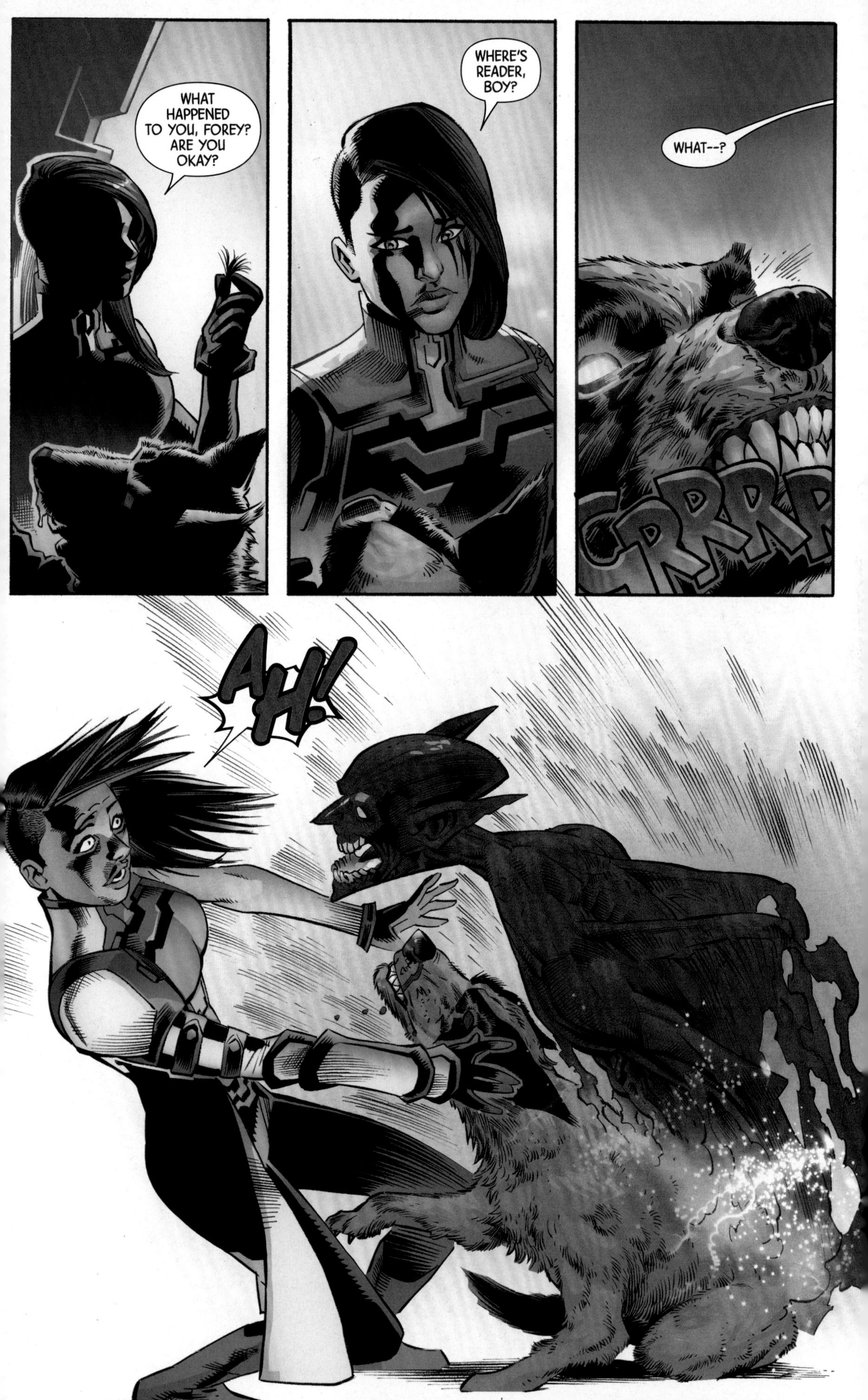
WHAT HAPPENED TO YOU, FOREY? ARE YOU OKAY?
WHERE'S READER, BOY?
WHAT--?
CRRR
AH!

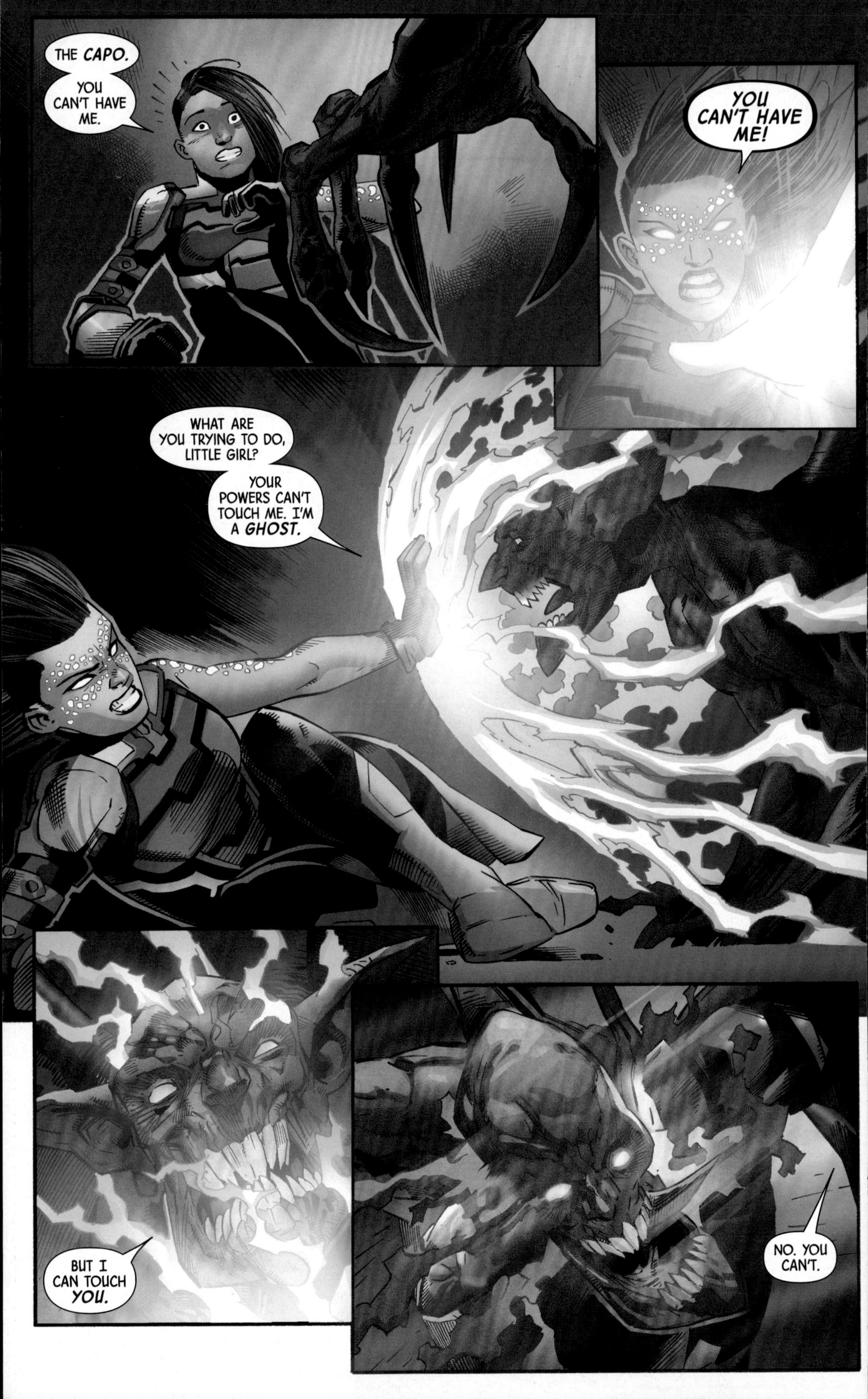
THE CAPO.
YOU CAN'T HAVE ME.
YOU CAN'T HAVE ME!
WHAT ARE YOU TRYING TO DO, LITTLE GIRL?
YOUR POWERS CAN'T TOUCH ME. I'M A GHOST.
BUT I CAN TOUCH YOU.
NO. YOU CAN'T.

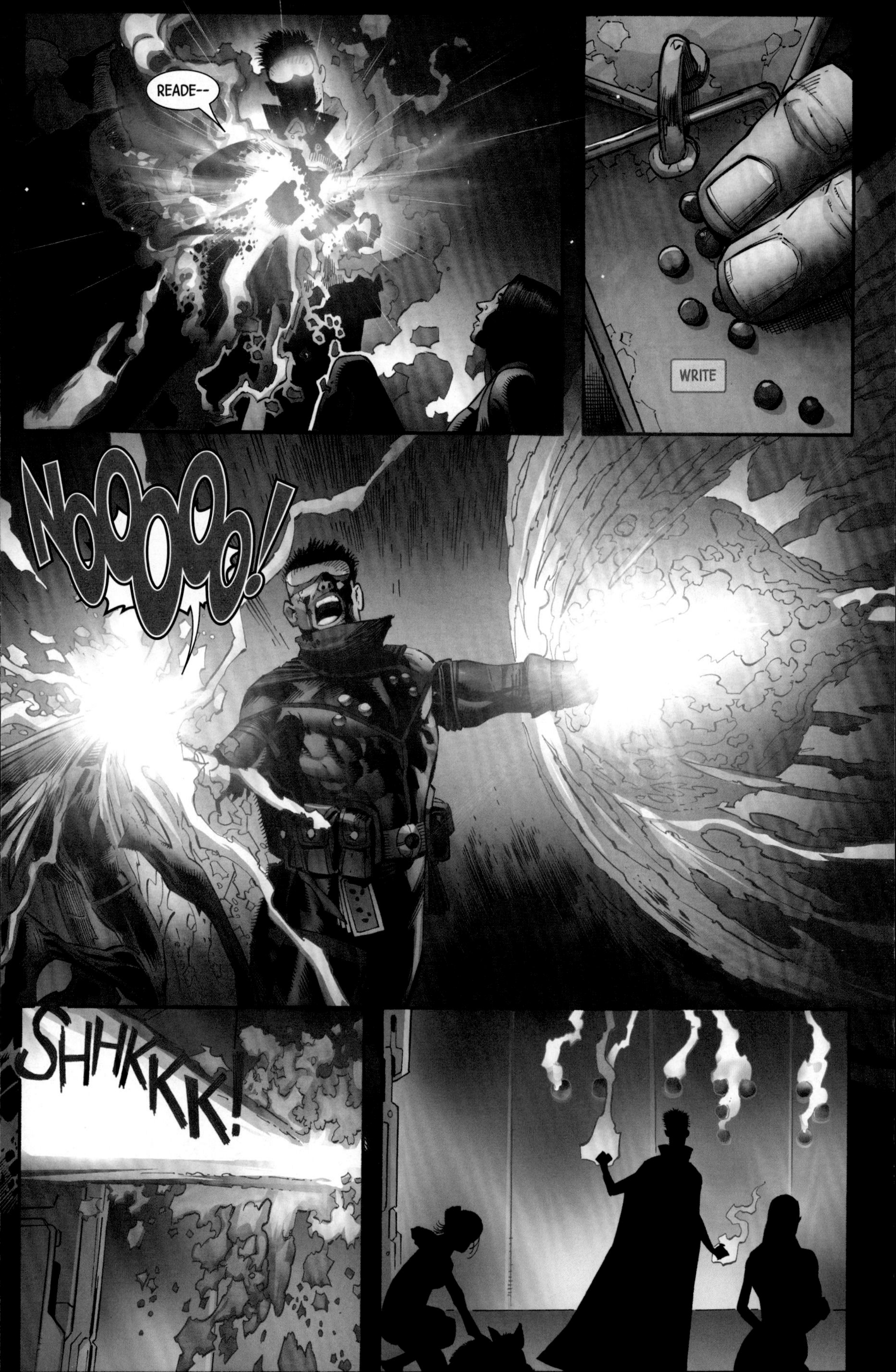
READE--
WRITE
NOOOOO!
SHHKKK!

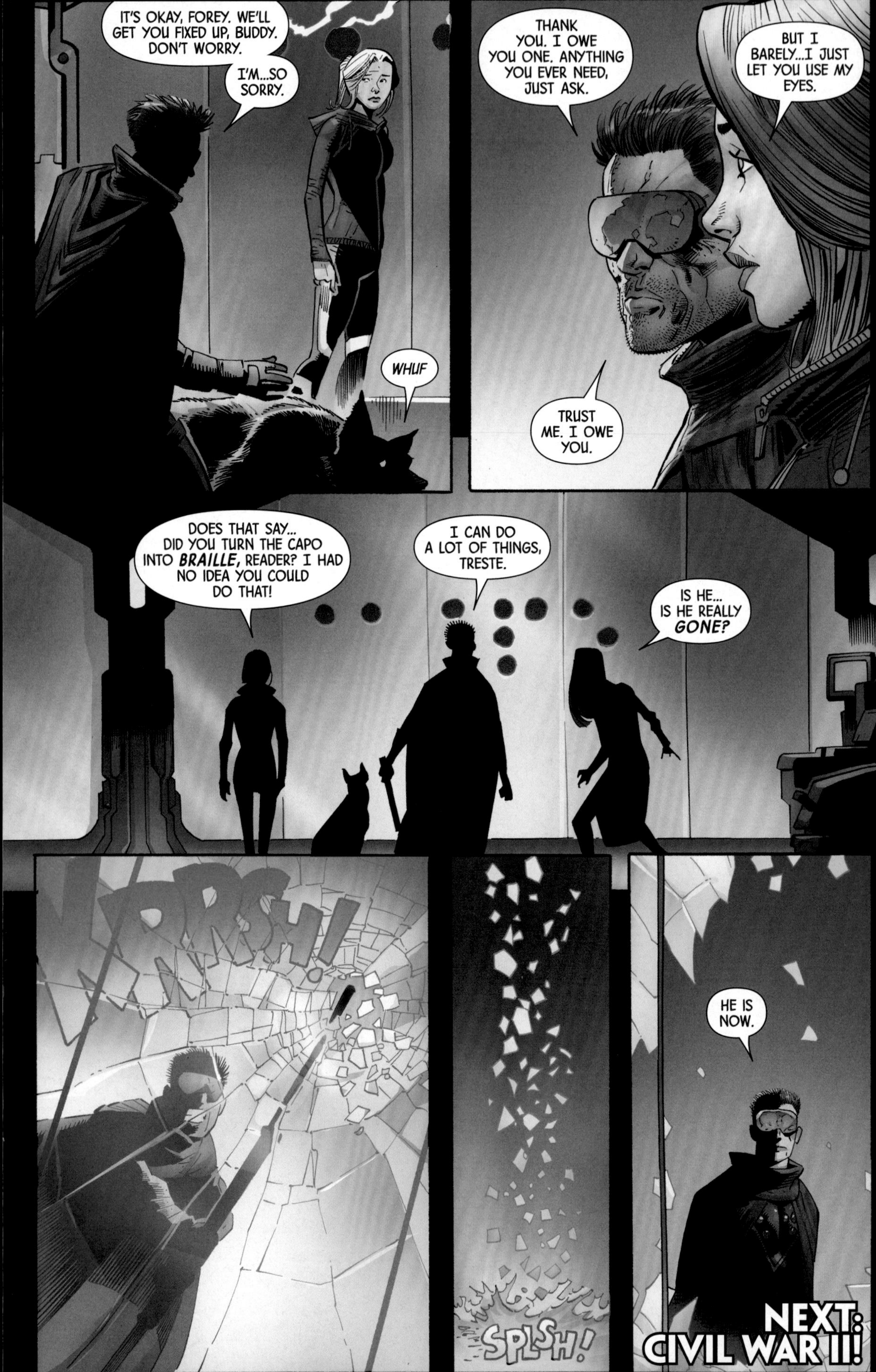
IT'S OKAY, FOREY. WE'LL GET YOU FIXED UP, BUDDY. DON'T WORRY.
I'M...SO SORRY.
WHUF
THANK YOU. I OWE YOU ONE. ANYTHING YOU EVER NEED, JUST ASK.
BUT I BARELY...I JUST LET YOU USE MY EYES.
TRUST ME. I OWE YOU.
DOES THAT SAY... DID YOU TURN THE CAPO INTO BRAILLE, READER? I HAD NO IDEA YOU COULD DO THAT!
I CAN DO A LOT OF THINGS, TRESTE.
IS HE... IS HE REALLY GONE?
KRSH!
SPLSH!
HE IS NOW.
NEXT: CIVIL WAR II!

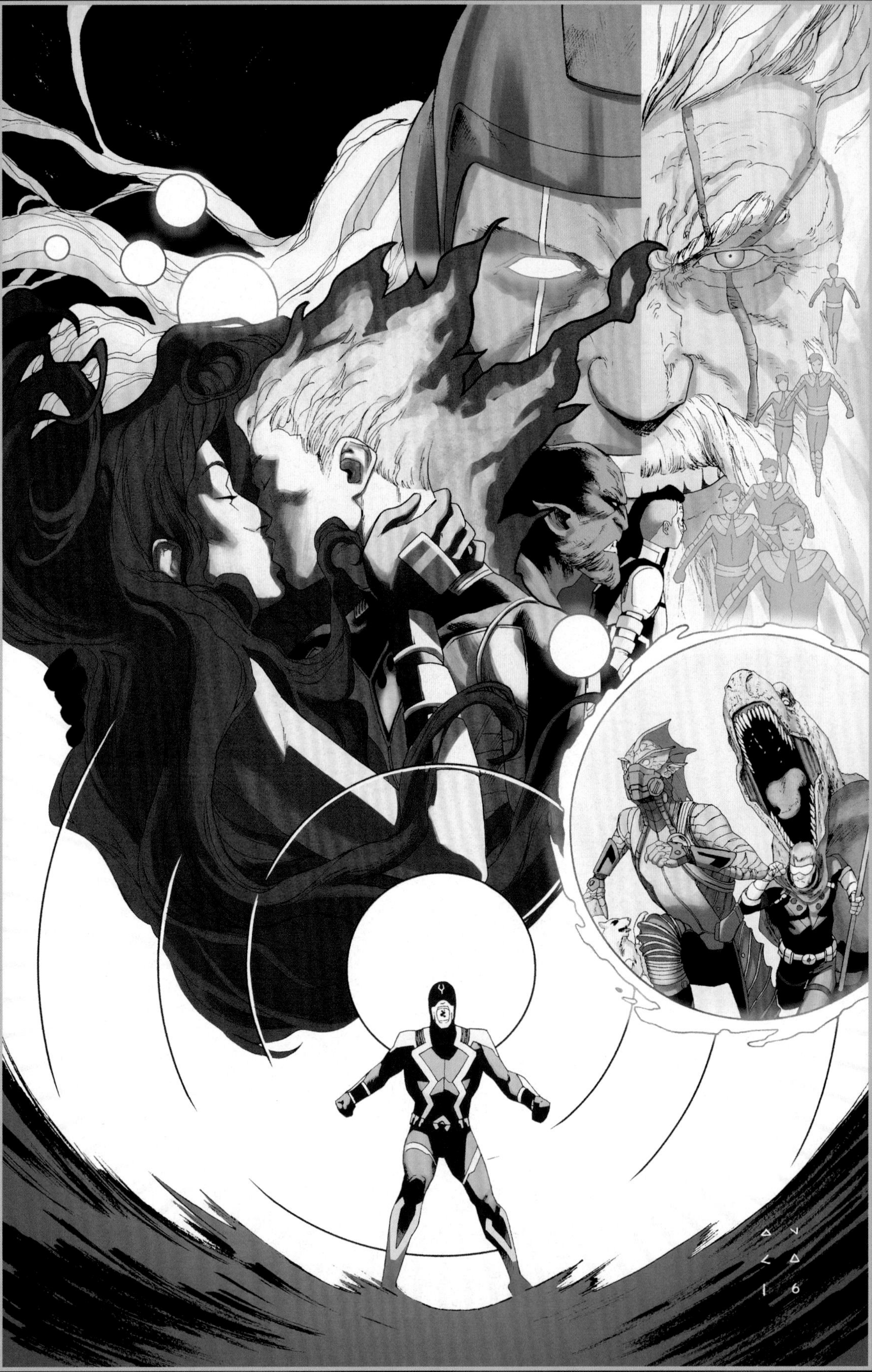

#5 STORY THUS FAR VARIANT BY KRIS ANKA

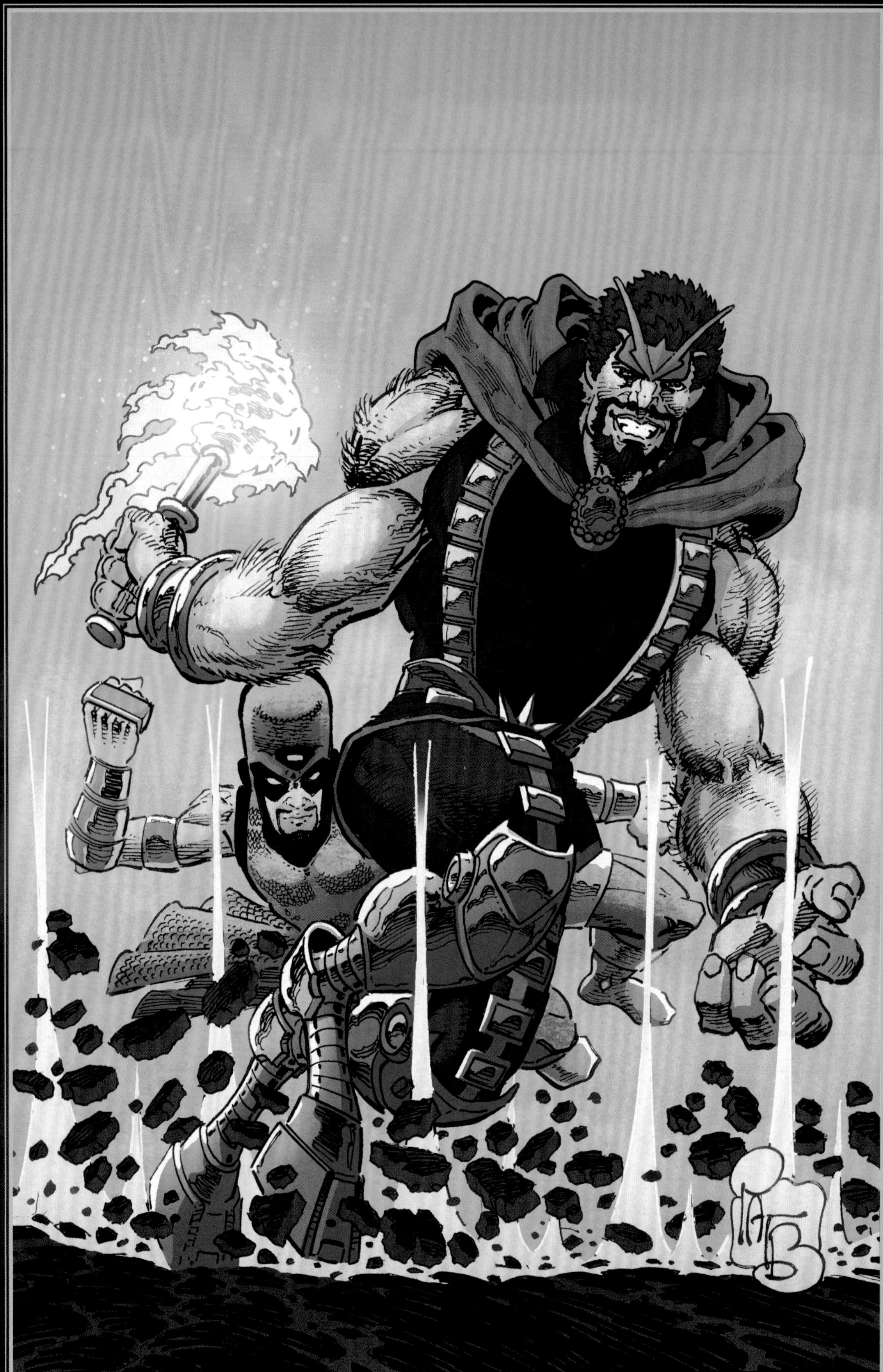

#5 VARIANT BY PAT BRODERICK & RACHELLE ROSENBERG

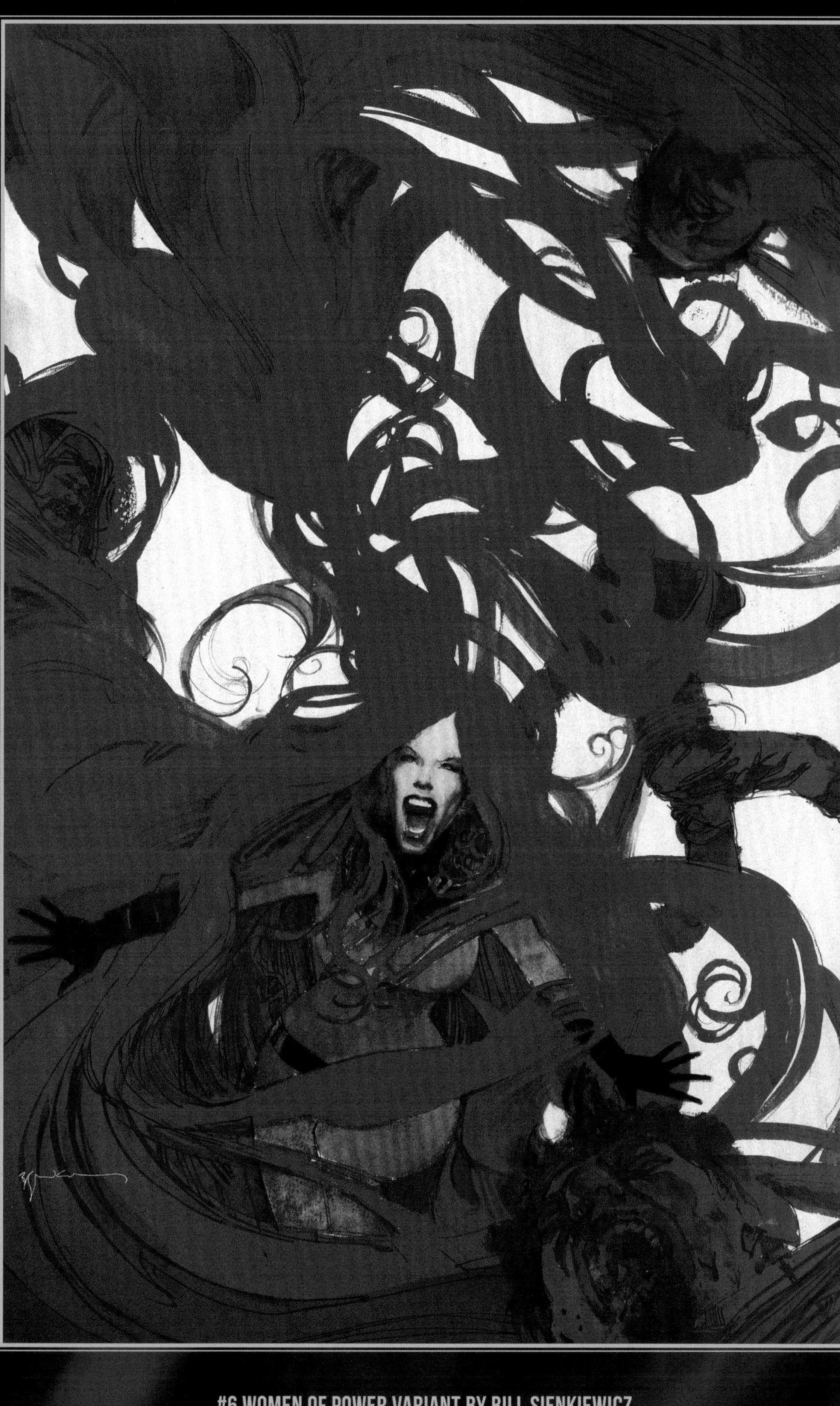

#6 WOMEN OF POWER VARIANT BY BILL SIENKIEWICZ

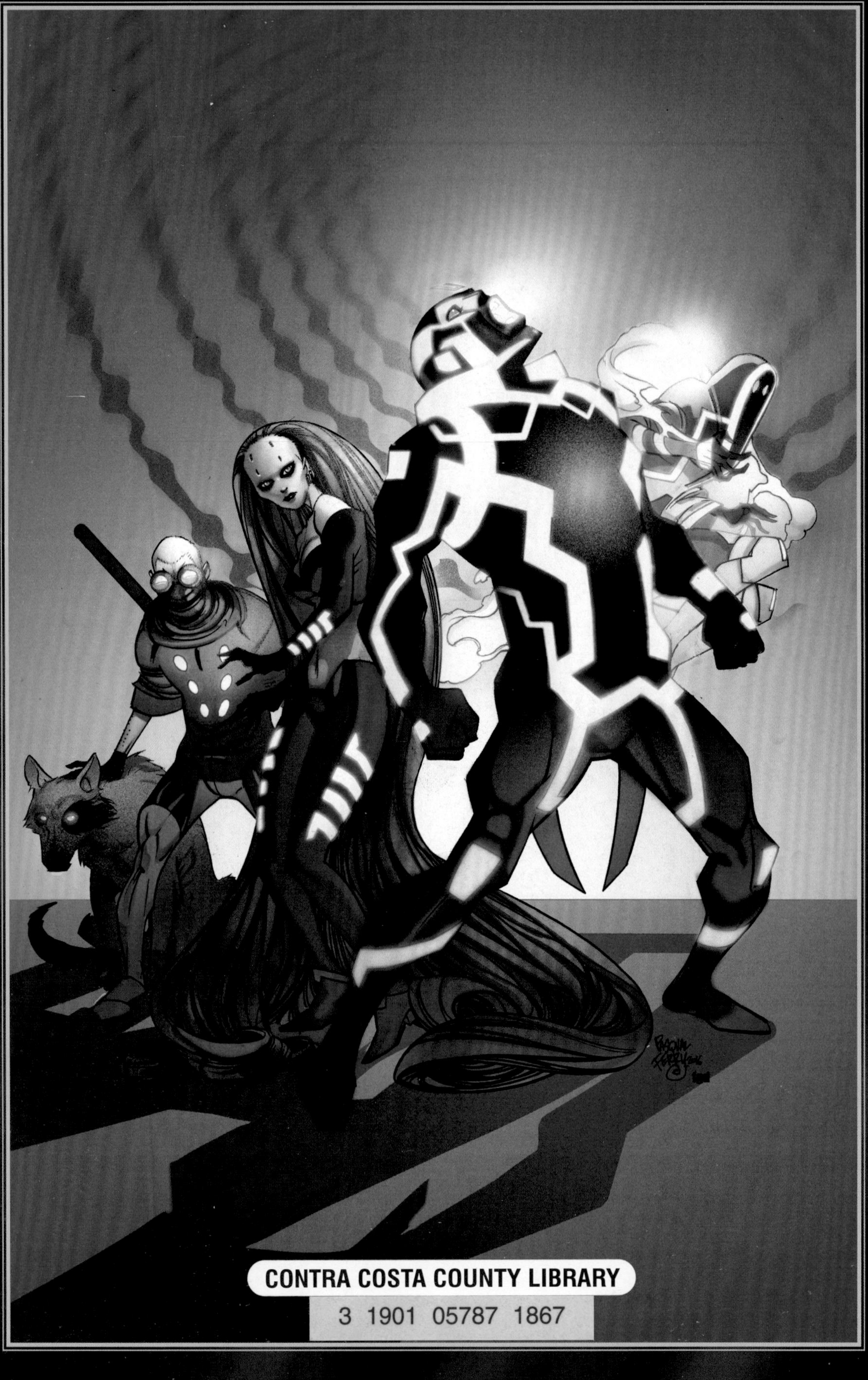

#8 AGE OF APOCALYPSE VARIANT BY PASQUAL FERRY & FRANK D'ARMATA